2012

THE BEST OF
COUNTRY COOKING

taste of home
THE #1 FOOD & ENTERTAINING MAGAZINE IN THE WORLD

For other Taste of Home books and products,
visit www.ShopTasteofHome.com.

DIG INTO THE GOODNESS OF COUNTRY COOKING

"Come and get it!" When the dinner bell rings, your gang will make double time, running to the table...particularly if the menu features the down-home flavors they love! With this edition of *Best of Country Cooking* at your fingertips, whipping up finger-licking favorites is easy as pie.

Inside you'll discover more than 300 succulent dishes sure to satisfy the biggest of appetites. Whether you rely on tasty classics such as Cornmeal-Crusted Walleye (p. 46) or enjoy new recipes like Apple Cider Cinnamon Rolls (p. 97), you can't go wrong with the heartwarming specialties found here. Take a look within and you'll also find:

 Prize Winners
Keep an eye out for the blue ribbon icon at left. That's your sign that a dish won a top spot in a national Taste of Home recipe contest.

Quick Fixes
In addition to a whole chapter of 30-minute main courses, *Best of Country Cooking* includes no-fuss appetizers, side dishes and desserts!

Tasty Twosomes
Cooking for two? Don't fill the fridge with leftovers. Just prepare any of the comforting delights from the "Cooking for Two" chapter. They're simply ideal for small households.

So go ahead! Pick a recipe, grab your favorite skillet and get ready to sink your teeth into the stick-to-your-ribs goodness the country has to offer!

■ **EDITORIAL**
Editor-in-Chief **Catherine Cassidy**
Executive Editor/Print & Digital Books **Stephen C. George**
Creative Director **Howard Greenberg**
Editorial Services Director **Kerri Balliet**

Senior Editor/Print & Digital Books **Mark Hagen**
Editor **Krista Lanphier**
Associate Creative Director **Edwin Robles Jr.**
Art Director **Gretchen Trautman**
Content Production Manager **Julie Wagner**
Layout Designers **Nancy Novak, Kathy Pieters**
Copy Chief **Deb Warlaumont Mulvey**
Copy Editors **Alysse Gear, Dulcie Shoener**
Project Copy Editor **Barb Schuetz**
Assistant Photo Coordinator **Mary Ann Koebernik**
Editorial Assistant **Marilyn Iczkowski**
Recipe Testing & Editing **Taste of Home Test Kitchen**
Food Photography **Taste of Home Photo Studio**

■ **BUSINESS**
Vice President, Publisher **Jan Studin, jan_studin@rd.com**
Regional Account Director **Donna Lindskog, donna_lindskog@rd.com**
Eastern Account Director **Jennifer Dietz**
Midwest & Western Account Director **Jackie Fallon**
Midwest Account Manager **Lorna Phillips**
Western Account Manager **Joel Millikin**
Michigan Sales Representative **Linda C. Donaldson**

Corporate Integrated Sales Director **Steve Sottile**
Vice President, Digital Sales and Development **Dan Meehan**
Digital/Integrated Director **Kelly Paxson**

General Manager, Taste of Home Cooking Schools **Erin Puariea**

Direct Response **Katherine Zito, David Geller Associates**

Executive Director, Brand Marketing **Leah West**
Vice President, Creative Director **Paul Livornese**
Marketing Manager **Katie Gaon Wilson**
Associate Marketing Manager **Emily Moore**
Public Relations Manager **Heidi Frank**

Vice President, Magazine Marketing **Dave Fiegel**

■ **READER'S DIGEST NORTH AMERICA**
President **Dan Lagani**

President, Canada **Tony Cioffi**
President, Books and Home Entertaining **Harold Clarke**
Chief Financial Officer **Howard Halligan**
Vice President, General Manager, Reader's Digest Media **Marilynn Jacobs**
Chief Marketing Officer **Renee Jordan**
Vice President, Chief Sales Officer **Mark Josephson**
Vice President, General Manager, RD Milwaukee **Lisa Karpinski**
Vice President, Chief Strategy Officer **Jacqueline Majers Lachman**
Vice President, Chief Content Officer **Liz Vaccariello**

■ **THE READER'S DIGEST ASSOCIATION, INC.**
President and Chief Executive Officer **Robert E. Guth**

■ **COVER PHOTOGRAPHY**
Photographer **Jim Wieland**
Senior Food Stylist **Kathryn Conrad**
Set Stylist **Pam Stasney**

Taste of Home Books
© 2012 Reiman Media Group, LLC
5400 S. 60th St. Greendale, WI 53129

International Standard Book Number (10): 1-61765-066-8
International Standard Book Number (13): 978-1-61765-066-6
International Standard Serial Number: 1097-8321

Taste of Home is a registered trademark of
The Reader's Digest Association, Inc.

All rights reserved. Printed in U.S.A.
1 3 5 7 9 10 8 6 4 2

ON THE FRONT COVER Herbed Chicken (p. 59), Triple-Layer Lemon Cake (p. 119), Bacon and Garlic Green Beans (p. 79).

ON THE BACK COVER Blueberry Muffins (p. 93), Zucchini Fries for 2 (p. 137), Steak au Poivre for 2 (p. 139).

CONTENTS

Snacks & Beverages   4

Soups, Salads & Sandwiches   18

Main Dishes   42

Side Dishes & Condiments   72

Breads, Rolls & More   84

Cookies, Bars & Candies   100

Dazzling Desserts   112

Cooking for Two   132

Meals in Minutes   152

Memorable Meals   166

The Cook's Quick Reference   180

Index   182

SNACKS & BEVERAGES

The savory dips and spreads, hot breads, cool drinks and more in this chapter make perfect starters and sippers for weekend gatherings, tailgating parties and other friendly get-togethers.

FAST CLAM DIP

ANNIE LEE MACDONALD
BORDEN-CARLTON, PRINCE EDWARD ISLAND

This simple appetizer comes together fast. I like to bring it to special-occasion parties.

2 cans (6-1/2 ounces *each*) minced clams
1 package (8 ounces) cream cheese, softened
1 tablespoon onion soup mix
1 tablespoon lemon juice
Assorted crackers or chips

Drain clams, reserving 2 tablespoons juice. In a small bowl, beat the cream cheese, soup mix, lemon juice and reserved clam juice until blended; fold in clams. Refrigerate until serving. Serve with crackers. YIELD: 1-1/2 cups.

QUICK KRAUT SNACKS

THE FREMONT COMPANY

It's so easy to make this special appetizer for friends and family. Bite-size pieces are flavorful from tasty sauerkraut.

1 package (8 ounces) cream cheese, softened
3/4 cup sauerkraut, drained
1/3 cup diced fully cooked smoked sausage
2 tablespoons finely chopped onion
4 teaspoons Worcestershire sauce
1/2 cup toasted rye bread crumbs

In a large bowl, combine the cream cheese, sauerkraut, sausage, onion and Worcestershire sauce. Shape into 1-in. balls; roll in bread crumbs. Refrigerate until serving. YIELD: about 3 dozen.

BRUNCH TIDBITS BREAD

LINDA LAMBERTH ✤ TYLER, TEXAS

I really enjoy cooking but rarely have the time during the week. So we treasure our weekend breakfasts, when I prepare special recipes like these tasty tidbits.

1-1/2 cups (6 ounces) shredded cheddar cheese
3/4 cup chopped green olives
3/4 cup chopped ripe olives
1/2 cup mayonnaise
1/4 cup sliced green onions
1/4 teaspoon pepper
4 English muffins, split

In a large bowl, combine the cheese, olives, mayonnaise, onions and pepper. Spread on English muffins; cut into fourths.

Place on an ungreased baking sheet and bake at 350° for 8-10 minutes or until bubbly. Or freeze and bake frozen at 350° for 18-20 minutes. YIELD: 8 servings.

ARTICHOKE-CHEESE FRENCH BREAD

BECKY GRONDAHL ❖ FOOTHILL RANCH, CALIFORNIA

You'll love this amazing French bread appetizer. The creamy artichoke mixture is heaped on top of lightly toasted bread and then sprinkled with cheddar. Be prepared to double the recipe, because it will go fast!

    1 loaf (1 pound) unsliced French bread
    3 jars (6-1/2 ounces *each*) marinated quartered artichoke
       hearts, drained
1-1/2 cups (6 ounces) shredded pepper Jack cheese
    1 cup (8 ounces) sour cream
    1 can (4 ounces) chopped green chilies
    2 garlic cloves, minced
    2 cups (8 ounces) shredded cheddar cheese, *divided*

Cut bread in half lengthwise; carefully hollow out top and bottom of loaf, leaving 1/2-in. shells. Cube removed bread; set aside.

In a large bowl, combine the artichokes, pepper Jack cheese, sour cream, green chilies, minced garlic and 1 cup cheddar cheese. Add the bread cubes and toss to coat. Spoon filling into bread shells; sprinkle with remaining cheddar cheese.

Place the bread on an ungreased baking sheet. Cover with foil. Bake at 350° for 15 minutes. Remove the foil and bake 10-15 minutes longer or until heated through. Slice and serve warm. YIELD: 16 servings.

SAY "CHEESE!"

Store cheese in airtight containers, plastic bags or plastic wrap in the refrigerator (about 4 months for soft cheeses and 6 months for hard cheeses). When buying bulk cheese, 4 ounces equals 1 cup shredded.

2 cans (14-1/2 ounces *each*) diced tomatoes, drained
1 medium onion, chopped
1/4 cup canned diced jalapeno peppers
2 tablespoons minced fresh cilantro
1/2 to 1 teaspoon salt
1 garlic clove, minced
1 teaspoon sugar
1 teaspoon dried basil
1/2 teaspoon dried oregano
1/4 teaspoon dried tarragon
1/4 teaspoon ground cumin
2 tablespoons lime juice
1 teaspoon red wine vinegar
1 can (4 ounces) chopped green chilies, optional
Tortilla chip scoops

In a large bowl, combine the first 11 ingredients. Stir in the lime juice, vinegar and chilies if desired. Cover and refrigerate for 8 hours or overnight. Serve with tortilla chips. YIELD: 3 cups.
EDITOR'S NOTE: Wear disposable gloves when cutting hot peppers; the oils can burn skin. Avoid touching your face.

SNAPPY COCKTAIL MEATBALLS

NANCY MEANS ✤ MOLINE, ILLINOIS

This recipe was given to me more than 20 years ago by a German friend. The meatballs are easy to prepare and can be made ahead of time.

2 eggs, lightly beaten
1-1/4 cups soft bread crumbs
1 teaspoon salt
1/2 teaspoon garlic salt
1/2 teaspoon onion powder

SWISS CHEESE BREAD

KARLA BOICE ✤ MAHTOMEDI, MINNESOTA

This bread will receive rave reviews, whether you serve it as an appetizer or with a meal. For real convenience, you can make it ahead of time and freeze it!

1 loaf (18-20 inches) French bread
8 ounces (2 sticks) butter, softened
2 cups (8 ounces) shredded Swiss cheese
3/4 teaspoon celery seed
3/4 teaspoon garlic powder
3 tablespoons dehydrated parsley flakes

Trim top and side crusts from bread, leaving bottom crust intact. Make diagonal cuts, 1 in. thick, through the bread but not through the bottom. Combine all remaining ingredients. Spread half the butter mixture between bread slices. Spread remaining mixture over top and sides of bread.

Place bread in foil boat; cover loosely with another sheet of foil. Bake at 425° for 20-30 minutes. For last 5 minutes, remove foil to allow bread to brown. YIELD: 18-24 servings.

BIG DIPPER SALSA

STACY TROUTNER ✤ MONROEVILLE, INDIANA

I often make this incredible zesty salsa when we have a barn party. You can adjust the spice level by increasing or decreasing the amount of jalapeno peppers.

    1/2 teaspoon pepper
    2 pounds lean ground beef (90% lean)
SAUCE
    1 can (28 ounces) diced tomatoes, undrained
    1/2 cup packed brown sugar
    1/4 cup vinegar
    1/2 teaspoon salt
    1 teaspoon grated onion
    10 gingersnaps, finely crushed

In a large bowl, combine the first six ingredients. Crumble beef over mixture and mix well. Shape into 1-1/4-in. balls. Place meatballs on a greased rack in a shallow baking sheet. Bake at 450° for 15 minutes. Drain on paper towels.

Meanwhile, for sauce, combine the tomatoes, brown sugar, vinegar, salt and onion in large saucepan. Bring to a boil. Stir in gingersnaps, continuing to boil until sauce is thick and clear. Reduce heat to simmer; add meatballs. Heat through. YIELD: About 5 dozen.

MEXICAN LAYER DIP

SHEILA FRASHER ✦ CROWN CITY, OHIO

This adaptable dip is like a magnet to hungry guests at our family gatherings and casual parties. It's tasty served hot or cold. Just one scoop and you're hooked!

    1 pound ground beef
    1 medium onion, chopped, *divided*
    1 can (15 ounces) tomato sauce
    2 teaspoons sugar
    1 teaspoon chili powder
    1/8 teaspoon salt
    1/8 teaspoon pepper
    1 can (16 ounces) refried beans
    2 medium tomatoes, seeded and chopped
    1 small green pepper, finely chopped
    2 cups (16 ounces) sour cream
    3 cups (12 ounces) shredded Mexican cheese blend
Corn chips

In a large skillet, cook beef and half of the onion over medium heat until meat is no longer pink; drain. Stir in the tomato sauce, sugar, chili powder, salt and pepper. Bring to a boil. Reduce heat; simmer, uncovered, for 20 minutes or until thickened.

Spread refried beans into a 13-in. x 9-in. dish; top with beef mixture, tomatoes, green pepper and remaining onion. Layer with sour cream and cheese. Serve with chips. YIELD: 8 cups.

CHOCOLATE SODA

TASTE OF HOME TEST KITCHEN

Poodle skirts may be out, but the old-fashioned ice cream soda our Test Kitchen concocted is still a simply perfect way to cool down on a hot summer day.

    3 tablespoons chocolate syrup
    1 tablespoon half-and-half cream
    3/4 cup carbonated water
    1/4 cup vanilla ice cream

In a tall glass, combine chocolate syrup and cream. Stir in water; top with ice cream. Serve immediately. YIELD: 1 serving.

SOFTENING ICE CREAM
Transfer ice cream from the freezer to the refrigerator 20-30 minutes before using, or let stand at room temperature for 10-15 minutes. Soften hard ice cream in the microwave at 30% power for about 30 seconds.

CAJUN SHRIMP SPREAD

LISA HUFF ❖ WILTON, CONNECTICUT

Just for fun, I mixed my favorite recipes for spinach dip and shrimp spread together in one bowl. Our snack-loving family is crazy about the Cajun-flavored combination!

 1 package (8 ounces) cream cheese, softened
 2/3 cup sour cream
 2/3 cup mayonnaise
 2 garlic cloves, minced
 1-1/2 teaspoons Cajun seasoning
Dash hot pepper sauce
 2 cups chopped cooked peeled shrimp
 1 package (10 ounces) frozen chopped spinach, thawed and squeezed dry
 2 tablespoons chopped sweet red pepper
 2 tablespoons chopped green onion
Assorted crackers

In a large bowl, whisk the first six ingredients until blended. Stir in the shrimp, spinach and sweet red pepper. Chill until serving. Sprinkle with chopped green onion. Serve with crackers. YIELD: 4-1/2 cups.

SESAME OMELET SPINACH SPIRALS

ROXANNE CHAN ❖ ALBANY, CALIFORNIA

These pretty little spirals would be perfect for a buffet of international hors d'oeuvres. They remind me of sushi. The dipping sauce is an exotic accompaniment to this fun finger food.

 4 tablespoons tahini
 4 spinach tortillas (8 inches), warmed
 6 eggs
 2 tablespoons *each* finely chopped green onion, sweet red pepper and canned water chestnuts
 2 tablespoons shredded carrot
 1 teaspoon minced fresh gingerroot
 1/4 teaspoon crushed red pepper flakes
 2 teaspoons sesame oil, *divided*
DIPPING SAUCE
 1/4 cup reduced-sodium soy sauce
 1 tablespoon minced fresh cilantro
 1 garlic clove, minced
 1 teaspoon sesame seeds, toasted
 1 teaspoon rice vinegar
 1 teaspoon sesame oil
 1/4 teaspoon grated orange peel

Spread tahini over tortillas; set aside. In a small bowl, whisk the eggs, onion, red pepper, water chestnuts, carrot, ginger and pepper flakes.

Heat a large nonstick skillet over medium heat; lightly brush with some of the oil. Pour 1/3 cup egg mixture into the pan; cook for 1 minute or until set. Flip egg mixture and cook 30 seconds to 1 minute longer or until lightly browned. Place omelet on a tortilla; roll up. Repeat three times, brushing skillet as needed with remaining oil. Cut wraps into 1-in. slices.

Combine the sauce ingredients; serve with spirals. YIELD: about 2-1/2 dozen (1/3 cup sauce).

 # CRAB PESTO CHEESECAKE

CAROLYN BUTTERFIELD ❖ LAKE STEVENS, WASHINGTON

This savory cheesecake is a sure hit for entertaining. Serve it with crackers or baguette slices. Pesto brings out the best in the crabmeat.

1 cup crushed roasted vegetable-flavored butter crackers
3 tablespoons butter, melted
3 packages (8 ounces *each*) cream cheese, softened
1 cup sour cream
3/4 cup shredded Asiago cheese
3 tablespoons prepared pesto
1 teaspoon grated lemon peel
1/2 teaspoon salt
2 eggs, lightly beaten
1 cup fresh crabmeat
1 cup canned water-packed artichoke hearts, chopped
Additional prepared pesto
Assorted crackers

Place a greased 9-in. springform pan on a double thickness of heavy-duty foil (about 18 in. square). Securely wrap the foil around the pan.

In a small bowl, combine the crushed cracker crumbs and melted butter. Press onto the bottom of the prepared pan. Place the pan on a baking sheet. Bake at 350° for 8 minutes. Cool on a wire rack.

In a large bowl, beat the softened cream cheese, sour cream, shredded Asiago cheese, pesto, grated lemon peel and salt until smooth. Add the eggs; beat on low speed just until combined. Fold in the crab and chopped artichokes. Pour over the crust. Place the springform pan in a large baking pan; add 1 in. of hot water to larger pan.

Bake at 325° for 55-65 minutes or until the center is just set and the top appears dull. Remove the springform pan from the water bath. Cool on a wire rack for 10 minutes. Carefully run a knife around the edge of the pan to loosen; cool 1 hour longer. Refrigerate overnight.

Remove sides of pan. Drizzle with additional pesto; serve with crackers. YIELD: 24 servings.

CANTALOUPE BANANA SMOOTHIES

JANICE MITCHELL ✤ AURORA, COLORADO

This is one of my favorite flavor combinations for a smoothie. Cool, fruity and delicately sweet, a full glass satisfies my evening munchies.

1/2 cup fat-free plain yogurt
4-1/2 teaspoons orange juice concentrate
2 cups cubed cantaloupe
1 large firm banana, cut into 1-inch pieces and frozen
2 tablespoons nonfat dry milk powder
2 teaspoons honey

In a blender, combine all the ingredients. Cover and process until blended. Pour into chilled glasses; serve immediately. YIELD: 3 cups.

NORWEGIAN MEATBALLS

JEANE JENSON ✤ STILLWATER, MINNESOTA

These meatballs are a favorite around our area. On May 17, Norwegian Independence Day, many people serve them with a mashed rutabaga and potato dish. So this recipe is both delicious and very traditional.

2 eggs, lightly beaten
1 cup milk
1 cup dry bread crumbs
1/2 cup finely chopped onion
2 teaspoons salt
2 teaspoons sugar
1/2 teaspoon *each* ground ginger, nutmeg and allspice
1/4 teaspoon pepper
2 pounds extra-lean ground beef (95% lean)
1 pound ground pork
GRAVY
2 tablespoons finely chopped onion
3 tablespoons butter
5 tablespoons all-purpose flour
4 cups beef broth
1/2 cup heavy whipping cream
Dash cayenne pepper
Dash white pepper

In a large bowl, combine the eggs, milk, bread crumbs, chopped onion and seasonings. Let stand until the crumbs absorb the milk. Add the ground beef and pork; stir until well blended. Shape into 1-in. meatballs.

Place meatballs on a greased rack in a shallow baking pan. Bake at 400° until browned, about 18 minutes or until a thermometer reads 160°; drain. Set aside.

For gravy, in a large skillet, saute onion in butter until tender. Stir in flour and brown lightly. Slowly add broth; cook and stir until smooth and thickened. Blend in the cream, cayenne and white pepper. Gently stir in meatballs; heat through but do not boil. YIELD: about 16 servings.

HOMEMADE CREAM SODA

SHELLY BEVINGTON-FISHER ❖ HERMISTON, OREGON

When your gang's thirsty, it's time to break out this bubbly, cherry-flavored refresher. Bright pink and creamy, it's instant happiness in a glass.

3/4 cup grenadine syrup
1/4 cup half-and-half cream
1-1/2 cups club soda, chilled
Ice cubes

In a blender, combine grenadine and cream; cover and process until blended. Stir in club soda; serve immediately over ice. YIELD: 2 servings.

EDITOR'S NOTE: This recipe was tested with Rose's grenadine.

HAM 'N' CHEESE PUFFS

JOYCE SCHOTTEN ❖ RENNER, SOUTH DAKOTA

A full-time job, farm life and our kids' activities keep me busy. These easy puffs are a real down-home delight.

1 cup water
1/2 cup butter
1 cup all-purpose flour
1/2 teaspoon ground mustard
4 eggs
1 cup finely chopped fully cooked ham
1/2 cup shredded sharp cheddar cheese
Warm prepared cheese sauce, optional

In a large heavy saucepan over medium heat, bring water and butter to a boil. Add flour and mustard all at once; stir until a smooth ball forms. Remove from the heat; let stand for 5 minutes. Add eggs, one at a time, beating well after each addition. Beat until smooth. Stir in the ham and cheese (cheese does not have to melt).

Drop batter by tablespoonfuls 2 in. apart onto greased baking sheets. Bake at 400° for 30-35 minutes or until golden brown. Serve warm or cold with cheese sauce for dipping if desired. YIELD: about 4-1/2 dozen.

CHEESE AND GRAPE APPETIZERS

ELEANOR GROFVERT ❖ KALAMAZOO, MICHIGAN

This appetizer is well worth the time it takes to make. The grapes look especially attractive on a bed of lettuce surrounded with crackers and cheese.

2 packages (2 ounces *each*) ground almonds
1 package (8 ounces) cream cheese, softened
2 ounces crumbled blue cheese, room temperature
2 tablespoons heavy whipping cream, room temperature
2 tablespoons minced fresh parsley
1 to 1-1/4 pounds red *or* green seedless grapes
Chilled greens

Spread almonds on baking pan. Bake at 275° until golden brown, stirring twice.

In a small bowl, combine the cheeses, heavy cream and minced parsley until blended. Place the cheese mixture in a shallow dish. Roll the grapes in the mixture to thoroughly coat, then in the toasted almonds.

Place on a waxed paper-lined tray; refrigerate until serving. Refrigerate leftovers. Serve with greens. YIELD: about 5 dozen.

In a large bowl, combine the egg, corn, cracker crumbs, sugar and baking powder (batter will be soft).

In an electric skillet or deep-fat fryer, heat oil to 375°. Drop batter by rounded teaspoonfuls; fry in batches until golden brown, about 1 minute on each side. Drain on paper towels. Serve warm. YIELD: 2-1/2 dozen.

CRABMEAT-CHEESE APPETIZERS

MARION BEDIENT ❖ CAMERON, WISCONSIN

This recipe is based on one I developed for a contest. I've changed it somewhat since, and it's become a favorite of my family and friends.

1 jar (5 ounces) Old English cheese spread
1 tablespoon Miracle Whip
1 teaspoon lemon juice
2 tablespoons finely minced green onion (white portion)
1 can (6 ounces) crabmeat, well-drained
1 tube (8 ounces) refrigerated crescent rolls
1 tablespoon green onion tops, thinly sliced
Paprika

In a large bowl, combine the cheese spread, Miracle Whip, lemon juice, white part of onion and crabmeat. Remove crescent rolls from tube; do not unroll.

Cut each section into 12 slices. Place slices on ungreased baking sheet. Divide crab mixture over 24 crescent roll slices. Sprinkle with green onion tops and paprika.

Bake at 375° for 10-12 minutes or until puffed and lightly browned on bottom. Serve immediately. YIELD: 2 dozen.

COOL LIME PIE FRAPPES

MARIE RIZZIO ❖ INTERLOCHEN, MICHIGAN

I love serving this light and luscious drink to guests on hot days. It has the taste and creamy texture of key lime pie without the unwanted calories.

1/4 cup fat-free milk
2 tablespoons lime juice
2 cups fat-free vanilla frozen yogurt, softened
1/2 teaspoon grated lime peel
2 teaspoons graham cracker crumbs

In a blender, combine the milk, lime juice, frozen yogurt and lime peel; cover and process until blended. Stir if necessary. Pour into chilled glasses; sprinkle with cracker crumbs. Serve immediately. YIELD: 2 servings.

FRIED CORN BALLS

RONNIE-ELLEN TIMONER ❖ MIDDLETOWN, NEW YORK

These bite-size treats are so easy to make. Serve them as an appetizer or as a side to a beef or chicken entree.

1 egg, lightly beaten
1 can (8-1/4 ounces) cream-style corn
3/4 cup crushed saltines (about 22 crackers)
1/2 teaspoon sugar
1/2 teaspoon baking powder
Oil for deep-fat frying

 # THREE-CHEESE FONDUE

BETTY MANGAS ❖ TOLEDO, OHIO

I got this easy recipe from my daughter, who lives in France. It's become my go-to fondue, and I make it often for our family.

1/2 pound *each* Emmentaler, Gruyere and Jarlsberg cheeses, shredded
2 tablespoons cornstarch, *divided*
4 teaspoons cherry brandy
2 cups dry white wine
1/8 teaspoon ground nutmeg
1/8 teaspoon paprika
Dash cayenne pepper
Cubed French bread baguette, boiled red potatoes and/or tiny whole pickles

In a large bowl, combine cheeses and 1 tablespoon cornstarch. In a small bowl, combine remaining cornstarch with cherry brandy; set aside. In a large saucepan, heat wine over medium heat until bubbles form around sides of pan.

Reduce the heat to medium-low; add a handful of cheese mixture. Stir mixture constantly, using a figure-eight motion, until almost completely melted. Continue adding cheese, one handful at a time, allowing cheese to almost completely melt between additions.

Stir brandy mixture; gradually stir into the cheese mixture. Add spices; cook and stir until mixture is thickened and smooth.

Transfer to a fondue pot and keep warm. Serve with bread cubes, potatoes and/or pickles. YIELD: 4 cups.

CHEESES FROM AROUND THE WORLD

Emmentaler is a medium-hard cheese from Switzerland with a savory, mellow flavor. Gruyere, also from Switzerland, is a rich, salty cheese that is aged 10-12 months. Jarlsberg from Norway is semi-firm, mild and buttery.

MOCK CHICKEN LEGS

JEANNE HERDA ❖ BURNSVILLE, MINNESOTA

When I was young, my mother made this recipe for us. I was recently going through her cookbook collection and found it. Now I make this tasty, fun appetizer for my own family and enjoy mixing the old memories with new ones.

   1 egg, lightly beaten
1/2 cup cornflake crumbs
1/4 cup milk
   2 tablespoons finely chopped green pepper
   1 teaspoon salt
3/4 pound ground pork
3/4 pound ground veal
  12 Popsicle sticks

COATING
   1 egg
1/4 cup milk
   2 cups cornflake crumbs
Oil for frying

In a large bowl, combine the first five ingredients. Crumble ground meat over mixture and mix well. Shape a 1/4 cupful of meat mixture around each Popsicle stick to resemble a 3-in. log.

In a shallow bowl, whisk egg and milk. Place cornflake crumbs in another shallow bowl. Coat each leg in crumbs, then dip in egg mixture and recoat in crumbs. Let stand for 5 minutes.

In an electric skillet, heat 1/4 in. oil to 375°. Fry legs, a few at a time, for 1 minute on each side or until golden brown. Drain on paper towels.

Arrange on an ungreased baking sheet. Bake at 350° for 15-20 minutes or until no pink remains and a thermometer reads 160°. YIELD: 1 dozen.

HOT WINGS

DAWN WRIGHT ❖ MOLINE, MICHIGAN

You'll find these wings have just the right amount of "zip." But if you want them a little hotter—like we often do—just add more hot pepper sauce.

   4 pounds whole chicken wings
Oil for deep-fat frying
1/4 cup butter
1/4 cup honey
1/4 cup barbecue sauce
   4 to 6 tablespoons hot pepper sauce
   3 tablespoons vinegar
   3 tablespoons prepared mustard
1/4 teaspoon garlic salt
Celery and carrot sticks
Blue cheese *or* ranch salad dressing

Cut wings into three sections; discard wing tip section. In an electric skillet or deep-fat fryer, heat oil to 350°. Fry chicken wings, a few at a time, about 9 minutes or until golden. Drain on paper towels; place in a large bowl.

In a small saucepan, combine the next seven ingredients; cook and stir 5-10 minutes. Pour over cooked wings; let stand 10 minutes. With a slotted spoon, remove wings from sauce and place in a single layer on greased baking sheets.

Bake at 350° for 15 minutes. Serve hot with vegetable sticks and dressing for dipping. YIELD: 12-16 servings.

DAIRY HOLLOW HOUSE HERBAL COOLER

TINA PLOWMAN ❖ EUREKA SPRINGS, ARKANSAS

For a refreshing drink for your next summer party, try this cooler. Everyone will be asking for the recipe.

   8 bags Red Zinger tea
   1 quart (4 cups) boiling water
   1 can (12 ounces) frozen apple juice concentrate, thawed
4-1/2 cups cold water
   1 medium orange, sliced
1/2 lemon, sliced
Mint sprig to garnish

Steep tea in boiling water in a large container; cool until lukewarm. Discard tea bags.

Add the apple juice concentrate, cold water and orange and lemon slices. Chill thoroughly. Serve coolers over ice with a sprig of mint. YIELD: 8 servings.

AUNT SHIRLEY'S LIVER PATE

SHIRLEY BROWNELL ❖ AMSTERDAM, NEW YORK

While living in San Francisco, I developed this recipe to serve at our many get-togethers with friends. Now my nieces and nephews request the pate at family gatherings!

3/4 cup butter, *divided*
1-1/4 pounds chicken livers, halved
1/4 cup chopped onion
2 teaspoons Worcestershire sauce
1 tablespoon minced fresh parsley
1/4 cup sliced pimiento-stuffed olives
Additional parsley, optional
Crackers

In a large skillet, melt 1/2 cup butter. Add the chicken livers, onion, Worcestershire sauce and parsley. Saute over medium heat for 6-8 minutes or until chicken is no longer pink. Remove from the heat; cool for 10 minutes.

Transfer to blender; process until smooth. Melt remaining butter; cool to lukewarm. Add to blender; process until blended.

Pour into a 2-1/2-cup mold that has been lined with plastic wrap. Cover and chill for 8 hours or overnight.

Before serving, unmold pate onto a chilled plate. Press olives on top of pate; garnish with parsley if desired. Serve with crackers. YIELD: 8-10 servings (2-1/4 cups).

CHEESY OLIVE SNACKS

ALMA HARDY ❖ TULSA, OKLAHOMA

When guests stop by unexpectedly, this is an ideal recipe to whip up. The olives and onion provide a unique flavor. Many people have complimented me on it.

1 cup grated process American cheese
1 can (4-1/2 ounces) chopped ripe olives, drained
1/2 cup chopped onion
5 to 6 English muffins, split

Combine the cheese, olives and onion. Spread over muffin halves. Broil 4 in. from the heat for 5 minutes or until the cheese is melted. Serve immediately. Yield: 10-12 servings.

APPETIZER PARTY

For an appetizer buffet that serves as the meal, offer five or six different appetizers and plan on eight to nine pieces per guest. If you'll also be serving a meal, two to three pieces per person is sufficient.

SECRET-INGREDIENT STUFFED EGGS

KEYNIBEAR ❖ TASTE OF HOME ONLINE COMMUNITY

My take on deviled eggs is unique and full of surprises. The down-home appetizer Mom used to make gets an upscale touch from mango, goat cheese and pecans. People love these tempting treats.

6 hard-cooked eggs
4 tablespoons crumbled goat cheese, *divided*
3 tablespoons finely chopped pecans, *divided*
3 tablespoons mayonnaise
2 tablespoons finely chopped celery
2 tablespoons mango chutney
1/4 teaspoon salt
1/8 teaspoon pepper

Cut eggs in half lengthwise. Remove yolks; set whites aside. In a small bowl, mash yolks. Add 3 tablespoons goat cheese, 2 tablespoons pecans, mayonnaise, celery, chutney, salt and pepper; mix well. Stuff into egg whites. Refrigerate until serving. Just before serving, sprinkle with remaining goat cheese and pecans. YIELD: 1 dozen.

SOUPS, SALADS & SANDWICHES

For a tasty lunch menu, dinner on the light side or a dish to go along with the main course, consider this chapter! It's full of the hearty favorites and refreshing ideas you're sure to turn to time and again.

VEGETABLE SOUP WITH DUMPLINGS

REV. WILLIS PIEPENBRINK ❖ OSHKOSH, WISCONSIN

This nutritious soup is never boring because the vegetables can vary depending on what's in season or on hand. The dumplings are optional.

2 to 3 meaty beef soup bones
3 quarts water
2 small onions, *divided*
1 bay leaf
4 medium potatoes, peeled and cubed
2 medium carrots, cubed
1-1/2 cups canned diced tomatoes, undrained
2 cups cubed cabbage
2 celery ribs, sliced
2 cups cut green beans
3/4 cup medium pearl barley
Minced fresh parsley
Salt and pepper to taste
DUMPLINGS
1 cup all-purpose flour
2 teaspoons baking powder
Pinch salt
1/2 cup milk

In a stockpot, place the beef bones, water, one onion and bay leaf. Bring to a boil. Skim off foam. Reduce heat to simmer. Cover and cook for 3 hours or until meat falls off the bones.

Discard bones, onion and bay leaf. Remove meat from the bones and dice. Skim fat from broth. Add the meat, remaining onion quartered, remaining vegetables, barley and parsley to the pot. Season to taste. Cover and cook for 1 hour or until barley and vegetables are tender.

For dumplings, combine the flour, baking powder and salt. Add milk and stir just until moistened. Drop by teaspoonfuls onto simmering liquid. Cover and simmer for 10-15 minutes or until a toothpick inserted in a dumpling comes out clean (do not lift the cover while simmering). YIELD: 5 quarts.

MEATY MEXICAN SANDWICHES

TERI SPAULDING ❖ DURHAM, CALIFORNIA

I like to serve these hearty sandwiches during football-watching parties along with a salad and beans. Everyone raves about the great combination of flavors and textures.

1/2 pound ground pork
1/2 pound ground beef
1 small onion, chopped
1 garlic clove, minced
3/4 cup ketchup
1/2 cup raisins
1 teaspoon red wine vinegar
1/2 teaspoon ground cinnamon
1/2 teaspoon chili powder
1/2 teaspoon salt
1/4 teaspoon pepper
1/8 teaspoon ground cumin
Pinch ground cloves
1/2 cup slivered almonds, toasted
6 hard rolls, split
1-1/2 cups (6 ounces) shredded cheddar cheese
2 cups shredded lettuce

In a large skillet, cook the pork, beef and onion over medium heat until meat is no longer pink. Add the garlic; cook 1 minute longer. Drain. Stir in the ketchup, raisins, vinegar and seasonings. Cover and simmer for 20-25 minutes, stirring occasionally. Stir in almonds.

Hollow out the top and bottom of each roll, leaving a 1/2-in. shell. (Discard removed bread or save for another use.) Fill each roll with about 1/2 cup meat mixture. Top with cheese and lettuce; replace top of roll. YIELD: 6 servings.

BUYING GROUND MEAT

Ground meat is labeled based on the percentage of fat by weight. Lean meat has less than 10% fat by weight. Any package, whether ground beef or turkey, with the same fat percentage has the same calorie count and total fat grams.

THAI TURKEY BURGERS

SHELBY GODDARD ❖ BATON ROUGE, LOUISIANA

When we're tired of everyday burgers, I make these turkey patties for a taste of Thailand. The slaw is a fun switch from traditional burger garnishes.

SPICY PEANUT SLAW
- 1 tablespoon rice vinegar
- 1 tablespoon Thai chili sauce
- 1 tablespoon peanut butter
- 1 tablespoon Thai red chili paste
- 1 cup shredded cabbage
- 1 small carrot, shredded
- 1 radish, finely chopped
- 1 green onion, finely chopped
- 3 tablespoons dry roasted peanuts, chopped
- 1-1/2 teaspoons minced fresh mint *or* 1/2 teaspoon dried mint

BURGERS
- 1 small onion, finely chopped
- 2 tablespoons minced fresh cilantro
- 2 garlic cloves, minced
- 2 to 3 teaspoons Thai red chili paste
- 1 pound ground turkey
- 4 hamburger buns, split and toasted

In a small bowl, combine the vinegar, chili sauce, peanut butter and chili paste. Add the remaining slaw ingredients; toss to coat. Set aside.

In a large bowl, combine the onion, cilantro, garlic and chili paste. Crumble turkey over mixture and mix well. Shape into four patties.

Using long-handled tongs, moisten a paper towel with cooking oil and lightly coat the grill rack. Grill burgers, covered, over medium heat or broil 4 in. from the heat for 5-7 minutes on each side or until a thermometer reads 165° and juices run clear. Serve on buns with slaw. YIELD: 4 servings.

MOTHER'S POTATO SOUP

LOUELLA KIGHTLINGER ❖ ERIE, PENNSYLVANIA

Many of our favorite family recipes came from my mother-in-law, who was a wonderful cook. My husband inherited her love of cooking, and he enjoys stirring up her recipes, including this fabulous soup. Rivels, which are similar to spaetzle, are small dumplings that are cooked in broth.

RIVELS
- 1 egg white, lightly beaten
- Pinch salt
- 6 tablespoons all-purpose flour

SOUP
- 1-1/2 cups cubed peeled potatoes , cut into 3/4-inch pieces
- 1 large carrot, sliced
- 1/2 cup chopped onion
- 1/2 teaspoon salt
- 1/8 teaspoon pepper
- 1-1/2 cups water
- 1 egg yolk
- 1/2 cup 2% milk
- Minced fresh parsley

In a small bowl, combine the egg white, salt and flour (mixture will be slightly dry); set aside. In a large saucepan, combine the potatoes, carrot, onion, salt, pepper and water. Bring to a boil; cover and cook for 3 minutes.

With a knife, cut the rivel batter by the teaspoonful into the soup. Cook, partially covered, over medium heat for 10 minutes. Beat egg yolk and milk; add to the soup. Bring to a boil. Remove from the heat and sprinkle with parsley. Serve immediately. YIELD: 2 servings.

3 quarts water
2 pounds broiler/fryer chicken pieces, skin removed
2 large onions, halved
3 teaspoons chicken bouillon granules
3 cups cooked long grain rice
Pepper to taste

Cut vegetables into 2-in. pieces; place in a Dutch oven. Add the water, chicken, onions and bouillon. Bring to a boil; skim fat. Reduce heat; cover and simmer for 2 hours.

Set chicken aside until cool enough to handle. Let broth cool for 1 hour; skim fat. Remove meat from bones; discard bones and cut chicken into chunks.

In a blender, puree the vegetables and broth in batches; strain. Return chicken and broth to Dutch oven. Stir in rice. Cook over medium heat until bubbly, stirring occasionally. Season with pepper. YIELD: 20 servings (5 quarts).

GOLDEN SQUASH SOUP

NANCY MCFADYEN ✤ SMITHS FALLS, ONTARIO

I served this unusual soup last Thanksgiving and received rave reviews—even people who don't usually like squash enjoyed its hearty flavor. To dress it up, I sometimes add a dollop of yogurt on top.

3 cups coarsely chopped onion
2 tablespoons canola oil
1/4 teaspoon ground nutmeg
1/4 teaspoon ground cinnamon
1/4 teaspoon dried thyme
2 bay leaves
1-1/2 cups water
2 celery ribs, chopped
1 medium carrot, chopped

ONION ITALIAN SAUSAGE

RUTH VAN DER LEEST ✤ LYNDON, ILLINOIS

When my five children were all still at home, this was one of their most-requested meals. I've long had this recipe among my standbys, and, like all cooks who improvise and experiment, I've changed it as our tastes changed.

6 medium onions, peeled and sliced 1/4 inch thick
2 tablespoons butter
6 Italian sausage links
1 small green pepper, chopped
1-1/2 tablespoons Italian seasoning
Dash reduced-sodium soy sauce
Italian rolls, split

In a large skillet, saute onions in butter until lightly browned. Remove from pan; set aside. In the same skillet, lightly brown sausage, turning frequently. Remove; set aside with onions.

Add more butter to skillet if necessary; saute pepper until crisp-tender. Add the onions, sausages, Italian seasoning and soy sauce. Add water to 1-in. depth and simmer until a thermometer inserted in the sausages reads 140° and water is cooked away. Serve on rolls. YIELD: 6 servings.

HARVEST CHICKEN RICE SOUP

DIANE WINNINGHAM ✤ UNIONTOWN, MISSOURI

Because the produce in this soup is pureed, you can easily get children to eat their vegetables without them knowing it! Kids of all ages will savor it with a loaf of crusty bread.

2 celery ribs with leaves
2 medium carrots
1 pound white potatoes, peeled
1 pound sweet potatoes, peeled

2 cups mashed cooked butternut squash, *divided*
1-1/2 cups tomato juice, *divided*
1 cup apple juice, *divided*
1 cup orange juice, *divided*
Salt and pepper to taste

In a large saucepan, saute onion in oil with nutmeg, cinnamon, thyme and bay leaves until onion is tender. Stir in the water, celery and carrot; cover and simmer until carrot is tender. Discard bay leaves.

In a blender, place half of the squash and half of the tomato, apple and orange juices; add half of the vegetable mixture. Puree; return to pan. Repeat with the remaining squash, juices and vegetable mixture; return to pan. Add salt and pepper. Heat through. YIELD: 6-8 servings (2 quarts).

CILANTRO BEAN BURGERS

DOROTHY ANDREWS ❖ GRAFTON, WISCONSIN

Seasoned with cilantro and cumin, bean patties make a tempting alternative to beef burgers. Jazz them up with a little salsa or guacamole.

1/2 cup canned pinto beans, rinsed and drained
1/2 cup canned black beans, rinsed and drained
1/4 cup shredded carrots
1 tablespoon minced fresh cilantro
3/4 teaspoon dried minced onion
3/4 teaspoon lime juice
1 small garlic clove, minced
1/4 teaspoon ground cumin
1/8 teaspoon salt
1/8 teaspoon pepper
1/4 cup soft bread crumbs
2 tablespoons egg substitute
1-1/2 teaspoons cornmeal
1-1/2 teaspoons canola oil
Salsa, guacamole and tortilla chips, optional

In a food processor, combine the first 10 ingredients; cover and pulse until blended. Stir in bread crumbs and egg substitute; refrigerate for 30 minutes.

Shape bean mixture into two patties; sprinkle each side with cornmeal. In a large nonstick skillet, cook patties in oil for 4-5 minutes on each side or until lightly browned. Serve with salsa, guacamole and tortilla chips if desired. YIELD: 2 servings.

Eat Your Vegetables

When you have a bushel of fresh vegetables to use after the summer harvest, or you just want to eat on the lighter side, you'll love having these veggie-packed recipes on hand.

GERMAN VEGETABLE SOUP

GUDRUN BRAKER ❖ BURNETT, WISCONSIN

My sister-in-law gave me the recipe for this nice, thick soup. Don't be scared off by the number of ingredients—the taste is well worth the effort!

1-1/2 pounds ground beef
  2 medium onions, diced
  2 tablespoons beef bouillon granules
  1 cup water
Salt and pepper to taste
  1/2 to 1 teaspoon garlic powder
  1 bay leaf
  1 can (46 ounces) tomato *or* vegetable juice
  3 celery ribs, diced
  6 medium carrots, sliced
  3 medium potatoes, peeled and diced
  3 cups shredded cabbage
  1 small green pepper, chopped
  1 can (15-1/4 ounces) whole kernel corn, drained
  1 can (8-1/2 ounces) peas, drained
  1 can (8 ounces) cut green beans, drained

In a large Dutch oven, cook beef and onions over medium heat until meat is no longer pink; drain.

Dissolve bouillon in water; add to the beef mixture. Add the salt, pepper, garlic, bay leaf, tomato juice, celery, carrots, potatoes, cabbage and green pepper.

Simmer, uncovered, for 25 minutes or until vegetables are tender. Stir in the corn, peas and beans; heat through. Discard bay leaf before serving. YIELD: 16 servings (4 quarts).

VEGETABLE TUNA SANDWICHES

MRS. ALLAN MILLER ❖ ST. JOHN, NEW BRUNSWICK

I packed lunches for a husband and seven children for years and tried many different recipes to keep things new and exciting. I hope you enjoy these fun sandwiches.

  2 packages (3 ounces *each*) cream cheese, softened, *divided*
  6 tablespoons mayonnaise, *divided*
  1/4 teaspoon salt
  1/8 teaspoon pepper
  1 can (6 ounces) tuna, drained and flaked
  3 tablespoons finely chopped celery
  3 tablespoons finely chopped green pepper
  1 cup shredded carrots
  2 tablespoons finely chopped onion
  8 slices white bread
  4 slices whole wheat bread

In a large bowl, combine one package of cream cheese, 3 tablespoons mayonnaise, salt and pepper until smooth. Stir in the tuna, celery and green pepper. In another bowl, combine the carrots, onion and remaining cream cheese and mayonnaise. Spread 1/3 cup tuna mixture on four slices of white bread; top with a slice of whole wheat bread. Spread 1/4 cup carrot mixture on the whole wheat bread; top with a slice of white bread. YIELD: 4 servings.

GRILLED VEGETABLE RANCH SALAD

TRISHA KRUSE ❖ EAGLE, IDAHO

We're thrilled when the garden starts providing the goodies needed for this simple salad. It's wonderful alongside grilled salmon or basic burgers and hot dogs.

  1 yellow summer squash
  1 medium zucchini

In a small bowl, whisk the sour cream, mayonnaise, milk, dressing mix, garlic salt and pepper. Divide salad greens among six serving plates; top with grilled vegetables. Serve with dressing. YIELD: 6 servings (1 cup dressing)

EDITOR'S NOTE: If you do not have a grill wok or basket, use a disposable foil pan. Poke holes in the bottom of the pan with a meat fork to allow liquid to drain.

SUMMER GARDEN SALAD

JESSICA JOSEPH ✤ KISSIMMEE, FLORIDA

When it's time to raid your garden and herb patch, put together this healthy salad! A touch of mint will make your mouth water.

   1 medium tomato, thinly sliced
1/2 small cucumber, thinly sliced
   3 tablespoons chopped celery
   2 tablespoons sliced ripe olives
   2 tablespoons chopped sweet onion
   1 tablespoon minced fresh mint
   2 teaspoons minced fresh parsley
   2 teaspoons olive oil
   2 teaspoons balsamic vinegar
   1 small garlic clove, minced
Dash salt
Dash pepper
   1 tablespoon crumbled feta cheese
Fresh mint leaves, optional

Place tomato and cucumber in a small bowl; add the celery, olives, onion, mint and parsley. Toss to combine.

In another small bowl, whisk the oil, vinegar, garlic, salt and pepper; pour over tomato mixture and toss to coat. Divide vegetables between two plates; sprinkle with cheese. Garnish with mint leaves if desired. YIELD: 2 servings.

   1 small red onion
   1 small eggplant
   1 small sweet red pepper
   2 teaspoons olive oil
   2 teaspoons balsamic vinegar
   2 teaspoons reduced-sodium soy sauce
1/2 teaspoon dried oregano
1/4 teaspoon dried rosemary, crushed
1/3 cup sour cream
1/3 cup mayonnaise
1/4 cup 2% milk
   4 teaspoons ranch salad dressing mix
1/2 teaspoon garlic salt
1/4 teaspoon pepper
   6 cups spring mix salad greens

Slice the squash, zucchini and red onion; cube the eggplant and cut the red pepper into 1-in. pieces. Place in a large bowl; add the oil, vinegar, soy sauce, oregano and rosemary. Toss to coat.

Transfer to a grill wok or basket. Grill, covered, over medium heat for 10-12 minutes or until tender, stirring once.

ABOUT EGGPLANT

Select eggplant with smooth skin. To store, refrigerate for up to 5 days in a plastic bag. Young and tender eggplants do not need to be peeled before using, but larger eggplants may be bitter and will taste better when peeled.

TASTY ITALIAN BURGERS

SHARON NOVIN ✤ WEST HILLS, CALIFORNIA

The best flavors of Italy are celebrated in my tempting turkey burgers—pesto, basil, tomato and mozzarella. Grill some up for an international cookout.

        3 tablespoons shredded Parmesan cheese
        1 garlic clove, minced
        1 pound lean ground turkey
    1/2 pound Italian turkey sausage links, casings removed
        6 hamburger buns, split
        3 tablespoons olive oil
        6 tablespoons prepared pesto
        6 ounces fresh mozzarella cheese, sliced
        6 lettuce leaves
        6 slices tomato
    1/4 cup thinly sliced fresh basil leaves

In a large bowl, combine Parmesan cheese and garlic. Crumble turkey and turkey sausage over mixture and mix well. Shape into six patties.

Grill burgers, covered, over medium heat or broil 4 in. from the heat for 5-8 minutes on each side or until a thermometer reads 165° and juices run clear.

Brush buns with oil; grill, uncovered, for 1-2 minutes or until toasted. Serve burgers on buns with pesto, mozzarella cheese, lettuce, tomato and basil. YIELD: 6 servings.

CALICO MAIN DISH SOUP

JOSIE PRITCHARD ✤ ATKINSON, ILLINOIS

Serve this hearty soup with a pan of corn bread on a cold winter's night. It'll warm you right down to your toes!

    1-1/2 pounds ground beef
    1/2 cup diced green pepper
    1/3 cup chopped onion
        2 tablespoons chili powder
        1 teaspoon salt
        1 teaspoon ground cumin
        2 cans (10-3/4 ounces each) condensed golden mushroom soup, undiluted
    1-1/3 cups water
        1 can (15-1/4 ounces) whole kernel corn, drained
        1 can (14-1/2 ounces) diced tomatoes, undrained
        1 can (14-1/2 ounces) cut green beans, drained
        1 cup uncooked instant rice
        1 to 2 cups tomato juice, optional

In a large saucepan, cook beef over medium heat until no longer pink; drain. Add the green pepper, onion, chili powder, salt and cumin. Cook and stir over medium heat for 5 minutes.

Add the soup, water, corn, tomatoes, beans and rice. Bring to a boil. Reduce heat; simmer, uncovered, for 20 minutes, stirring occasionally. Thin with tomato juice if desired. YIELD: 6-8 servings (2 quarts).

QUINOA VEGETABLE SALAD

MERWYN GARBINI ✤ TUCSON, ARIZONA

Protein-rich quinoa has been called the nutritional supergrain. Its light and crunchy texture makes it terrific in salads, like this well-dressed mix of colorful veggies.

        1 cup water
    1/2 cup quinoa, rinsed
        1 cup grape tomatoes, halved
    1/2 cup frozen peas, thawed
        1 small carrot, shredded
        1 shallot, minced
        2 tablespoons lemon juice
        1 tablespoon white balsamic vinegar
        1 tablespoon minced fresh parsley

1 tablespoon minced fresh thyme *or* 1 teaspoon dried thyme
2 teaspoons olive oil
1-1/2 teaspoons Dijon mustard
1/4 teaspoon sugar
1/4 teaspoon salt
1/8 teaspoon pepper
2 cups fresh spinach

In a small saucepan, bring water to a boil. Add quinoa. Reduce heat; cover and simmer for 12-15 minutes or until water is absorbed. Remove from the heat; fluff with a fork. Transfer to a large bowl; cool completely. Add the tomatoes, peas, carrot and shallot.

In a small bowl, combine the lemon juice, vinegar, parsley, thyme, oil, mustard, sugar, salt and pepper. Drizzle over quinoa mixture; toss to coat. Chill until serving.

Place the spinach on a serving plate; top with quinoa salad. YIELD: 4 servings.

EDITOR'S NOTE: Look for quinoa in the cereal, rice or organic food aisle.

RAMEN-VEGGIE CHICKEN SALAD

LINDA GEARHART ❖ GREENSBORO, NORTH CAROLINA

Like a salad with plenty of crunch? This refreshing recipe is sure to please. Toasted noodles, delicate almonds and sesame seeds provide the crunchy topping. The chicken makes it a main dish.

1/4 cup sugar
1/4 cup canola oil
2 tablespoons cider vinegar
1 tablespoon reduced-sodium soy sauce
1 package (3 ounces) ramen noodles
1 tablespoon butter
1/3 cup sliced almonds
1 tablespoon sesame seeds
1 boneless skinless chicken breast half (6 ounces)
4 cups shredded Chinese *or* napa cabbage
1/2 large sweet red pepper, thinly sliced
3 green onions, thinly sliced
1 medium carrot, julienned

In a small saucepan, combine the sugar, oil, vinegar and soy sauce. Bring to a boil, cook and stir for 1 minute or until sugar is dissolved; set aside to cool.

Meanwhile, break noodles into small pieces (save seasoning packet for another use). In a small skillet, melt butter over medium heat.

Add the noodles, almonds and sesame seeds to the skillet; cook and stir for 1-2 minutes or until lightly toasted.

Grill chicken, covered, over medium heat for 4-6 minutes on each side or until a thermometer reads 170°.

Meanwhile, arrange the cabbage, red pepper, onions and carrot on two serving plates. Slice the chicken; place chicken over the salad. Top chicken and salad with the noodle mixture; drizzle all with the dressing. YIELD: 2 servings.

CHERRY-CHICKEN PASTA SALAD

TINA MATRO ❖ SUTTONS BAY, MICHIGAN

The Women in Mission group at my church always receives compliments for this sweet and savory salad. The dried cherries lend sweetness and the celery adds crunch.

2-1/2 cups uncooked bow tie pasta
3-1/2 cups shredded cooked chicken
    3 celery ribs, chopped
    6 green onions, chopped
3/4 cup dried cherries
    1 cup mayonnaise
    2 teaspoons sugar
1/2 teaspoon salt
1/2 teaspoon Dijon mustard
1/8 teaspoon pepper
Dash dried tarragon

Cook pasta according to package directions. Meanwhile, in a large bowl, combine the chicken, celery, onions and cherries. Drain pasta and rinse in cold water; add to chicken mixture.

In a small bowl, whisk the mayonnaise, sugar, salt, mustard, pepper and tarragon. Pour over salad and toss to coat. Chill until serving. YIELD: 6 servings.

SIMPLE SOUP GARNISHES

Topping soup with a garnish adds color, flavor and texture. Try finely chopped green onions or chives, minced fresh parsley, shredded cheddar, grated or shredded Parmesan, a dollop of sour cream or croutons.

LIVER DUMPLINGS

SARA LINDLER ❖ IRMO, SOUTH CAROLINA

These delicious dumplings can be served in beef broth, or you can thicken the broth like gravy and serve this dish as a stew. Either way, they are hearty, delicious and different!

1/2 pound uncooked beef liver
    1 large onion, cut into eighths
    1 teaspoon salt
1-1/2 teaspoons ground sage, *divided*
1/2 teaspoon ground coriander
1/2 teaspoon dried basil
1/2 teaspoon pepper, *divided*
    3 cups all-purpose flour
1/4 teaspoon baking powder
    3 egg whites
    1 egg yolk
    5 cans (14-1/2 ounces *each*) beef broth
1/2 cup cornstarch

In a food processor, combine the liver, onion, salt, 1 teaspoon sage, coriander, basil and 1/4 teaspoon pepper; cover and process until smooth. Add the flour, baking powder, egg whites and yolk; process until well mixed. Batter should be thick and spoonable. (Add a little water if too thick or a little flour if too thin.) Set batter aside.

In a 5-qt. Dutch oven, combine the broth, cornstarch and remaining sage and pepper; bring to a rolling boil, stirring constantly. Reduce heat to a gentle boil. Drop batter by heaping teaspoonfuls onto broth, dipping spoon in broth to release dough. Gently boil, uncovered, for 20 minutes or until dumplings are no longer sticky. Stir occasionally. YIELD: 8-10 servings.

Let stand for 10 minutes; thinly slice across the grain. Layer with beef, lettuce mixture, pineapple and nuts on each tortilla. Fold one end over filling, then fold in sides. Tie with an onion top. YIELD: 8 servings.

GARLIC RANCH POTATO SALAD

AMY KOWAL ❖ PITTSBURGH, PENNSYLVANIA

The hint of garlic in the dressing and the addition of fresh herbs add just the right flavor for this unique potato salad. As my official taste tester, my husband usually tells me to "add this" or "add that" to spice things up, but this was the first recipe I experimented with that already called for the perfect flavor balance.

3/4 pound medium red potatoes, cubed
1/4 teaspoon salt
1/8 teaspoon pepper
1/2 cup garlic ranch salad dressing
1/4 cup chopped sweet red pepper
2 tablespoons grated Parmesan cheese
1 tablespoon minced fresh basil or 1 teaspoon dried basil
1/2 teaspoon minced fresh rosemary or 1/8 teaspoon dried rosemary, crushed

Place the potatoes in a saucepan; cover with water. Bring to a boil. Reduce heat; cover and cook for 8-10 minutes or until tender. Drain and cool. Transfer to a large bowl; sprinkle with salt and pepper.

In a small bowl, whisk the remaining ingredients; pour over potatoes and toss to coat. Cover and refrigerate for at least 2 hours before serving. YIELD: 2 servings.

SPECIAL BEEF WRAPS

DIANE HALFERTY ❖ TUCSON, ARIZONA

These satisfying bundles burst with grilled steak, tangy pineapple and crunchy nuts.

1 cup white wine vinegar
1/4 cup reduced-sodium soy sauce
2 tablespoons lime juice
2 tablespoons canola oil
1 tablespoon honey
1 beef flank steak (1-1/2 pounds)
2 cups torn mixed salad greens
1/2 cup sliced green onions
1 cup water
8 green onion tops
3/4 cup pineapple tidbits, drained
1 cup honey-roasted peanuts, coarsely chopped
8 flour tortillas (8 inches), warmed

In a 2-cup measuring cup, combine the vinegar, soy sauce, lime juice, oil and honey. Pour 1-1/4 cups into a large resealable plastic bag; add steak. Seal bag and turn to coat. Refrigerate for 1-2 hours. In a large bowl, combine the lettuce, sliced green onions and remaining marinade. Cover and refrigerate.

In a small skillet, bring water to a boil. Add onion tops; boil for 30-60 seconds. Drain and immediately place in ice water. Drain and pat dry; set aside.

Drain and discard marinade from steak. Grill, uncovered, over medium heat, or broil 4-6 in. from the heat for 7-10 minutes on each side or until meat reaches desired doneness (for medium-rare, a thermometer should read 145°; medium, 160°; well-done, 170°).

CHICKEN AND PINEAPPLE SALAD

RYMA SHOHAMI ✦ MONTREAL, QUEBEC

I serve this entree salad in hollowed-out pineapple halves as a pretty company dish. Tender chicken tossed with fruit, nuts and veggies is delicious with a mild curry dressing.

1 fresh pineapple
4 cups sliced cooked chicken breast
1 medium onion, chopped
1 celery rib, chopped
1/3 cup golden raisins
1/3 cup slivered almonds, toasted
2/3 cup mayonnaise
1/4 cup unsweetened pineapple juice
1 tablespoon Dijon mustard
3/4 teaspoon curry powder
1/4 teaspoon salt
Leaf lettuce, optional

PINEAPPLE SERVING BOWL

Stand a medium fresh pineapple upright and cut in half lengthwise, leaving the top attached. Cut the pineapple from inside each half, leaving a 1-in. shell. Use pineapple pieces as directed and/or save the remaining for later.

Cut pineapple in half; remove fruit, leaving 1-in. shells. Set shells aside for serving; cut fruit into cubes.

In a large bowl, combine the chicken, onion, celery, raisins, almonds and 1 cup cubed pineapple (refrigerate remaining pineapple for another use).

In a small bowl, whisk the mayonnaise, pineapple juice, mustard, curry and salt; add to chicken salad and toss to coat. Refrigerate until chilled.

Line pineapple shells with lettuce if desired; fill with chicken salad. YIELD: 7 servings.

CREAMY CLOUD NINE SALAD

JANICE HENSLEY ✦ OWINGSVILLE, KENTUCKY

Everyone will love this traditional "fluff" salad, chock-full of pineapple, marshmallows and bits of maraschino cherries.

1 package (8 ounces) cream cheese, softened
1 can (14 ounces) sweetened condensed milk
1/4 cup lemon juice
2 cans (20 ounces *each*) pineapple tidbits, drained
1-1/2 cups multicolored miniature marshmallows, *divided*
1 carton (8 ounces) frozen whipped topping, thawed
1/2 cup chopped nuts
1/3 cup maraschino cherries, chopped

In a large bowl, beat cream cheese, milk and juice until smooth. Add pineapple and 1 cup marshmallows; fold in whipped topping. Top with nuts, cherries and remaining marshmallows. Refrigerate leftovers. YIELD: 16 servings (1/2 cup each).

BEET SALAD WITH ORANGE-WALNUT DRESSING

MARIAN PLATT ✧ SEQUIM, WASHINGTON

Light and refreshing, this salad goes nicely with the heavier dishes of the autumn season. Your family and friends will also appreciate the tasty homemade dressing. It'll add festive color to any feast!

1 pound fresh beets
6 cups torn Bibb or Boston lettuce
3 medium navel oranges, peeled and sectioned
2 cups torn curly endive
2 cups watercress
2/3 cup chopped walnuts, toasted

DRESSING
1/2 cup canola oil
1/3 cup orange juice
3 tablespoons white wine vinegar
1 green onion, finely chopped
1 tablespoon lemon juice
1 tablespoon Dijon mustard
1/2 teaspoon salt
1/8 teaspoon white pepper

Place beets in a 13-in. x 9-in. baking dish; add 1 in. of water. Cover and bake at 400° for 40-45 minutes or until tender. Cool; peel and julienne.

In a serving bowl, combine the lettuce, oranges, endive and watercress. Add beets and walnuts.

In a small bowl, whisk the oil, orange juice, vinegar, green onion, lemon juice, Dijon mustard, salt and pepper. Drizzle over the salad; toss gently to coat. YIELD: 12 servings (about 1 cup dressing).

CAULIFLOWER AND HAM CHOWDER

PATTY WOYTASSEK ❖ HAVANA, NORTH DAKOTA

For great, quick meals during those cool fall and winter days, try this easy soup. The cauliflower and ham complement each other well, and you will always want a second helping.

- 2 cups chopped fresh or frozen cauliflower
- 1 cup thinly sliced celery
- 1 can (14-1/2 ounces) chicken broth
- 1 can (10-3/4 ounces) condensed cream of potato soup, undiluted
- 1 cup half-and-half cream or evaporated milk
- 1/8 teaspoon white pepper
- 2 tablespoons cornstarch
- 1/4 cup water
- 2 cups diced fully cooked ham
- 1/2 cup shredded cheddar cheese
- Minced fresh parsley

In a large saucepan, cook cauliflower and celery in broth for 4-5 minutes or until vegetables are crisp-tender. Do not drain. Stir in the soup, cream and pepper.

Combine the cornstarch and water until smooth; gradually stir into the cauliflower mixture. Bring to a boil; cook and stir for 2 minutes or until thickened. Reduce the heat. Add the ham; cook and stir for 2 minutes or until heated through. Just before serving, stir in the cheese. Garnish with minced parsley. YIELD: 6-8 servings.

SPINACH-ONION SALAD WITH HOT BACON DRESSING

LEIGH GALLAGHER ❖ ASOTIN, WASHINGTON

I knew this spinach salad was something special when my picky husband asked for seconds! The sweet-tart bacon dressing with a hint of honey is a real treat.

- 4 bacon strips, chopped
- 1 medium red onion, chopped, *divided*
- 1/4 cup balsamic vinegar
- 5 teaspoons honey
- 1/4 teaspoon salt
- 1/8 teaspoon pepper
- 1/4 cup canola oil
- 1 package (6 ounces) fresh baby spinach
- 1/2 cup crumbled feta cheese

In a large skillet, cook bacon and half of the onion over medium heat until bacon is crisp. Stir in the vinegar, honey, salt and pepper; heat through. Transfer to a small bowl; gradually whisk in the oil.

Place spinach in a large bowl. Drizzle warm dressing over spinach and toss to coat. Sprinkle with cheese and remaining onion. YIELD: 6 servings.

CHICKEN SALAD SUPREME

ELEANOR GROFVERT ❖ KALAMAZOO, MICHIGAN

Now that my husband and I are retired, we live in Florida for most of the winter. I often prepare this creamy, fruity chicken salad for a wonderful warm-weather lunch.

- 5 cups cubed cooked chicken
- 2 tablespoons canola oil
- 2 tablespoons orange juice
- 2 tablespoons vinegar
- 1 teaspoon salt
- 3 cups cooked rice
- 1-1/2 cups mayonnaise
- 1-1/2 cups sliced celery
- 1-1/2 cups small seedless green grapes
- 1 can (20 ounces) pineapple chunks, drained
- 1 can (11 ounces) mandarin oranges, drained
- 1 cup slivered almonds, toasted

In a large bowl, combine the chicken, oil, orange juice, vinegar and salt. Fold in the rice, mayonnaise, celery, grapes, pineapple and oranges. Cover and chill until ready to serve; stir in almonds. YIELD: 12 servings.

BEEF 'N' CHEESE BRAID

SHARON EULISS ❖ MCLEANSVILLE, NORTH CAROLINA

I love to experiment with foods and baking, and I thought that by putting beef and cheese in the middle of a baked loaf it would taste like a sub sandwich—and it does! It may sound complicated, but it's actually easy to make.

      1 package (1/4 ounce) active dry yeast
  3/4 cup warm water (110° to 115°)
  1/4 cup butter, *divided*
2-3/4 to 3 cups all-purpose flour
      1 tablespoon sugar
  1/2 teaspoon salt
      1 egg
  1/2 cup shredded dried beef
  1/2 cup shredded Swiss cheese
1-1/2 teaspoons dried basil

In a large bowl, dissolve yeast in water. Soften 2 tablespoons butter; add to yeast mixture with 1-1/2 cups flour, sugar, salt and egg; beat until smooth. Add enough remaining flour to make a soft dough.

Turn out onto a floured surface; knead until smooth and elastic, about 6-8 minutes. Place in a greased bowl, turning once to grease top. Cover and let rise in a warm place until doubled, about 1 hour.

In a small bowl, combine the beef, cheese and basil; set aside. Punch dough down. Roll into a 12-in. x 9-in. rectangle. Cut dough lengthwise into three 12-in. x 3-in. strips. Melt remaining butter; brush some over strips.

Divide the beef mixture in thirds and sprinkle down the center of each strip. Bring the long sides together and pinch to seal,

forming a rope. Place the ropes on a greased baking sheet, seam side down. Secure one end and braid the ropes together; secure other end. Cover and let rise in a warm place until doubled, about 30 minutes.

Brush loaf with the remaining melted butter. Bake at 375° for 25 minutes or until golden brown. Slice and serve warm. YIELD: 1 loaf.

BACON BREAKFAST SANDWICHES

ROSE CAROL BROWN ❖ PARK FOREST, ILLINOIS

This recipe is a standby when I need to make dinner in a snap. Our five children eat these sandwiches eagerly without complaint and agree they're better than any fast-food variety.

      1 tablespoon butter
      4 eggs
      2 tablespoons minced chives
      1 tablespoon water
  1/4 teaspoon salt
Dash pepper
      2 English muffins, split and toasted
      8 bacon strips, cooked and drained
      4 slices tomato
      4 slices American cheese
Additional minced chives, optional

In a large nonstick skillet, melt butter. Beat the eggs, chives, water, salt and pepper; pour into skillet. Cook and stir gently until eggs are set.

Top each muffin half with eggs, bacon, tomato and cheese. Place on a baking sheet. Broil 2-3 in. from the heat for 1-2 minutes or until cheese is melted. Garnish with chives if desired. YIELD: 2 servings.

An Apple a Day

There's something about the sweet-tart flavor and irresistible crunch of apples that instantly adds "yum!" to any salad. If you're a fan of apples, then you'll love these recipes!

PICNIC SWEET POTATO SALAD

MARY MARLOWE LEVERETTE ❖ COLUMBIA, SOUTH CAROLINA

A homemade vinaigrette coats this colorful salad that is full of sweet potato cubes. It's ideal for warm-weather picnics and patio parties, but my family loves it all year long!

    4 medium sweet potatoes, peeled and cubed
    3 medium apples, chopped
    6 bacon strips, cooked and crumbled
1/4 cup chopped onion
    3 tablespoons minced fresh parsley
1/2 teaspoon salt
1/4 teaspoon pepper
2/3 cup canola oil
    2 tablespoons red wine vinegar

Place sweet potatoes in a Dutch oven and cover with water. Bring to a boil. Reduce heat; cover and cook for 10-15 minutes or just until tender. Drain.

Transfer to a large bowl; cool to room temperature. Add the apples, bacon, onion, parsley, salt and pepper to the potatoes. In a small bowl, whisk oil and vinegar. Pour over salad; toss gently to coat. Chill until serving. YIELD: 13 servings (3/4 cup each).

APPLE CAMEMBERT SALAD

TRISHA KRUSE ❖ EAGLE, IDAHO

I like to serve this refreshing main-dish salad with thinly sliced pork roast or diced chicken breast.

    3 cups torn Boston lettuce
1/2 cup chopped apple
    2 ounces Camembert cheese, cubed
    2 tablespoons dried cherries
    2 tablespoons glazed pecans

DRESSING
    2 tablespoons mayonnaise
    1 tablespoon white wine vinegar
    1 tablespoon canola oil
    1 tablespoon maple syrup
Dash *each* sugar, salt and pepper

In a large bowl, combine the first five ingredients. In a small bowl, whisk the dressing ingredients. Pour over salad and toss to coat. YIELD: 4 servings.

 ## TURKEY WALDORF SALAD

TRISHA KRUSE ❖ EAGLE, IDAHO

A perfect combination of refreshing and filling, this scrumptious salad is ideal for days when you don't want to heat up the kitchen. Serve it stuffed in pita bread for a yummy lunch with lots of crunch!

- 1/4 cup sour cream
- 1/4 cup mayonnaise
- 1 tablespoon rice vinegar
- 2 teaspoons brown sugar
- 1 teaspoon soy sauce
- 1/4 teaspoon salt
- 1/4 teaspoon lemon-pepper seasoning
- 2 cups cubed cooked turkey breast
- 2 celery ribs, thinly sliced
- 1/4 cup dried cranberries
- 1 large apple, diced
- 2/3 cup chopped walnuts, toasted
- 4 Bibb lettuce leaves

In a small bowl, whisk together the first seven ingredients.

In a large bowl, combine the turkey, celery and cranberries. Pour dressing over mixture; toss to coat. Cover and refrigerate for at least 1 hour.

Just before serving, stir in apple and walnuts. Serve on lettuce leaves. YIELD: 4 servings.

APPLE AND GORGONZOLA SALAD

PAT FERJANCSIK ❖ SANTA ROSA, CALIFORNIA

This dressing is from my grandma, but I add Gorgonzola. One day, I marinated the apples in the dressing for a few hours, and it tasted so good, I do it every time now.

- 1/2 cup heavy whipping cream
- 1/4 cup red wine vinegar
- 1/4 teaspoon salt
- 1/4 teaspoon pepper
- 1 medium red apple, thinly sliced
- 1/2 cup crumbled Gorgonzola cheese
- 2 cups torn curly endive

In a small bowl, whisk the cream, vinegar, salt and pepper. Stir in the apple and cheese. Cover and refrigerate for at least 1 hour.

Divide endive between two plates; top with apple mixture. YIELD: 2 servings.

NUTRITIOUS APPLES

Apples are rich in vitamins A, B1, B2 and C. They also contain minerals, such as calcium, phosphorous, magnesium and potassium.

SPICED ORANGE GELATIN SALAD

JENNIFER KAUFFMAN FIGUEROA
GREENVILLE, SOUTH CAROLINA

This lovely molded salad looks and tastes festive. Its orange and cinnamon flavor combination will make it a popular side dish for most any entree.

    2 packages (3 ounces *each*) orange gelatin, *divided*
1-3/4 cups boiling water, *divided*
    3/4 cup cold water
    1 cup sweetened applesauce
    1 cup (8 ounces) sour cream
    1/4 teaspoon ground cinnamon
Lettuce leaves and sliced apples, optional

In a large bowl, dissolve one package of gelatin in 1 cup boiling water. Stir in cold water. Pour into a 6-cup ring mold coated with cooking spray. Refrigerate until set but not firm, about 1 hour.

Meanwhile, in a large bowl, dissolve remaining package of gelatin in remaining boiling water. Stir in the applesauce, sour cream and cinnamon. Refrigerate for 1 hour or until thickened. Gently spread over gelatin in mold. Refrigerate until firm.

Line a serving plate with lettuce leaves if desired; unmold gelatin onto plate. Garnish with apples and additional lettuce if desired. YIELD: 8 servings.

WINNING CREAM OF LEEK SOUP

YVONNE CRIMBRING ❖ CANTON, PENNSYLVANIA

I got this recipe from an old family friend, who gave me my first batch of leeks, too! This soup quickly became our family favorite.

    1 pound medium leeks (white portion only)
    1 cup butter, cubed
    1 cup all-purpose flour
    1 quart chicken stock *or* 4 bouillon cubes dissolved in 1 quart hot water
    1 quart half-and-half cream
1/2 teaspoon salt *or* to taste
1/4 teaspoon pepper
    1 cup cooked potato, diced
    1 cup diced fully cooked ham

Clean the leeks carefully, rinsing the layers well to remove any soil. Cut into 1/2-in. pieces. Steam in a covered container with 1/2 cup water until tender (you can do this in a microwave). Do not drain. Set aside.

Melt butter in a large saucepan; add flour, stirring constantly until smooth. Cook 2-4 minutes over low heat, stirring constantly until flour is thoroughly cooked. Gradually add chicken stock, stirring with wire whisk; bring to boil. Turn heat to low; add cream, seasonings, leeks, potato and ham. Do not boil. YIELD: about 4 quarts.

HAM 'N' CHEESE MELTS

MYRA INNES ❖ AUBURN, KANSAS

These one-of-a-kind sandwiches are a new twist on traditional ham and cheese sandwiches. The crunchy coating tastes great, but is easy to do. Prepared spaghetti sauce provides a delicious dipping sauce.

8 slices Italian bread (1/2 inch thick)
4 slices provolone cheese, halved
4 slices (1 ounce *each*) fully cooked ham
2 eggs
2 tablespoons milk
1/4 cup fine dry bread crumbs
1/4 cup grated Parmesan cheese
1/4 cup butter
1 cup spaghetti sauce, warmed

On four slices of Italian bread, layer with half the amount of provolone cheese, sliced ham, then remaining cheese slices. Top with remaining bread.

In a shallow dish, beat together the eggs and milk. In another shallow dish, combine the dry bread crumbs and the Parmesan cheese. Dip the sandwiches into the egg mixture, then into the crumb mixture.

In a large skillet over low heat, first melt the butter, then cook the assembled sandwiches in the butter for 4 minutes on each side or until golden brown. Serve with the spaghetti sauce for dipping. YIELD: 4 servings.

WATERCRESS & ORANGE SALAD

ALPHA WILSON ❖ ROSWELL, NEW MEXICO

Keep this recipe handy when you need to make a special salad quickly. The flavorful vinaigrette adds a refreshing touch to the greens and oranges. And watercress, with its peppery zing, is unique.

3 bunches watercress, trimmed (about 10 cups)
4 medium oranges, peeled and sectioned
1/4 cup olive oil
3 tablespoons orange juice
2 teaspoons grated orange peel
1/2 teaspoon lemon juice
1/4 teaspoon sugar
1/8 teaspoon salt
Dash pepper

In a large bowl, combine watercress and oranges. In a small bowl, whisk the remaining ingredients. Drizzle over salad; toss to coat. YIELD: 12 servings.

Meanwhile, tap clams; discard any that do not close. Place in a large saucepan; cover with water. Bring to a boil. Reduce heat; cover and simmer for 5-6 minutes or until clams open. Drain. Remove meat from clams; chop and set aside.

In a Dutch oven, cook bacon over medium heat until crisp. Add the butter, onion, celery and shallot; cook until vegetables are tender. Add garlic; cook 1 minute longer. Stir in flour until blended; cook and stir for 10 minutes or until browned (do not burn). Gradually add water and clam juice. Bring to a boil; cook and stir for 2 minutes or until thickened.

Remove corn from cobs. Stir the corn, potatoes, clam stock, parsley, bay leaf, salt, pepper and thyme into soup. Bring to a boil. Reduce heat; simmer, uncovered, for 30 minutes.

Add the scallops, shrimp and clams; cook 3-4 minutes longer or until shrimp turn pink and scallops are opaque. Stir in cream; heat through. Discard bay leaf. YIELD: 8 servings (2 quarts).

HEARTY OXTAIL SOUP

MARGIE GERNDT ✣ GILLETT, WISCONSIN

I created this recipe on the spur of the moment for a friend who was coming to visit. I knew she enjoyed soup, so I decided to liven up my usual vegetable soup by adding oxtails. Little did I know, oxtails were her favorite and she hadn't had them for years! She was so pleased when I sent the leftovers home with her!

    2 pounds oxtails *or* meaty beef shanks
1-1/2 cup sliced carrots
    1 cup chopped onion
    1 cup chopped celery
    1 cup sliced leeks
  1/2 green pepper, chopped
    3 tablespoons butter
    1 can (28 ounces) crushed tomatoes

NORTHWEST SEAFOOD CORN CHOWDER

BARBARA SIDWAY ✣ BAKER CITY, OREGON

This chowder showcases the best of Northwest seafood; it's all in here, from bay scallops to snapper.

    2 large ears sweet corn in husks
   14 fresh cherrystone clams
    6 bacon strips, chopped
  1/3 cup butter, cubed
    2 large onions, chopped
    1 celery rib, chopped
    1 tablespoon chopped shallot
    2 garlic cloves, minced
  1/2 cup all-purpose flour
    2 cups water
    1 bottle (8 ounces) clam juice
  3/4 pound potatoes, cubed
  1/4 cup clam stock
    2 tablespoons minced fresh parsley
    1 bay leaf
  1/2 teaspoon salt
  1/2 teaspoon white pepper
  1/4 teaspoon dried thyme
  1/2 pound bay scallops
  1/2 pound uncooked small shrimp, peeled and deveined
1-1/2 cups heavy whipping cream

Carefully peel back husks from corn to within 1 in. of bottom; remove silk. Rewrap corn in husks. Place on a baking sheet. Bake at 375° for 30-35 minutes or until tender.

4 beef bouillon cubes
2 teaspoons onion powder
1-1/2 teaspoons garlic powder
1 teaspoon pepper
Salt to taste
6 quarts water
1 cup medium pearl barley
Chopped fresh parsley

In a stockpot, saute the oxtails, carrots, onion, celery, leeks and green pepper in butter until vegetables are crisp-tender. Add the tomatoes, bouillon, onion and garlic powder, pepper, salt and water. Bring to a boil. Skim off any foam. Reduce heat; cover and simmer for 2-3 hours or until the meat is tender.

Stir in barley; cover and continue to simmer until tender, about 1 hour. Add additional water if necessary.

Remove bones; set aside until cool enough to handle. Remove meat from bones; discard bones and cut meat into cubes. Return meat to soup. Garnish with parsley. YIELD: 20-24 servings.

BACON BROCCOLI SALAD

ALAN ALSPAUGH ❖ MELBOURNE, FLORIDA

Here in the hot Florida sun, we appreciate refreshing no-fuss salads like this. It's a popular side dish at church potlucks and picnics.

10 bacon strips, cooked and crumbled
1 cup fresh broccoli florets
1/2 cup raisins
1/2 cup sunflower kernels
1/2 cup mayonnaise
1/4 cup sugar
2 tablespoons vinegar

In a large bowl, combine the bacon, broccoli, raisins and sunflower kernels; set aside.

In a small bowl, whisk the mayonnaise, sugar and vinegar; pour over broccoli mixture and toss to coat. Cover and chill for 1 hour. Stir before serving. YIELD: 4 servings.

 # GRILLED TURKEY PITAS

PENELOPE MALCOLM ❖ AMERICUS, GEORGIA

Move over, hamburgers! My Greek-style turkey sandwich filling is hearty enough to make a meal in a pita pocket. The yogurt adds creaminess and substance.

1 cup fat-free plain Greek yogurt
2 tablespoons olive oil
1 tablespoon lemon juice
1 tablespoon honey
2 garlic cloves, minced
1 teaspoon minced fresh oregano *or* 1/4 teaspoon dried oregano

1/4 teaspoon salt
1/8 teaspoon pepper
1 package (20 ounces) turkey breast tenderloins
3 medium tomatoes, seeded and chopped
1 small cucumber, chopped
1 small red onion, chopped
1 small green pepper, chopped
1/2 cup crumbled feta cheese
1/3 cup Greek olives, chopped
8 pita pocket halves

In a small bowl, combine the first eight ingredients. Pour 1/4 cup yogurt mixture into a large resealable plastic bag; add turkey. Seal bag and turn to coat; refrigerate turkey for 8 hours or overnight. Cover and refrigerate remaining yogurt mixture.

Drain and discard the yogurt marinade. Using long-handled tongs, moisten a paper towel with cooking oil and lightly coat the grill rack.

Grill, covered, over medium heat or broil 4 in. from the heat for 15-20 minutes or until a thermometer reads 170°, turning occasionally. Let stand for 5 minutes before slicing.

To remaining yogurt mixture, add the tomatoes, cucumber, onion, green pepper, cheese and olives.

Grill pita halves, uncovered, over medium heat for 1-2 minutes on each side or until warm. Fill each pita half with sliced turkey and 1/3 cup yogurt mixture. YIELD: 4 servings.

EDITOR'S NOTE: If Greek yogurt is not available in your area, line a strainer with a coffee filter and place over a bowl. Place 2 cups fat-free yogurt in prepared strainer; refrigerate overnight. Discard liquid from bowl; proceed as directed.

TABBOULEH SALAD

DEIRDRE DEE COX ❖ MILWAUKEE, WISCONSIN

The highlight of our neighborhood potluck has long been my mother-in-law's tabbouleh. It satisfies the healthiest appetites with filling bulgur wheat, parsley, mint and tomatoes brightened up with olive oil and lemon juice.

    1 cup bulgur
    2 cups boiling water
    4 medium tomatoes, chopped
    2 medium cucumbers, peeled and sliced
    1 cup minced fresh parsley
    1 cup minced fresh mint
    4 green onions, finely chopped
  1/3 cup lemon juice
  1/3 cup olive oil
    1 tablespoon chopped seeded jalapeno pepper
    2 garlic cloves, minced
  1/2 teaspoon salt
  1/2 teaspoon ground allspice
  1/4 teaspoon pepper
Bibb *or* Boston lettuce leaves

Place bulgur in a small bowl; stir in boiling water. Cover and let stand for 30 minutes or until most of the liquid is absorbed; drain well.

Place in a large bowl. Add the tomatoes, cucumbers, parsley, mint and onions. In a small bowl, whisk the lemon juice, oil, jalapeno, garlic, salt, allspice and pepper. Pour over bulgur mixture and toss to coat.

Cover and refrigerate for at least 2 hours. Serve over lettuce leaves. YIELD: 10 servings.

EDITOR'S NOTE: Wear disposable gloves when cutting hot peppers; the oils can burn skin. Avoid touching your face.

RADISH & GARBANZO BEAN SALAD

GRACE STRUTHERS ❖ CALGARY, ALBERTA

This recipe came about when we had a surprise visit from relatives. I didn't have time to get to the grocery story so I worked with what I had on hand—a can of chickpeas and produce from my garden.

    1 can (15 ounces) garbanzo beans *or* chickpeas, rinsed and
      drained
    6 radishes, halved and thinly sliced
  1/4 cup chopped red onion
    2 tablespoons minced fresh parsley
  1/4 cup prepared Italian salad dressing

In a small bowl, combine the beans, radishes, onion and parsley. Drizzle with dressing; toss to coat. Cover and refrigerate for at least 1 hour before serving. YIELD: 3 servings.

BULGUR BITS

Bulgur is a quick-cooking form of whole wheat that is ready to eat with minimal cooking. It has a nutlike flavor and is high in fiber. Look for bulgur in the cereal, rice or organic food aisle of your grocery store.

COLORADO LAMB CHILI

KAREN GORMAN ❖ GUNNISON, COLORADO

This hearty stew is made delicious with ingredients such as
fresh garlic, chili powder, Worcestershire and cumin. It
also tastes great with fresh rolls and a crisp green salad.

    1 pound lamb stew meat, cut into 1-inch pieces
    2 tablespoons canola oil, *divided*
    1 large onion, chopped
    1 large sweet yellow pepper, chopped
    4 garlic cloves, minced
    1 can (30 ounces) black beans, rinsed and drained
    1 can (28 ounces) diced tomatoes, undrained
    1 can (14-1/2 ounces) reduced-sodium
      beef broth
    1 tablespoon dried oregano
    1 tablespoon chili powder
    1 tablespoon brown sugar
    2 teaspoons Worcestershire sauce
    1 teaspoon ground cumin
    1/2 teaspoon fennel seed, crushed
Sliced green onions, chopped tomatoes and corn chips, optional

In a Dutch oven, brown the lamb stew meat in 1 tablespoon oil.
Remove and set aside.

In the same pan, saute onion and pepper in remaining oil until
tender. Add garlic; cook 1 minute longer. Add the beans,
tomatoes, broth, oregano, chili powder, brown sugar,
Worcestershire sauce, cumin and fennel. Return lamb to the pan.
   Bring to a boil. Reduce heat; cover and simmer for 1-1/4 to
1-1/2 hours or until lamb is tender. Garnish each serving with
green onions, tomatoes and corn chips if desired. YIELD: 6
servings (2-1/4 quarts).

SIMPLE LIME GELATIN SALAD

CYNDI FYNAARDT ❖ OSKALOOSA, IOWA

Looking for a festive dish to light up the holiday spread?
This pretty pale-green gelatin salad is eye-catching and has
a delightful, tangy flavor.

    2 packages (3 ounces *each*) lime gelatin
    2 cups boiling water
    1 quart lime sherbet
    1 carton (8 ounces) frozen whipped topping, thawed

In a large bowl, dissolve gelatin in boiling water. Beat in sherbet
until melted. Add whipped topping; beat well.
   Pour into an 8-cup ring mold coated with cooking spray.
Refrigerate for 4 hours or until set. Unmold onto a serving
platter. YIELD: 10 servings.

MAIN DISHES

Three words describe the recipes in this chapter: simple, hearty and wholesome. From bubbling casseroles to succulent roasts, these family-pleasing main courses are full of down-home goodness.

PORK TENDERLOIN NECTARINE SALAD

ROBYN LIMBERG-CHILD ❖ ST. CLAIR, MICHIGAN

A bag of fresh nectarines shared by my neighbor inspired this grilled pork recipe. The salad is delicious served with corn bread as a quick lunch or light, summer supper.

    1/4 cup balsamic vinegar
    1/4 cup maple syrup
      2 tablespoons olive oil
      1 pound pork tenderloin, cut into 1/4-inch slices

SALADS
      6 cups spring mix salad greens
      4 medium nectarines, sliced
      4 ounces Havarti cheese, cubed
    1/2 cup sliced sweet onion
    1/4 cup honey-roasted almonds
      1 cup honey mustard salad dressing

In a large resealable plastic bag, combine the vinegar, syrup and oil. Add the pork; seal bag and turn to coat. Refrigerate for 8 hours or overnight.

Drain and discard marinade. Using long-handled tongs, moisten a paper towel with cooking oil and lightly coat the grill rack. Grill pork, covered, over medium heat or broil 4 in. from the heat for 2-3 minutes on each side or until tender.

Divide the salad greens among six plates; top with pork, nectarines, cheese, onion and almonds. Drizzle with dressing. YIELD: 6 servings.

GREEN CHILI BEEF BURRITOS

JENNY FLAKE ❖ NEWPORT BEACH, CALIFORNIA

This recipe gets rave reviews every time I make it. The shredded beef has a luscious, slow-cooked flavor that you can't get anywhere else.

      1 boneless beef chuck roast (3 pounds)
      1 can (14-1/2 ounces) beef broth
      2 cups green enchilada sauce
      1 can (4 ounces) chopped green chilies
    1/2 cup Mexican-style hot tomato sauce
    1/2 teaspoon salt
    1/2 teaspoon garlic powder
    1/2 teaspoon pepper
     12 flour tortillas (12 inches)
Optional toppings: shredded lettuce, chopped tomatoes, shredded cheddar cheese and sour cream

Cut roast in half and place in a 3- or 4-qt. slow cooker. Add broth. Cover and cook on low for 8-9 hours or until meat is tender.

Remove beef. When cool enough to handle, shred meat with two forks. Skim fat from cooking liquid; reserve 1/2 cup cooking juices.

Return shredded beef and reserved liquid to the slow cooker. Stir in the enchilada sauce, green chilies, tomato sauce, salt, garlic powder and pepper.

Cover and cook on low for 1 hour or until heated through. Spoon beef mixture down the center of tortillas; add toppings of your choice. Roll up. YIELD: 12 servings.

EDITOR'S NOTE: This recipe was tested with El Pato brand Mexican-style hot tomato sauce. If you cannot find Mexican-style hot tomato sauce, you may substitute 1/2 cup tomato sauce, 1 teaspoon hot pepper sauce, 1/8 teaspoon onion powder and 1/8 teaspoon chili powder.

BEEF TIPS & CARAMELIZED ONION CASSEROLE

LINDA STEMEN ✤ MONROEVILLE, INDIANA

The robust flavor of beef sweetened by onions makes this a recipe you'll repeat. Fix a double batch, serving half tonight and freezing the rest. It's great with mashed potatoes.

4 pounds beef sirloin tip roast, cut into 1-inch cubes

1/2 teaspoon salt

1/2 teaspoon pepper

2 tablespoons olive oil

4 large sweet onions, halved and thinly sliced

3 tablespoons butter

4 garlic cloves, minced

2/3 cup all-purpose flour

2 cans (10-1/2 ounces *each*) condensed beef consomme, undiluted

1 can (14-1/2 ounces) reduced-sodium beef broth

2 tablespoons Worcestershire sauce

2 bay leaves

1/2 cup heavy whipping cream

8 slices French bread (1/2 inch thick), toasted

1 cup (4 ounces) shredded part-skim mozzarella cheese

Sprinkle beef with salt and pepper. In a large skillet, brown meat in oil in batches; drain. Transfer to a greased 13-in. x 9-in. baking dish.

In the same skillet, cook onions in butter over medium-low heat for 25-30 minutes or until golden brown, stirring occasionally. Add garlic; cook 1 minute longer.

Stir in flour until blended; gradually add consomme and broth. Stir in Worcestershire sauce and bay leaves. Bring to a boil; cook and stir for 1 minute or until thickened. Pour over beef.

Cover and bake at 325° for 1 hour. Carefully stir in cream; discard bay leaves. Bake, uncovered, 25-35 minutes longer or until meat is tender. Place toast over beef mixture; sprinkle with cheese. Bake for 5 minutes or until cheese is melted. YIELD: 8 servings.

CORNMEAL-CRUSTED WALLEYE

ALLEN PLUNGIS ❖ HARTLAND, MICHIGAN

These moist, tender fillets are a terrific option when you want a meal that's not too heavy. The corn and roasted pepper condiment goes perfectly with the walleye.

    2 large sweet red peppers
    4 large ears sweet corn, husks removed
    3 tablespoons canola oil, *divided*
    1/2 cup yellow cornmeal
1-3/4 teaspoons salt, *divided*
    1/2 teaspoon white pepper
Dash cayenne pepper
    4 walleye fillets (6 ounces *each*)
    1/2 pound sliced fresh mushrooms
    3 tablespoons butter

Broil the red peppers 4 in. from the heat until skins blister, about 15 minutes. With tongs, rotate peppers a quarter turn. Broil and rotate until all sides are blistered and blackened. Immediately place the peppers in a large bowl; cover and let them stand for 15-20 minutes.

Meanwhile, brush corn with 1 tablespoon oil. Transfer to an ungreased 13-in. x 9-in. baking dish. Cover and bake at 350° for 30-40 minutes or until tender. Peel off and discard charred skin from peppers. Remove stems and seeds. Finely chop peppers. Cut corn from cobs.

In a shallow bowl, combine the cornmeal, 1 teaspoon salt, pepper and cayenne. Coat walleye in cornmeal mixture.

In a large skillet, saute mushrooms in butter until tender. Add peppers, corn and remaining salt; saute 2-3 minutes longer.

In another large skillet, fry fillets in remaining oil for 2-3 minutes on each side or until fish flakes easily with a fork. Serve with corn salsa. YIELD: 4 servings (about 4 cups corn salsa).

HAM 'N' SWISS RING

BOBBIE LOPEZ ❖ BUCYRUS, OHIO

My family loves ham and cheese together, so I came up with this recipe. I like to serve this rich, creamy dish with rice and steamed broccoli.

    1 tube (8 ounces) refrigerated crescent rolls
    1 cup sliced fresh mushrooms
    2 tablespoons chopped onion
    1 tablespoon butter
    1 cup chopped fully cooked ham
    3/4 cup shredded Swiss cheese
    1/4 cup chopped fresh parsley
    1 tablespoon Dijon mustard
    1/2 teaspoon lemon juice

Arrange crescent rolls on a 13-in. round pizza pan, forming a ring with wide ends overlapping and pointed ends facing the outer edge of pan.

In a large skillet, saute mushrooms and onion in butter for 8 minutes or until juices are absorbed. Add remaining ingredients; stir well. Spoon over wide ends of rolls. Fold points of rolls over filling and tuck under wide ends at center (filling will be visible).

Bake at 350° for 20-25 minutes or until golden brown. YIELD: 4 servings.

BROCCOLI BEEF PIE

MARIE GIEGERICH ❖ DUBUQUE, IOWA

I received this recipe from my daughter-in-law. It makes a delicious dish for a potluck—everyone loves it!

2 cups chopped fresh broccoli
1 pound ground beef
1 can (4 ounces) mushroom stems and pieces, drained
2 cups (8 ounces) shredded cheddar cheese, *divided*
1/3 cup chopped onion
2 cups biscuit/baking mix
1/2 cup water
4 eggs
1/2 cup milk
1/4 cup grated Parmesan cheese
1/2 teaspoon salt
1/2 teaspoon pepper

In a small saucepan bring 1 in. of water to a boil. Add broccoli; cover and boil for 3-5 minutes or until crisp-tender; drain and set aside.

In a large skillet, cook beef over medium heat until no longer pink; drain. Stir in mushrooms, 1-1/2 cups cheddar cheese and onion. Remove from the heat and set aside.

Combine the biscuit mix and water to form a soft dough. Add remaining cheddar cheese; stir until blended. With well-floured hands, pat dough onto the bottom and 1 in. up the sides of a greased 13-in. x 9-in. baking dish.

Spoon meat mixture over dough; top with broccoli. Combine the eggs, milk, Parmesan cheese, salt and pepper; pour over broccoli. Bake, uncovered, at 350° for 35 minutes or until a knife inserted near the center comes out clean. YIELD: 8 servings.

EDITOR'S NOTE: To make a Spinach Beef Pie, substitute spinach for the broccoli and Swiss cheese for the cheddar cheese.

PORK TENDERLOIN WITH PEAR CREAM SAUCE

JOYCE MOYNIHAN ❖ LAKEVILLE, MINNESOTA

Pork's mild taste goes well with sweet flavors and many seasonings. Here, I've teamed it with both luscious pears and a refreshing herb blend.

1 pork tenderloin (1 pound)
1 tablespoon herbes de Provence
1/2 teaspoon salt
1/4 teaspoon pepper
4 tablespoons butter, *divided*
4 medium pears, peeled and sliced
1 tablespoon sugar
4 shallots, chopped
1-1/4 teaspoons dried thyme
1/4 cup pear brandy *or* pear nectar
1 cup heavy whipping cream
1/3 cup pear nectar

Sprinkle pork with the herbes de Provence, salt and pepper. In a large ovenproof skillet, brown pork in 1 tablespoon butter on all sides. Bake at 425° for 18-22 minutes or until a thermometer reads 145°. Remove pork from skillet and keep warm. Let meat stand for 5 minutes before slicing.

Meanwhile, in a large skillet, saute pears and sugar in 2 tablespoons butter until golden brown. Remove from pan and keep warm. In the same pan, melt remaining butter. Add shallots; saute until tender. Stir in thyme.

Remove from the heat. Add brandy; cook over medium heat until liquid is almost evaporated, stirring to loosen browned bits from pan. Add cream and nectar; cook and stir until slightly thickened. Slice pork; serve with pears and cream sauce. YIELD: 4 servings.

EDITOR'S NOTE: Look for herbes de Provence in the spice aisle.

SOUTHWESTERN POTPIE WITH CORNMEAL BISCUITS

ANDREA BOLDEN ❖ UNIONVILLE, TENNESSEE

My Southwestern-inspired potpie is full of sweet and spicy pork, corn, beans and chilies. It's a surefire winner for any gathering. The cornmeal gives the biscuits a little crunch.

> 1/4 cup all-purpose flour
> 1-1/2 pounds boneless pork loin roast, cut into 1/2-inch cubes
> 2 tablespoons butter
> 1 jalapeno pepper, seeded and chopped
> 2 garlic cloves, minced
> 2 cups beef broth
> 1 can (14-1/2 ounces) diced tomatoes, undrained
> 1 teaspoon ground cumin
> 1/2 teaspoon chili powder
> 1/4 to 1/2 teaspoon ground cinnamon
> 1 can (15-1/4 ounces) whole kernel corn, drained
> 1 can (15 ounces) pinto beans, rinsed and drained
> 1 can (4 ounces) chopped green chilies

BISCUITS
> 3 cups biscuit/baking mix
> 3/4 cup cornmeal
> 1/2 cup shredded cheddar cheese
> 4-1/2 teaspoons sugar
> 1 cup 2% milk

Place flour in a large resealable plastic bag. Add pork, a few pieces at a time, and shake to coat. In a Dutch oven, brown pork in butter in batches. Remove and set aside.

In the same pan, saute jalapeno and garlic in the drippings for 1 minute. Stir in the broth, tomatoes, cumin, chili powder, cinnamon and pork. Bring to a boil. Reduce heat; cover and simmer for 1 hour or until pork is tender.

Add the corn, beans and chilies; heat through. Transfer to a greased 13-in. x 9-in. baking dish.

In a large bowl, combine the biscuit mix, cornmeal, cheese and sugar; stir in milk just until moistened. Turn onto a lightly floured surface; knead 8-10 times.

Pat or roll out to 1/2-in. thickness; cut with a floured 2-1/2-in. biscuit cutter. Arrange over meat mixture. Bake at 400° for 15-18 minutes or until golden brown. Let stand for 10 minutes before serving. YIELD: 12 servings.

EDITOR'S NOTE: Wear disposable gloves when cutting hot peppers; the oils can burn skin. Avoid touching your face.

CHICKEN IN THE GARDEN

GERRY GRACKEN ❖ CLEARWATER, FLORIDA

Enjoy this comforting casserole with rice, noodles or biscuits. It's easy to prepare and mouthwatering, too. Your family will love it!

> 3 cups frozen chopped broccoli, thawed and drained
> 1 package (10 ounces) frozen mixed vegetables, thawed and drained
> 3 cups cubed cooked chicken *or* turkey
> 2 cans (10-3/4 ounces *each*) reduced-fat reduced-sodium condensed cream of mushroom soup, undiluted
> 1/2 cup 2% milk
> 1/2 cup mayonnaise
> 1/2 teaspoon curry powder
> 1 cup (4 ounces) shredded cheddar cheese

Hot cooked rice, noodles *or* biscuits

Place broccoli and mixed vegetables in a greased 2-qt. baking dish. Top with chicken. Combine the soup, milk, mayonnaise and curry; pour over top.

Bake, uncovered, at 350° for 35 minutes. Sprinkle with cheese. Bake 5-10 minutes longer or until cheese is melted. Serve with rice, noodles or biscuits. YIELD: 6 servings.

PORK CHOPS WITH MUSHROOM GRAVY

LOIS CHAMBERS ✤ RENO, NEVADA

These golden-brown pork chops are tender and moist after cooking in a savory gravy. It's an easy and elegant dish that will impress guests.

6 boneless pork loin chops (6 ounces *each*)
6 tablespoons butter, *divided*
1/2 pound sliced fresh mushrooms
2 tablespoons lemon juice
1 medium onion, chopped
1 small garlic clove, minced
1/4 cup all-purpose flour
1 teaspoon salt
1/4 teaspoon dried tarragon
1 can (10-1/2 ounces) condensed beef broth, undiluted
3/4 cup white wine *or* beef broth
1 teaspoon browning sauce, optional

In a large skillet, brown pork chops in 2 tablespoons butter for 2-3 minutes on each side. Remove and keep warm.

Toss mushrooms with lemon juice. In the same skillet, saute the mushrooms and onion in remaining butter until tender. Add garlic; cook 1 minute longer.

Stir the flour, salt and tarragon into the skillet until blended. Gradually stir in broth, wine and browning sauce if desired, scraping up any browned bits from the bottom of pan. Bring to a boil. Return the chops to skillet. Reduce heat; cover and simmer for 10-15 minutes or until a thermometer reads 145°. Let stand 5 minutes before serving. YIELD: 6 servings.

DEFINITION OF DEGLAZING

The Pork Chops with Mushroom Gravy recipe utilizes a technique called "deglazing." Water, broth or wine is added to a pan in which meat has been cooked, and the browned bits and drippings are scraped up to make a gravy.

Outstanding Entrees

For a memorable experience around the dinner table at your next celebration, try one of these impressive main dishes. It will be the succulent star of your festive feast.

🎀 GRILLED STUFFED SALMON

CATHIE BEARD ✤ PHILOMATH, OREGON

For years, my husband worked for the U.S. Fish and Wildlife Service—so I've prepared fish all kinds of different ways. This variation of stuffed salmon gets high marks from my family.

1 whole salmon (8 pounds)
2 teaspoons salt, *divided*
1-1/4 teaspoons pepper, *divided*
2 cups unseasoned stuffing cubes
1 cup shredded carrots
1 cup sliced mushrooms
1 large onion, finely chopped
1/2 cup minced fresh parsley
3/4 cup butter, melted, *divided*
1/4 cup egg substitute
4-1/2 teaspoons plus 1/4 cup lemon juice, *divided*
1 garlic clove, minced
2 tablespoons canola oil

Remove head and tail from salmon if desired. Sprinkle the cavity with 1 teaspoon each salt and pepper.

In a large bowl, combine the stuffing cubes, carrots, mushrooms, onion, parsley, 1/4 cup butter, egg substitute, 4-1/2 teaspoons

lemon juice, garlic and remaining salt and pepper; stuff cavity. Secure with metal skewers. Drizzle salmon with oil. Using long-handled tongs, moisten a paper towel with cooking oil and lightly coat the grill rack.

Prepare grill for indirect heat using a drip pan. Place salmon over drip pan and grill, covered, over indirect medium heat for 40-50 minutes or until fish flakes easily with a fork and a thermometer reads 165° for stuffing.

In a small bowl, combine remaining butter and lemon juice. Serve with salmon. YIELD: 12 servings.

HOLIDAY BAKED HAM

STACY DUFFY ✤ CHICAGO, ILLINOIS

Nothing is better at the holidays than a delicious ham baking in the oven. The preserves mixture will be sure to please all of your guests.

1 fully cooked smoked half ham (6 to 7 pounds)
1 tablespoon whole cloves
1/4 cup apricot preserves
1 tablespoon butter
2 teaspoons Dijon mustard

Place ham with fat side up in a shallow roasting pan. Score fat in a diamond pattern; insert cloves into cuts. Bake, uncovered, at 325° for 1 hour and 15 minutes.

In a small saucepan, combine the preserves, butter and mustard; heat through. Spoon over the ham. Bake, uncovered, 30 minutes longer or until a thermometer reads 140°. Remove cloves before slicing ham. YIELD: 8-10 servings.

Remove the roast to a serving platter; let stand for 10 minutes before slicing.

Skim the fat from pan drippings. Transfer the drippings and vegetables to a food processor; cover and process until smooth. Pour into a small saucepan. Add browning sauce if desired and remaining water; heat through. Slice roast; serve with gravy. YIELD: 16 servings.

ROAST LEG OF LAMB WITH ROSEMARY

SUZY HORVATH ❖ GLADSTONE, OREGON

Roast lamb is perfect for Eastertime or any special occasion. This succulent entree calls for a flavorful rosemary, garlic and onion rub.

      1/3 cup olive oil
      1/4 cup minced fresh rosemary
      1/4 cup finely chopped onion
        4 garlic cloves, minced
      1/2 teaspoon salt
      1/4 teaspoon pepper
        1 bone-in leg of lamb (5 to 6 pounds), trimmed

Combine the oil, rosemary, onion, garlic, salt and pepper; rub over lamb. Place fat side up on a rack in a shallow roasting pan.

Bake, uncovered, at 325° for 2 to 2-1/2 hours or until meat reaches desired doneness (for medium-rare, a thermometer should read 145°; medium, 160°; well-done, 170°), basting occasionally with pan juices. Let stand for 15 minutes before slicing. YIELD: 10-12 servings.

HOLIDAY PORK ROAST

MARY ANN DELL ❖ PHOENIXVILLE, PENNSYLVANIA

This special dish is perfect for Christmas or New Year's Eve. A mouthwatering ginger gravy and tender vegetables complement the moist herbed roast.

        1 boneless whole pork loin roast (5 pounds)
        1 tablespoon minced fresh gingerroot
        2 garlic cloves, minced
        1 teaspoon rubbed sage
      1/4 teaspoon salt
      1/3 cup apple jelly
      1/2 teaspoon hot pepper sauce
        2 medium carrots, sliced
        2 medium onions, sliced
  1-1/2 cups water, *divided*
        1 teaspoon browning sauce, optional

Place pork roast on a rack in a shallow roasting pan. Combine the ginger, garlic, sage and salt; rub over meat. Bake, uncovered, at 350° for 1 hour.

Combine jelly and pepper sauce; brush over roast. Arrange carrots and onions around roast. Pour 1/2 cup water into pan. Bake 40-50 minutes longer or until a thermometer reads 145°.

GARLIC-ROSEMARY CORNISH HEN

JANE ASHWORTH ❖ BEAVERCREEK, OHIO

I've served these hens for backyard cookouts as well as for formal dinner entrees. The garlic is mild and pleasant and, combined with rosemary and lemon, results in tender, moist meat.

1 Cornish game hen (20 to 24 ounces), split lengthwise
1/2 medium lemon, cut into wedges
2 fresh rosemary sprigs
1 tablespoon olive oil
1/4 teaspoon salt
1/8 teaspoon pepper
10 garlic cloves
2 tablespoons chicken broth
1/4 cup white wine or additional chicken broth

Place hens, breast side up, over lemon and rosemary in an ungreased 11-in. x 7-in. baking dish. Brush with oil and sprinkle with salt and pepper. Add garlic to pan. Bake, uncovered, at 450° for 20 minutes. Reduce heat to 350°.

WHAT IS A CORNISH GAME HEN?

Also known as a poussin, a Cornish game hen is a small broiler/fryer chicken that is less than 30 days old and weighs 1-1/2 to 2 pounds. Despite the name, it's a domestic chicken, not a game bird, and can be either male or female.

Pour broth and wine over hen and bake 10-15 minutes longer or until a thermometer reads 180°, basting twice with pan juices. Remove hen to serving plates and keep warm.

Transfer pan juices to a saucepan. Bring to a boil. Reduce heat; simmer, uncovered, for 5-7 minutes or until pan juices reach desired consistency. Strain juices and serve with hen. YIELD: 2 servings.

PRONTO PINWHEELS

EILEEN OWEN ❖ JOHNSTOWN, COLORADO

Serve this pretty dish with a crisp lettuce salad and top it off with fresh fruit or a lemony dessert, and you have a complete meal your family will love!

1-1/2 pounds lean ground beef (90% lean)
1/4 cup finely chopped onion
5 ounces condensed vegetable beef soup, undiluted
1/2 teaspoon chili powder
1 can (4 ounces) chopped green chilies, drained
1/2 cup quick-cooking oats
2 tubes (7-1/2 ounces each) refrigerated biscuits
16 thin tomato slices
1/2 cup sliced ripe olives
1 medium green pepper, chopped
1-1/2 cups (6 ounces) shredded cheddar cheese

In a large bowl, combine the first six ingredients; set aside. Roll biscuits into an 18-in. x 9-in. rectangle and top with meat mixture. Roll rectangle, jelly-roll style, starting from wide end. Seal seams. Cut into 1-in. slices.

Place slices in two greased 9-in. pie plates. Cover with foil and bake at 350° for 15 minutes. Uncover and bake 10 minutes longer. Remove from oven; top each pinwheel with a tomato slice, olives, green pepper and cheese. Return to oven for a few minutes or until cheese is melted. YIELD: 16 servings.

CHICKEN WITH CRANBERRY-BALSAMIC SAUCE

SUSAN CORTESI ❖ NORTHBROOK, ILLINOIS

Here's a quick and delicious way to make ordinary chicken breasts into elegant specialties. The fruity sauce also livens up roasted pork and turkey.

    4 boneless skinless chicken breast halves (6 ounces *each*)
1-1/4 teaspoons salt, *divided*
  1/2 teaspoon pepper
    1 tablespoon olive oil
    1 cup cranberry juice
  1/3 cup balsamic vinegar
  1/4 cup whole-berry cranberry sauce
    2 tablespoons finely chopped shallot
    3 tablespoons butter

Sprinkle chicken with 1 teaspoon salt and the pepper. In a large skillet, brown chicken in oil on both sides. Transfer to a greased 13-in. x 9-in. baking pan. Bake at 425° for 12-15 minutes or until a thermometer reads 170°.

Add the cranberry juice, vinegar, cranberry sauce and shallot to the skillet, stirring to loosen browned bits from pan. Bring to a boil; cook until liquid is reduced to about 1/2 cup. Stir in butter and remaining salt until butter is melted. Serve with chicken. YIELD: 4 servings.

CHICK-A-RONI

ROSEMARY ELAINE FENTON ❖ WEST SALEM, ILLINOIS

This dish is guaranteed to be a hit in your home! It has a wonderful cheesy flavor that everyone will love—including the kids.

    2 cups cubed cooked chicken
    2 cups cooked macaroni
    1 can (10-3/4 ounces) condensed cream of chicken soup, undiluted
    1 jar (4 ounces) diced pimientos, drained
    4 ounces process American cheese (Velveeta), cubed
    1 cup (4 ounces) shredded cheddar cheese
    1 package (3 ounces) cream cheese, cubed

In a large bowl, combine all ingredients. Transfer to a greased 3-qt. baking dish. Cover and bake at 350° for 20 minutes. Uncover; bake 20 minutes longer or until heated through. YIELD: 6-8 servings.

BAKED SPINACH SUPREME

BETTY CLAYCOMB ❖ ALVERTON, PENNSYLVANIA

This healthful recipe makes a lovely brunch bake or main dish for lunch. The cheese mix will convince anyone to eat their spinach, plus it adds extra protein.

  1 cup reduced-fat biscuit/baking mix
  2 egg whites
  1 egg
  1/4 cup fat-free milk
  1/4 cup finely chopped onion

FILLING
  1 package (10 ounces) frozen chopped spinach, thawed and squeezed dry
  1-1/2 cups fat-free cottage cheese
  3/4 cup shredded Monterey Jack cheese
  1/2 cup grated Parmesan cheese
  2 egg whites
  1 egg
  1 teaspoon dried minced onion

In a small bowl, combine the biscuit mix, egg whites, egg, milk and onion. Spread into a greased 11-in. x 7-in. baking dish.

In another bowl, combine the filling ingredients. Gently spoon over biscuit mixture.

Bake, uncovered, at 350° for 28-32 minutes or until golden brown and a knife inserted near the center comes out clean. YIELD: 6 servings.

BRAISED PORK WITH TOMATILLOS

MATTHEW LAWRENCE ❖ VASHON, WASHINGTON

A pork braise is a sure way to make people's mouths water. The tomatillos in this dish offer a subtle hint of openness and lightness to the meat. For ultimate flavor, make the dish one day ahead and reheat.

  1 tablespoon coriander seeds
  1 tablespoon cumin seeds
  1 bone-in pork shoulder roast (3 to 4 pounds)
  1/4 teaspoon salt
  1/4 teaspoon pepper
  1 tablespoon canola oil
  15 tomatillos, husks removed, and chopped
  1 medium onion, chopped
  2 garlic cloves, peeled and halved
  1 cup white wine
  8 cups chicken broth

POLENTA
  4 cups chicken broth
  1 cup yellow cornmeal

In a small dry skillet over medium heat, toast coriander and cumin seeds until aromatic, about 1-2 minutes. Remove from skillet. Crush seeds using a spice grinder or mortar and pestle; set aside.

Sprinkle pork with salt and pepper. In a Dutch oven, brown roast in oil on all sides. Remove and set aside. Add tomatillos and onion to the pan; saute until tomatillos are tender and lightly charred. Add the garlic and crushed spices; cook 1 minute longer.

Add wine, stirring to loosen browned bits from pan. Stir in broth and return roast to pan. Bring to a boil. Cover and bake at 350° for 3 to 3-1/2 hours or until pork is tender.

Meanwhile, in a large heavy saucepan, bring broth to a boil. Reduce heat to a gentle boil; slowly whisk in cornmeal. Cook and stir with a wooden spoon for 15-20 minutes or until polenta is thickened and pulls away cleanly from the sides of the pan. Serve with pork. YIELD: 6 servings.

CHICKEN CASSEROLE

RUTH VAN DYKE ❖ TRAVERSE CITY, MICHIGAN

The original family recipe for this casserole called for the sauce to be made from scratch. Through the years, I developed this version that takes less time to prepare and still tastes great. It's an attractive main dish.

1/2 cup chopped celery
1/4 cup chopped onion
2 tablespoons chopped green pepper
2 tablespoons butter
2 cups cubed cooked chicken
1 jar (4-1/2 ounces) sliced mushrooms, drained
6 pimiento-stuffed olives, sliced
1 can (10-3/4 ounces) condensed cream of chicken soup, undiluted
1 cup milk
5 cups cooked wide egg noodles

TOPPING
1/2 cup cornflake crumbs
1/4 cup shredded cheddar cheese
2 tablespoons butter, melted

In a large skillet, saute the celery, onion and green pepper in butter. Remove from the heat; stir in the chicken, mushrooms, olives, soup, milk and noodles.

Transfer to a 2-qt. baking dish. Cover and bake at 325° for 25 minutes. Meanwhile, combine topping ingredients. Sprinkle around edge of casserole; bake 5 minutes longer or until cheese is melted. YIELD: 4-6 servings.

MAC 'N' CHEESE WITH HAM

ANITA DURST ❖ MADISON, WISCONSIN

This hearty and comforting casserole features ingredients that everyone loves. It has a satisfying homemade aroma.

1 package (7 ounces) elbow macaroni
2 tablespoons butter
3 tablespoons all-purpose flour
1 teaspoon dried parsley flakes
3/4 teaspoon ground mustard
1/4 teaspoon pepper
2 cups 2% milk
1 package (16 ounces) process cheese (Velveeta), cubed
2 cups cubed fully cooked ham
1 package (10 ounces) frozen cut asparagus, thawed
1 jar (6 ounces) sliced mushrooms, drained
3 tablespoons dry bread crumbs

Cook macaroni according to package directions. Meanwhile, in a large saucepan, melt butter. Stir in the flour, parsley, mustard and pepper until blended. Gradually stir in milk. Bring to a boil; cook and stir for 2 minutes or until thickened. Stir in cheese until melted.

Drain macaroni; add to cheese sauce. Stir in the ham, asparagus and mushrooms. Transfer to a greased 2-1/2-qt. baking dish. Sprinkle with bread crumbs. Bake, uncovered, at 350° for 25-30 minutes or until bubbly. YIELD: 6 servings.

SWEET MUSTARD CHOPS

DEANN ALLEVA ❖ COLUMBUS, OHIO

These pork chops are perfect for company because they marinate overnight in a special barbecue sauce. Then just pop them on the grill when you're ready to eat. They're fast and flavorful.

1/2 cup mayonnaise
1/4 cup packed brown sugar
1/4 cup prepared mustard
2 teaspoons seasoned salt
1/3 cup red wine vinegar
4 bone-in pork loin chops (1 inch thick and 8 ounces *each*)

In a small bowl, combine the mayonnaise, brown sugar, mustard and seasoned salt. Whisk in vinegar. Pour into a large resealable plastic bag; add pork. Seal and refrigerate overnight.

Discard marinade. Grill, covered, over medium heat for 4-5 minutes on each side or until a thermometer reads 145°, turning occasionally. Let stand for 5 minutes. YIELD: 4 servings.

APPLE VENISON MEAT LOAF

LORRAINE MCCLAIN ❖ REPUBLICAN CITY, NEBRASKA

Venison is a nice change of pace from turkey for a holiday meal. This meat loaf doesn't taste gamey, and our guests enjoy it—especially the ones who stay with us during hunting season.

1 egg, lightly beaten
1/2 cup ketchup
1 tablespoon prepared horseradish
2 cups shredded peeled apples
2 cups unseasoned stuffing cubes
1/4 cup finely chopped onion
1 tablespoon ground mustard
2 pounds ground venison

In a large bowl, combine the first seven ingredients. Crumble venison over mixture and mix well. Pat into an ungreased 9-in. x 5-in. loaf pan.

Bake, uncovered, at 350° for 60-70 minutes or until no pink remains and a thermometer reads 160°. YIELD: 8 servings.

PRICELESS BBQ RIBS

EDGAR F. WRIGHT ❖ NEW ORLEANS, LOUISIANA

The tasty combination of seasonings and a mouthwatering barbecue sauce makes these ribs unforgettable.

16 cups water
2 racks pork baby back ribs (2-1/2 pounds *each*)
1/3 cup sugar
1/3 cup onion powder
1/3 cup seafood seasoning
2 tablespoons garlic powder
1 bay leaf

BARBECUE SAUCE
1 cup barbecue sauce
1/4 cup packed brown sugar
1 tablespoon honey
1 tablespoon Liquid Smoke, optional

In a stock pot, combine the first seven ingredients; bring to a boil. Reduce heat; cover and simmer for 1 hour or until tender.

Remove from the heat; let stand for 30 minutes. Drain and discard cooking liquid.

In a small bowl, combine the barbecue sauce ingredients. Brush half of sauce over ribs. Grill ribs, covered, over medium heat for 4-5 minutes or until heated through, basting with remaining barbecue sauce. YIELD: 5 servings.

BIG-BATCH MARINARA SAUCE

CYNDY GERKEN ❖ NAPLES, FLORIDA

I typically freeze part of this marinara sauce to have on hand for guests or when I'm craving a comforting pasta dish. It adds a fresh, herby layer of flavor.

  4 large onions, chopped
  2 tablespoons olive oil
10 garlic cloves, minced
  4 cans (28 ounces *each*) crushed tomatoes
  7 cans (15 ounces *each*) tomato sauce
  2 cans (6 ounces *each*) tomato paste
  1 cup grated Parmesan cheese
  1 cup minced fresh parsley
3/4 cup minced fresh basil *or* 1/4 cup dried basil
  2 tablespoons minced fresh oregano *or* 2 teaspoons dried oregano
  2 tablespoons herbes de Provence *or* Italian seasoning
Hot cooked spaghetti

In a stockpot, saute the onions in oil until tender. Add garlic; cook 2 minutes longer. Add the crushed tomatoes, tomato sauce, tomato paste, cheese and herbs. Bring to a boil. Reduce heat; simmer, uncovered, for 2-3 hours or until desired consistency, stirring occasionally.

Serve desired amount over spaghetti. Cool remaining sauce; transfer to freezer containers. Freeze for up to 3 months.
TO USE FROZEN SAUCE: Thaw in the refrigerator overnight. Place in a saucepan and heat through. YIELD: 6 quarts.
EDITOR'S NOTE: Look for herbes de Provence in the spice aisle.

HOMEMADE ITALIAN SEASONING

You can mix your own Italian seasoning. Try substituting 1/4 teaspoon each of basil, thyme, rosemary and oregano for each teaspoon of Italian seasoning called for in a recipe. You can blend just a few of these with good results.

PIZZA CASSEROLE

JUDY CHANDLER ❖ FRANKLIN, KENTUCKY

I discovered this hearty recipe in the reader's exchange page of our local electric cooperative's magazine.

1 pound ground beef
1 package (3-1/2 ounces) sliced pepperoni
1 medium onion, chopped
1 medium green pepper, chopped
1 jar (4-1/2 ounces) sliced mushrooms, drained
7 ounces vermicelli, cooked and drained
1/3 cup butter, melted
1 can (15 ounces) tomato sauce, *divided*
1 cup (4 ounces) shredded Swiss cheese
4 cups (16 ounces) shredded part-skim mozzarella cheese
1/2 teaspoon dried oregano
1/2 teaspoon dried basil

In a large skillet, cook the beef, pepperoni, onion and green pepper over medium heat until meat is no longer pink; drain. Stir in mushrooms; set aside.

Combine vermicelli and butter in a greased 13-in. x 9-in. baking dish; toss to coat. Pour 1 cup tomato sauce over pasta; top with half of meat mixture. Combine Swiss and mozzarella cheeses; sprinkle half over top. Sprinkle with oregano and basil. Layer with remaining meat and cheese mixtures. Pour remaining tomato sauce over top.

Bake, uncovered, at 350° for 25-30 minutes or until bubbly. YIELD: 8-10 servings.

CHICKEN ALFREDO STUFFED SHELLS

MICHELE SHEPPARD ❖ MASONTOWN, PENNSYLVANIA

Tender chicken, a rich sauce and pasta shells, filled with gooey cheese, make the dish oh-so satisfying.

1 package (12 ounces) jumbo pasta shells
1-1/2 pounds boneless skinless chicken breasts, cut into 1/2-inch cubes
2 tablespoons olive oil, *divided*
1/2 pound sliced baby portobello mushrooms
1 egg, beaten
1 carton (15 ounces) ricotta cheese
3-1/4 cups grated Parmesan cheese, *divided*
1 cup (4 ounces) shredded part-skim mozzarella cheese
1 teaspoon dried parsley flakes
3/4 teaspoon salt
1/2 teaspoon pepper
1/2 cup butter, cubed
2 garlic cloves, minced
2 cups heavy whipping cream

Cook pasta according to package directions. Meanwhile, in a large skillet, brown chicken in 1 tablespoon oil. Remove and set aside. In same pan, saute mushrooms in remaining oil until tender; set aside. Combine egg, ricotta, 1-1/2 cups Parmesan, mozzarella and seasonings.

Drain and rinse pasta with cold water; stuff each shell with about 1 tablespoon of cheese mixture. Place in a greased 13-in. x 9-in. baking dish. Top with chicken and mushrooms.

In a large saucepan over medium heat, melt butter. Add garlic; cook and stir for 1 minute. Add cream; cook 5 minutes longer. Add 1-1/2 cups Parmesan cheese; cook and stir until thickened.

Pour sauce over the casserole. Sprinkle with remaining Parmesan cheese. Cover and bake at 350° for 30 minutes. Uncover; bake 10-15 minutes longer or until bubbly. YIELD: 10 servings.

CURRIED BEEF

ANN MORGAN ❖ TALLAHASSEE, FLORIDA

Served with rice or noodles, this comforting beef dish hits the spot on a cool day.

    1 tablespoon all-purpose flour
    1 teaspoon salt
1/8 teaspoon pepper
    1 pound beef top round steak, cut into thin 3-inch strips
    3 tablespoons canola oil, *divided*
    2 cups sliced onions
    1 garlic clove, minced
    1 teaspoon curry powder
    1 teaspoon beef bouillon granules
    1 cup boiling water
1/2 cup tomato juice
    3 tablespoons tomato paste
Hot cooked noodles *or* rice

In a large resealable bag, combine the flour, salt and pepper; add beef. Seal bag and shake to coat. In a large skillet, brown beef in 2 tablespoons oil; drain.

Add the onions and remaining oil; saute until onions are golden brown. Add garlic; cook 1 minute longer. Sprinkle with curry. Dissolve bouillon in boiling water; pour over beef and onions. Bring to a boil. Reduce heat; cover and simmer for 1 hour or until meat is tender.

Add tomato juice and paste; cook for 5 minutes or until heated through. Serve with noodles or rice. YIELD: 4 servings.

HERBED CHICKEN

POLLY LLOYD ❖ BURLINGTON, WISCONSIN

My family and friends always comment on the wonderful herb flavors in my chicken recipe. The herbs make great seasoning for the vegetables, too! It's a great idea for busy cooks because it truly is a meal in one.

        1 broiler/fryer chicken (3-1/2 to 4 pounds)
    3/4 to 1 cup water
        1 tablespoon chicken bouillon granules
    3/4 teaspoon dried thyme
    1/2 teaspoon dried marjoram
    1/4 teaspoon lemon-pepper seasoning
        1 pound red potatoes, halved
        2 medium onions, cut into 1/2-inch pieces
1-1/2 to 2 cups fresh baby carrots

Place the chicken in a greased roasting pan. Combine the water, bouillon, thyme, marjoram, and lemon-pepper seasoning; pour over the chicken. Arrange the halved potatoes, onions and baby carrots around the chicken.

Cover and bake at 350° for 50 minutes. Uncover; bake for 20-30 minutes or until vegetables are tender and chicken juices run clear, basting once. Let chicken stand for 5-10 minutes before carving. YIELD: 4 servings.

OVERNIGHT CHICKEN CASSEROLE

JOHNIE MAE BARBER ❖ OKLAHOMA CITY, OKLAHOMA

I don't know where this casserole originated, but the recipe was given to me some 40 years ago. It's my family's all-time favorite. Not only is it a great "company" meal, it's also well-received at potluck dinners.

    8 slices day-old white bread
    4 cups chopped cooked chicken
    1 jar (4-1/2 ounces) sliced mushrooms, drained
    1 can (8 ounces) sliced water chestnuts, drained
    4 eggs, lightly beaten
    2 cups milk
  1/2 cup mayonnaise
  1/2 teaspoon salt
    6 to 8 slices process American cheese
    1 can (10-3/4 ounces) condensed cream of celery soup, undiluted
    1 can (10-3/4 ounces) condensed cream of mushroom soup, undiluted
    1 jar (2 ounces) chopped pimientos, drained
    2 tablespoons butter, melted

Remove the crusts from bread and set aside. Arrange bread slices in a greased 13-in. x 9-in. baking dish. Top with chicken; cover with the mushrooms and water chestnuts.

In a large bowl, whisk the eggs, milk, mayonnaise and salt. Pour over chicken. Arrange cheese on top. Combine soups and pimientos; pour over cheese. Cover and refrigerate overnight.

Remove from the refrigerator 30 minutes before baking. Crumble reserved crusts; toss with melted butter. Sprinkle over top. Bake, uncovered, at 325° for 1-1/4 hours or until a knife inserted near the center comes out clean. Let stand for 10 minutes before cutting. YIELD: 8-10 servings.

SMOKED SHRIMP & WILD MUSHROOM FETTUCCINE

BARBARA SIDWAY ❖ BAKER CITY, OREGON

We smoke these prawns in-house, but a grill works just as well. The broccoli and tomatoes add color to the flavorful prawns and mushrooms.

      2 cups soaked mesquite wood chips
     10 uncooked jumbo shrimp, peeled and deveined
      1 package (12 ounces) fettuccine
  1-1/2 cups fresh broccoli florets
      2 large portobello mushrooms, sliced
      2 tablespoons olive oil
      3 garlic cloves, minced
    1/4 teaspoon salt
    1/2 cup white wine or chicken broth
      2 cups heavy whipping cream
      1 medium tomato, chopped

Add wood chips to grill according to manufacturer's directions.

Using long-handled tongs, moisten a paper towel with cooking oil and lightly coat the grill rack. Thread shrimp onto two metal or soaked wooden skewers. Grill, covered, over medium heat for 5-8 minutes or until shrimp turn pink, turning once.

Meanwhile, cook fettuccine according to package directions. In a large skillet, saute broccoli and mushrooms in oil until tender. Add garlic and salt; cook 1 minute longer. Add wine, stirring to loosen browned bits from pan. Gradually stir in cream. Bring to a boil. Reduce heat; simmer, uncovered, for 10-12 minutes or until thickened.

Drain the fettuccine. Add to sauce mixture with shrimp. Cook and stir until heated through; gently stir in tomato. YIELD: 5 servings.

THREE-CHEESE SPINACH CALZONES

MARIE RIZZIO ❖ INTERLOCHEN, MICHIGAN

Our Italian mother used to whip up these yummy dough pockets when we came home from school for lunch. They're easy to pick up and dip into sauce.

- 1 package (10 ounces) frozen chopped spinach, thawed and squeezed dry
- 1 cup (4 ounces) shredded fontina cheese
- 1/2 cup part-skim ricotta cheese
- 1/2 cup crumbled Gorgonzola cheese
- 3 green onions, chopped
- 1/4 teaspoon salt
- 1/8 teaspoon pepper
- 1 tube (13.8 ounces) refrigerated pizza crust
- 1 egg, lightly beaten
- 1 teaspoon water
- 1 cup spaghetti sauce, warmed

In a large bowl, combine the first seven ingredients. On a lightly floured surface, unroll pizza crust into an 11-in. square. Cut into four squares. Transfer to a greased baking sheet. Spoon spinach mixture over half of each square to within 1/2 in. of edges.

For each calzone, fold one corner over filling to the opposite corner, forming a triangle; press edges with a fork to seal. Cut slits in top. Combine egg and water; brush over calzones.

Bake at 375° for 12-15 minutes or until golden brown. Serve with spaghetti sauce. YIELD: 4 servings.

Winning Casseroles

Every one of these stick-to-your-ribs casseroles is a contest winner, so you know they're good. Your family will love digging into the comforting goodness of these hot and hearty dinners!

🎗 THE BEST DERNED SOUTHWESTERN CASSEROLE

VALERIE IGAL ❖ OAK HILL, VIRGINIA

If you want to add a little spice to life—and to dinner—serve this hearty main dish. It's full of Tex-Mex goodness and looks colorful on the plate.

1-1/2 pounds uncooked chorizo, casings removed, *or* bulk spicy pork sausage
1 small onion, chopped
1 can (15 ounces) black beans, rinsed and drained
1 can (15 ounces) tomato sauce
1 can (11 ounces) Mexicorn, drained
2 cans (4 ounces *each*) chopped green chilies
1 cup salsa
1/4 cup minced fresh cilantro
3 teaspoons *each* ground cumin, chili powder and paprika
2 teaspoons garlic powder
12 corn tortillas (6 inches)
2 large tomatoes, sliced
2 cups (8 ounces) shredded Monterey Jack *or* cheddar-Monterey Jack cheese

Crumble chorizo into a large skillet; add onion. Cook over medium heat until meat is no longer pink; drain. Add beans, tomato sauce, corn, chilies, salsa, cilantro and seasonings; heat through.

Place six tortillas in the bottom of a greased 13-in. x 9-in. baking dish. Layer with 3-1/2 cups meat mixture, tomatoes and 1 cup cheese. Top with remaining tortillas, meat and cheese.

Cover and bake at 375° for 40 minutes. Uncover; bake 5-10 minutes longer or until heated through. Let stand for 10 minutes before cutting. YIELD: 12 servings.

🎗 CLASSIC COTTAGE PIE

SHANNON ARTHUR ❖ LUCASVILLE, OHIO

A combination of ground lamb or beef with mashed potatoes and a bubbling layer of cheese is the perfect comfort food. It's a good remedy for the winter chills.

1 pound ground lamb *or* beef
2 medium carrots, finely chopped
1 medium onion, finely chopped
2 tablespoons all-purpose flour
2 tablespoons minced fresh parsley
1 tablespoon Italian seasoning
3/4 teaspoon salt
1/4 teaspoon pepper
1-1/2 cups reduced-sodium beef broth
2 tablespoons dry red wine *or* additional reduced-sodium beef broth
1 tablespoon tomato paste
1 teaspoon brown sugar
1/2 cup frozen peas

TOPPING
4 medium potatoes, peeled and cubed
1/2 cup 2% milk
1/4 cup butter, cubed
3/4 cup shredded cheddar cheese, *divided*
1/4 teaspoon salt
1/8 teaspoon pepper

In a large skillet, cook lamb, carrots and onion over medium heat until meat is no longer pink and vegetables are tender; drain. Stir in flour, parsley, Italian seasoning, salt and pepper until blended. Gradually add broth and wine; stir in tomato paste and brown sugar. Bring to a boil. Reduce heat; simmer, uncovered, for 10-15 minutes or until thickened, stirring occasionally.

Meanwhile, for topping, place potatoes in a large saucepan and cover with water. Bring to a boil. Reduce heat; cover and cook for 10-15 minutes or until tender.

Stir peas into meat mixture; transfer to a greased 9-in. deep-dish pie plate. Drain potatoes; mash with milk and butter. Stir in 1/2 cup cheese, salt and pepper. Spread over meat mixture; sprinkle with remaining cheese.

Place pie plate on a foil-lined baking sheet (plate will be full). Bake at 400° for 20-25 minutes or until the top is golden brown. YIELD: 6 servings.

SHRIMP AND FONTINA CASSEROLE

EMORY DOTY ✦ JASPER, GEORGIA

Looking for a seafood casserole that tastes gourmet? Try this one. The Cajun flavor comes through the cheese topping and the confetti of green onions and red peppers makes it pretty enough for guests.

1/2 cup all-purpose flour
1 tablespoon Cajun seasoning
1/2 teaspoon pepper
2 pounds uncooked large shrimp, peeled and deveined
2 tablespoons olive oil
4 thin slices prosciutto or deli ham, cut into thin strips
1/2 pound medium fresh mushrooms, quartered
2 tablespoons butter
4 green onions, chopped
2 garlic cloves, minced
1 cup heavy whipping cream
8 ounces fontina cheese, cubed
1 jar (7 ounces) roasted sweet red peppers, drained and chopped
1/4 cup grated Parmigiano-Reggiano cheese
1/4 cup grated Romano cheese

In a large resealable plastic bag, combine the flour, Cajun seasoning and pepper. Add shrimp, a few at a time, and shake to coat.

In a large skillet over medium heat, cook shrimp in oil in batches until golden brown. Drain on paper towels. Transfer to an ungreased 13-in. x 9-in. baking dish; top with prosciutto. Set aside.

In the same skillet, saute mushrooms in butter until tender. Add onions and garlic; cook 1 minute longer. Add cream and fontina cheese; cook and stir until cheese is melted. Remove from the heat; stir in peppers. Pour over prosciutto. Sprinkle with remaining cheeses.

Bake, uncovered, at 350° for 15-20 minutes or until bubbly and cheese is melted. Let stand for 10 minutes before serving. YIELD: 8 servings.

ROASTED EGGPLANT LASAGNA

MARGARET WELDER ✦ MADRID, IOWA

With a vegetarian on my guest list, I was inspired to make this lasagna for a party. Watching the cheese bubbling and smelling roasting veggies, I couldn't wait for the party to start. Everyone went home with the recipe.

1 small eggplant
2 small zucchini
5 plum tomatoes, seeded
1 large sweet red pepper
1 large onion, cut into small wedges
1/4 cup olive oil
3 tablespoons minced fresh basil, *divided*
3 garlic cloves, minced
3/4 teaspoon salt, *divided*
1/2 teaspoon pepper, *divided*
2/3 cup pitted Greek olives, chopped
1/4 cup butter, cubed
1/4 cup all-purpose flour
2-3/4 cups milk
1 bay leaf
1/8 teaspoon ground nutmeg
5 tablespoons grated Parmesan cheese, *divided*
2 tablespoons shredded Asiago cheese
3/4 cup shredded part-skim mozzarella cheese
6 no-cook lasagna noodles

Cut eggplant, zucchini, tomatoes and red pepper into 1-in. pieces; place in a large bowl. Add onion, oil, 2 tablespoons basil, garlic, 1/2 teaspoon salt and 1/4 teaspoon pepper; toss. Transfer to two greased 15-in. x 10-in. x 1-in. baking pans. Bake at 450° for 20-25 minutes or until crisp-tender. Stir in olives.

In a large saucepan, melt butter; stir in flour until smooth. Gradually stir in milk. Add bay leaf and nutmeg. Bring to a boil; cook and stir for 2 minutes or until thickened. Remove from heat. Stir in 3 tablespoons Parmesan, Asiago and remaining basil, salt and pepper. Discard bay leaf.

Spread a fourth of the sauce in a greased 11-in. x 7-in. baking dish. Top with 2-1/3 cups vegetables, 1/4 cup mozzarella and three noodles. Repeat layers. Top with a fourth of the sauce, remaining vegetables, mozzarella, sauce and Parmesan. Cover and bake at 375° for 30-40 minutes or until bubbly. Let stand 15 minutes before serving. YIELD: 8 servings.

HASTY HEARTLAND DINNER

AMERICAN EGG BOARD ✤ PARK RIDGE, ILLINOIS

This easy dinner comes together in no time at all. It uses ingredients that you probably have on hand.

- 1 package (5-1/2 ounces) au gratin potatoes
- 4 hard-cooked eggs, chopped
- 1 cup chopped fully cooked ham
- 1 cup frozen peas

In a microwave, cook potatoes according to package directions. Add sauce packet and milk as directed. Stir in eggs, ham and peas.

Cover and cook on high, stirring occasionally, until heated through, about 3-5 minutes. Let stand for 5 minutes before serving. YIELD: 4 servings.

 SLOW-COOKED POT ROAST

VERA CARROLL ✤ MEDFORD, MASSACHUSETTS

I like to serve my fork-tender pot roast with sauteed tarragon carrots and rosemary-roasted red potatoes. This homey meal suits all tastes, and the aroma is captivating.

- 1 large sweet onion, chopped
- 1 cup sliced baby portobello mushrooms
- 1 beef rump roast *or* bottom round roast (3 pounds)
- 1/2 teaspoon salt
- 1/4 teaspoon pepper
- 1 cup dry red wine *or* beef broth
- 1 tablespoon brown sugar
- 1 tablespoon Dijon mustard
- 1 teaspoon Worcestershire sauce
- 2 tablespoons cornstarch
- 2 tablespoons cold water

SPANISH TURKEY TENDERLOINS

ROXANNE CHAN ✤ ALBANY, CALIFORNIA

If you're hungry for warm-weather fare, try this. The grilled turkey and the bright, sunny colors of the relish look and taste like summer.

- 1 package (20 ounces) turkey breast tenderloins
- 1 tablespoon olive oil
- 1/2 teaspoon salt
- 1/2 teaspoon pepper
- 1/4 teaspoon paprika

RELISH
- 1 plum tomato, chopped
- 1 large navel orange, peeled, sectioned and chopped
- 1/4 cup sliced pimiento-stuffed olives
- 1 green onion, finely chopped
- 2 tablespoons minced fresh oregano *or* 2 teaspoons dried oregano
- 2 tablespoons sliced almonds
- 2 tablespoons minced fresh parsley
- 1 large garlic clove, minced
- 1 tablespoon capers, drained
- 1 teaspoon lemon juice
- 1/2 teaspoon grated lemon peel
- 1/4 teaspoon salt

Rub turkey with oil; sprinkle with salt, pepper and paprika.

Grill, covered, over medium heat or broil 4 in. from the heat for 15-20 minutes or until a thermometer reads 170°, turning occasionally. Let stand for 5 minutes before slicing.

Meanwhile, in a small bowl, combine the relish ingredients. Serve with turkey. YIELD: 6 servings.

Place onion and mushrooms in a 5-qt. slow cooker. Rub roast with salt and pepper; cut in half and place over onion mixture. In a small bowl, combine the wine, brown sugar, mustard and Worcestershire sauce; pour over roast. Cover and cook on low for 6-8 hours or until meat is tender.

Mix cornstarch and water until smooth; stir into cooking juices. Cover and cook on high for 30 minutes or until gravy is thickened; serve with pot roast. YIELD: 6 servings.

ROSEMARY PORK WITH BERRY PORT SAUCE

HEATHER ZGALJARDIC ✤ LEAGUE CITY, TEXAS

Rosemary and blueberries pair flawlessly together and go great with a tenderloin of pork.

- 2 pork tenderloins (1 pound *each*)
- 2 teaspoons olive oil
- 1 teaspoon minced fresh rosemary *or* 1/4 teaspoon dried rosemary, crushed
- 1 teaspoon salt
- 1 teaspoon pepper

SAUCE
- 1 shallot, finely chopped
- 1 teaspoon olive oil
- 1-1/2 cups port wine *or* grape juice
- 1 cup reduced-sodium chicken broth
- 1 cup fresh *or* frozen blueberries
- 1/2 cup dried cherries
- 1/2 teaspoon minced fresh rosemary *or* 1/4 teaspoon dried rosemary, crushed

Rub pork with oil; sprinkle with rosemary, salt and pepper. Place on a rack in a shallow roasting pan. Bake at 425° for 20-30 minutes or until a thermometer reads 145°.

Meanwhile, in a small saucepan, saute shallot in oil. Stir in the remaining sauce ingredients. Bring to a boil; cook until liquid is reduced by half. Cool slightly. Transfer to a blender; cover and process until blended.

Let pork stand for 5 minutes; slice and serve with sauce. YIELD: 8 servings (1-3/4 cups sauce).

CHICKEN 'N' CHILIES CASSEROLE

LOIS KEEL ❖ ALBUQUERQUE, NEW MEXICO

This casserole is easy to prepare and can be made ahead if you have a busy day coming up. It makes good use of leftover meat and is very filling.

1 cup (8 ounces) sour cream
1 cup half-and-half cream
1 cup chopped onion
1 can (4 ounces) chopped green chilies
1 teaspoon salt
1/2 teaspoon pepper
1 package (2 pounds) frozen shredded hash brown potatoes
2-1/2 cups cubed cooked chicken
2-1/2 cups (10 ounces) shredded cheddar cheese, *divided*

In a large bowl, combine the sour cream, half-and-half cream, onion, chilies, salt and pepper. Stir in the potatoes, chicken and 2 cups cheese.

Pour into a greased 13-in. x 9-in. baking dish. Bake, uncovered, at 350° for 1-1/4 hours or until golden brown. Sprinkle with remaining cheese before serving. YIELD: 6-8 servings.

EDITOR'S NOTE: Cooked turkey or ham can be substituted for the chicken.

JERK PORK & PINEAPPLE KABOBS

AVA BRYAN ❖ EAST HARTFORD, CONNECTICUT

Here's a perfect way to spice up a barbecue. These kabobs are sure to please guests who like a little heat. I recommend using pina colada yogurt as a dip.

2 bunches green onions, coarsely chopped
1 medium onion, coarsely chopped
1 habanero pepper, halved and seeded
2 tablespoons white vinegar
2 tablespoons orange juice
1 tablespoon olive oil
1 tablespoon reduced-sodium soy sauce
2 teaspoons salt
2 teaspoons brown sugar
2 teaspoons ground allspice
2 garlic cloves, peeled
2 teaspoons minced fresh gingerroot
2 teaspoons minced fresh thyme
1/2 teaspoon pepper
1/4 teaspoon ground cinnamon
1/4 teaspoon ground nutmeg
1/4 teaspoon lime juice
1 pound pork tenderloin, cut into 1-inch pieces
1 can (8 ounces) unsweetened pineapple chunks, drained
1 large green pepper, cut into 1-inch pieces
1 large sweet red pepper, cut into 1-inch pieces

In a food processor, combine the first 17 ingredients; cover and process until blended. Transfer to a large resealable plastic bag; add the pork. Seal the bag and turn to coat; refrigerate for at least 3 hours.

Drain and discard marinade. On four metal or soaked wooden skewers, alternately thread the pork, pineapple and peppers. Grill, covered, over medium heat or broil 4 in. from the heat for 10-15 minutes or until meat is tender, turning occasionally. YIELD: 4 kabobs.

EDITOR'S NOTE: Wear disposable gloves when cutting hot peppers; the oils can burn skin. Avoid touching your face.

MARINATED PORK WITH CARAMELIZED FENNEL

GILDA LESTER ❖ MILLSBORO, DELAWARE

Fresh-flavored marinade turns this pork tender and juicy. I often complete the meal with simple cauliflower or Brussels sprouts, roasted so they're naturally sweet.

1/4 cup olive oil
1 tablespoon reduced-sodium soy sauce
2 garlic cloves, minced
2 teaspoons grated lemon peel
1 teaspoon ground cumin
1 teaspoon fennel seed, crushed
1/2 teaspoon salt
1/2 teaspoon pepper
1/2 teaspoon ground allspice
2 pork tenderloins (3/4 pound *each*)

FENNEL
2 medium fennel bulbs, halved and cut into 1/2-inch slices
4-1/2 teaspoons plus 1 tablespoon olive oil, *divided*
1/4 teaspoon salt
1/4 teaspoon pepper
Fennel fronds, optional

In a large resealable plastic bag, combine the first nine ingredients; add pork. Seal bag and turn to coat. Refrigerate for 8 hours or overnight.

Place fennel in a large bowl; drizzle with 4-1/2 teaspoons oil. Sprinkle with salt and pepper; toss to coat. Transfer to an ungreased 15-in. x 10-in. x 1-in. baking pan. Bake at 450° for 30-35 minutes or until tender, stirring once.

Meanwhile, drain and discard marinade. In a large ovenproof skillet, brown pork in remaining oil on all sides. Place skillet in oven; bake pork for 18-22 minutes or until a thermometer reads 145°.

Let stand for 5 minutes before slicing. Serve with roasted fennel. Garnish with fennel fronds if desired. YIELD: 6 servings.

SALMON WITH GINGERED RHUBARB COMPOTE

SUSAN ASANOVIC ❖ WILTON, CONNECTICUT

Rhubarb plays the role of lemon in this recipe, brightening and accenting the rich taste of the fish. I like to double the amount of compote and save half for another fast and healthy meal.

1 medium onion, thinly sliced
4 green onions, sliced
2 tablespoons butter
4 cups sliced fresh *or* frozen rhubarb
1/4 cup packed brown sugar
1/2 cup sweet white wine *or* white grape juice
1 tablespoon minced fresh gingerroot
1/2 teaspoon salt
1/4 teaspoon pepper
4 salmon fillets (6 ounces *each*)
Additional sliced green onions, optional

In a large ovenproof skillet, cook the sliced onions in the butter over medium heat for 15-20 minutes or until they are golden brown, stirring frequently.

Add rhubarb and brown sugar; cook 3 minutes longer. Stir in the wine, ginger, salt and pepper. Bring to a boil. Reduce heat; simmer, uncovered, for 5-10 minutes or until rhubarb is tender, stirring occasionally.

Place the salmon fillets over the rhubarb mixture. Bake, uncovered, at 350° for 20-25 minutes or until the fish flakes easily with a fork. Sprinkle with additional green onions if desired. YIELD: 4 servings.

POOR MAN'S DINNER

MILA ABNER ❖ VADA, KENTUCKY

Don't let the name fool you—this dish guarantees million-dollar taste with just a few ingredients!

1 pound ground beef
1/4 teaspoon pepper
1/4 teaspoon garlic powder
5 large potatoes, peeled and sliced
1 large onion, sliced
2 cans (10-3/4 ounces *each*) condensed cream of mushroom soup, undiluted
1/2 cup 2% milk
Minced fresh parsley

In a large skillet, cook beef over medium heat until no longer pink; drain. Season with pepper and garlic powder. Layer the beef, potatoes and onion slices in a shallow 2-qt. baking dish. Combine soup and milk; pour over all.

Cover and bake at 350° for 1-1/4 hours or until potatoes are tender. Garnish with parsley. YIELD: 6 servings.

EDITOR'S NOTE: For an extra-cheesy beef dinner, substitute 2 cans (11 oz. each) condensed cheddar cheese soup for the mushroom soup.

UNSTUFFED PORK CHOPS

SHERRI MELOTIK ❖ OAK CREEK, WISCONSIN

This is comfort food at its finest. The savory flavors of sage and onion in the stuffing infuse the chops while they bake. The pork comes out tender and moist.

2 bone-in pork loin chops (8 ounces *each*)
2 teaspoons olive oil
1-1/2 cups crushed chicken stuffing mix
3/4 cup 2% milk
2/3 cup condensed cream of mushroom soup, undiluted
1/8 teaspoon pepper

In a large skillet, brown pork chops in oil. Transfer to an 8-in. square baking dish; sprinkle with stuffing mix. In a small bowl, combine the milk, soup and pepper; pour over top.

Cover and bake dish at 350° for 30-35 minutes or until a thermometer reads 160°. YIELD: 2 servings.

OLD-FASHIONED SWISS STEAK

ELEANORE HILL ❖ FRESNO, CALIFORNIA

The kids enjoyed this Swiss steak so much they would eat it as leftovers the next day.

1/2 cup plus 2 tablespoons all-purpose flour, *divided*
2 teaspoons salt, *divided*
3/4 teaspoon pepper, *divided*
1/2 teaspoon garlic salt
2 pounds beef top round steak, cut into serving-size pieces
3 tablespoons canola oil
2 cups chopped green pepper
1 cup chopped celery
1 cup chopped onion
1 garlic clove, minced
2 cans (14-1/2 ounces *each*) diced tomatoes, undrained
1 cup beef broth
1 tablespoon reduced-sodium soy sauce
1/4 cup cold water

In a large plastic bag, combine 1/2 cup flour, 1 teaspoon salt, 1/2 teaspoon pepper and garlic salt. Add beef, a few pieces at a time, and shake to coat. Remove meat from bag and pound with a mallet to tenderize.

In a Dutch oven, brown meat in oil until no longer pink. Add the green pepper, celery and onions; cook and stir for 10 minutes. Add garlic; cook 1 minute longer. Stir in the tomatoes, broth, soy sauce and remaining salt and pepper. Cover and bake at 325° for 2 hours.

Remove from the oven and return to stovetop. In a small bowl, combine water and remaining flour until smooth; gradually stir into juices. Bring to a boil over medium heat. Cook and stir sauce for 2 minutes or until thickened. YIELD: 6-8 servings.

IF COOKING FOR TWO: Freeze serving-size portions in airtight containers or freezer bags.

PECAN PORK MEDALLIONS WITH CAMBOZOLA CREAM

MARIE RIZZIO ❖ INTERLOCHEN, MICHIGAN

You can treat your family to fine dining straight from your kitchen with these elegant medallions. The nut-crusted pork and silky cheese sauce make this a special dish that I'm proud to serve.

1/2 cup white wine
1 tablespoon chopped shallot
1-1/2 cups heavy whipping cream
3 ounces Cambozola cheese, chopped
1/2 teaspoon Worcestershire sauce
1/4 teaspoon hot pepper sauce
1/8 teaspoon salt
1/8 teaspoon white pepper

PORK
1/3 cup dried tart cherries
3 tablespoons port wine
1-1/2 pounds pork tenderloin
1/2 cup chopped pecans
1/3 cup dry bread crumbs
1/4 teaspoon salt
1/8 teaspoon pepper
2 tablespoons butter

In a small saucepan, combine white wine and shallot. Bring to a boil; cook until liquid is reduced to about 2 tablespoons. Add the heavy cream, cheese, Worcestershire sauce, pepper sauce, salt and white pepper. Return to a boil; cook until slightly thickened, about 15 minutes. In small bowl, combine cherries and port wine; set aside.

Meanwhile, cut pork into 12 slices; flatten slices to 1/2-in. thickness. Place pecans in a food processor; cover and process until finely chopped. In a large resealable plastic bag, combine the pecans, bread crumbs, salt and pepper. Add pork, a few pieces at a time; shake to coat.

In a large skillet over medium-high heat, cook pork in butter in batches for 3-4 minutes on each side or until tender. Drain cherries; serve with pork and sauce. YIELD: 6 servings.

EDITOR'S NOTE: You may substitute 2 ounces Brie and 1 ounce blue cheese for the Cambozola cheese.

COBRE VALLEY CASSEROLE

CAROLYN DEMING ❖ MIAMI, ARIZONA

We live in southeastern Arizona, in a part of the state known as Cobre Valley. "Cobre" is a Spanish word for copper, which is mined here. Variations of this recipe have been enjoyed in this area for many years.

  1 pound ground beef
  1 medium onion, chopped
  1 celery rib, chopped
  1 envelope taco seasoning
1/4 cup water
  2 cans (15 to 16 ounces *each*) refried beans
  1 can (4 ounces) chopped green chilies, optional
  1 cup (4 ounces) shredded cheddar cheese
  2 green onions, sliced
  1 large tomato, peeled, seeded and chopped
1/3 cup sliced ripe olives, chopped
1-1/2 cups crushed tortilla chips

In a large skillet, cook the beef, onion and celery over medium heat until meat is no longer pink; drain. Stir in the taco mix, water, beans and green chilies if desired.

Pour into a greased 2-1/2-qt. baking dish. Bake, uncovered, at 350° for 30 minutes or until heated through. Top with cheese, green onions, tomato, olives and chips. YIELD: 6-8 servings.

🎖 PESTO VEGGIE PIZZA

AGNES WARD ❖ STRATFORD, ONTARIO

A thoughtful granddaughter gave me the recipe for this wonderful pizza. It's delicious down to its whole wheat crust. One bite and I'm in veggie heaven!

  2 cups sliced fresh mushrooms
  1 cup fresh broccoli florets, chopped
3/4 cup thinly sliced zucchini
1/2 cup julienned sweet yellow pepper
1/2 cup julienned sweet red pepper
  1 small red onion, thinly sliced and separated into rings
  1 tablespoon prepared pesto
  1 prebaked 12-inch thin whole wheat pizza crust
1/3 cup pizza sauce
  2 tablespoons grated Romano *or* Parmesan cheese
1/4 cup sliced ripe olives
1/2 cup crumbled reduced-fat feta cheese
1/2 cup shredded part-skim mozzarella cheese

In a large nonstick skillet coated with cooking spray, saute the mushrooms, broccoli, zucchini, peppers and onion until tender. Remove from the heat; stir in pesto.

Place crust on a 12-in. pizza pan; spread with pizza sauce. Sprinkle with Romano cheese; top with vegetable mixture and olives. Sprinkle with feta and mozzarella.

Bake at 450° for 8-12 minutes or until crust is lightly browned and mozzarella is melted. YIELD: 6 slices.

SALMON WITH CARIBBEAN SALSA

MARY JONES ❖ WILLIAMSTOWN, WEST VIRGINIA

Salmon fillets smothered in tropical fruit salsa make an elegant main dish recipe. The cinnamon-spiced seasoning is a wonderful complement to grilled chicken, too.

SEASONING
1 tablespoon salt
1 tablespoon ground nutmeg
1 tablespoon pepper
1-1/2 teaspoons *each* ground ginger, cinnamon and allspice
1-1/2 teaspoons brown sugar

SALMON
1 salmon fillet (3 pounds)
4-1/2 teaspoons olive oil

SALSA
1 medium mango
1 medium papaya
1 medium green pepper
1 medium sweet red pepper
1 cup finely chopped fresh pineapple
1/4 cup finely chopped red onion
3 tablespoons minced fresh cilantro
2 tablespoons lime juice
1 tablespoon olive oil
1/2 teaspoon salt

Combine the seasoning ingredients. Place fillet in a greased 15-in. x 10-in. x 1-in. baking pan; sprinkle with 1 tablespoon seasoning. (Save remaining seasoning for another use.) Drizzle salmon with oil. Cover and refrigerate for at least 2 hours.

Peel and finely chop mango and papaya; place in a large bowl. Finely chop peppers; add to bowl. Add the remaining salsa ingredients and gently stir until blended. Cover and refrigerate for at least 2 hours. Bake salmon at 350° for 25-30 minutes or until fish flakes easily with a fork. Serve with salsa. YIELD: 8 servings (5 cups salsa).

CRAB-STUFFED FLOUNDER WITH HERBED AIOLI

BEVERLY OFERRALL ❖ LINKWOOD, MARYLAND

If you like seafood, you'll love this scrumptious flounder. The light and creamy aioli sauce tops it off with bright tones of chives and garlic.

1/4 cup egg substitute
2 tablespoons fat-free milk
1 tablespoon minced chives
1 tablespoon reduced-fat mayonnaise
1 tablespoon Dijon mustard
Dash hot pepper sauce
1 pound lump crabmeat
6 flounder fillets (6 ounces *each*)
Paprika

AIOLI
1/3 cup reduced-fat mayonnaise
2 teaspoons minced chives
2 teaspoons minced fresh parsley
2 teaspoons lemon juice
1 garlic clove, minced

In a small bowl, combine the first six ingredients; gently fold in crab. Cut the fillets in half widthwise; place six halves in a 15-in. x 10-in. x 1-in. baking pan coated with cooking spray. Spoon the crab mixture over the fillets; top with remaining fish. Sprinkle with paprika.

Bake at 400° for 20-24 minutes or until fish flakes easily with a fork. Meanwhile, combine the aioli ingredients. Serve with fish. YIELD: 6 servings.

SIDE DISHES & CONDIMENTS

What better way to balance a meal than with a bright and beautiful vegetable side dish or a hearty potato casserole. Here, you'll also find easy-to-make condiments, such as jam, relish and more!

GINGER FRIED RICE

BECKY MATHENY ❖ STRASBURG, VIRGINIA

For variety and color, I like to combine at least two types of vegetables. This is a flexible dish, limited only by what's in the fridge and your imagination.

2 teaspoons canola oil, *divided*
1 egg, lightly beaten
1/4 cup chopped sweet red pepper
1 tablespoon chopped green onion
1 garlic clove, minced
1 cup cold cooked instant rice
1/4 cup cubed cooked chicken
1 to 2 tablespoons soy sauce
1/2 teaspoon ground ginger
1 tablespoon shredded carrot

In a large skillet, heat 1 teaspoon oil over medium-high heat. Pour egg into skillet. As egg sets, lift edges, letting uncooked portion flow underneath. When egg is completely cooked, remove to plate. Set aside.

In the same skillet, saute the pepper and onion in remaining oil until tender. Add the garlic; cook 1 minute longer. Stir in the rice, chicken, soy sauce and ginger. Chop egg into small pieces; stir into the skillet and heat through. Garnish with shredded carrot. YIELD: 2 servings.

🏵 PEPPER JACK MAC

RIANNA STYX ❖ LIBERTYVILLE, ILLINOIS

When I want to make something hearty, creamy and cheesy, I go with this dish. It's comfort food at its finest.

2 cups uncooked elbow macaroni
1/4 cup butter, cubed
1/4 cup all-purpose flour
1/2 teaspoon salt
1/2 teaspoon ground mustard
1/2 teaspoon pepper
1/2 teaspoon Worcestershire sauce
1-1/2 cups milk
1/2 cup heavy whipping cream
3 cups (12 ounces) shredded pepper Jack cheese
1 package (8 ounces) cream cheese, cubed
1 cup (4 ounces) shredded sharp cheddar cheese
1/2 cup shredded Asiago cheese

TOPPING
3/4 cup panko (Japanese) bread crumbs
4 bacon strips, cooked and crumbled
1/4 cup grated Parmesan cheese
1 cup cheddar French-fried onions, crushed

Cook macaroni according to package directions; drain. Set aside. In a large saucepan, melt butter. Stir in flour, salt, mustard, pepper and Worcestershire saue until smooth; slowly add milk and cream. Bring to a boil; cook and stir for 1 minute or until thickened. Stir in cheeses until melted. Stir the macaroni into cheese mixture.

Transfer to a greased 2-qt. baking dish. Sprinkle with bread crumbs, bacon, Parmesan cheese and onions. Bake, uncovered, at 350° for 20-25 minutes or until bubbly and golden brown. YIELD: 6 servings.

BROCCOLI & HORSERADISH SAUCE

SUE CRAWLEY ❖ LANSING, MICHIGAN

This flavorful vegetable recipe is a family favorite. It's a great side dish that we usually serve alongside prime rib for holidays and special occasions.

1 bunch broccoli, cut into florets
1/4 cup sour cream
1/4 cup mayonnaise
2 teaspoons prepared horseradish
1/4 teaspoon Worcestershire sauce

Place broccoli in a steamer basket; place in a large saucepan over 1 in. of water. Bring to a boil; cover and steam for 3-4 minutes or until tender.

Meanwhile, in a small saucepan, combine the remaining ingredients. Heat over low heat until heated through. Serve with broccoli. YIELD: 4 servings (1/2 cup sauce).

APRICOT-GINGER ACORN SQUASH

TRISHA KRUSE ❖ EAGLE, IDAHO

It's a real treat digging into tender baked squash with a buttery apricot sauce. Natural fruit preserves add sweetness, and ginger makes it savory without unwanted calories.

1 small acorn squash
2 tablespoons apricot preserves
4 teaspoons butter, melted
1-1/2 teaspoons reduced-sodium soy sauce
1/4 teaspoon ground ginger
1/4 teaspoon pepper

Cut squash in half; discard seeds. Cut a thin slice from bottom of squash with a sharp knife to allow it to sit flat. Place hollow side up in a greased 11-in. x 7-in. baking dish.

Combine the remaining ingredients; spoon over squash. Cover and bake at 350° for 45 minutes. Uncover; bake 15 minutes longer or until tender. YIELD: 2 servings.

MATOKE IN PEANUT SAUCE

AMY YANDA ❖ BOULDER, COLORADO

This African recipe comes from BeadforLife, an organization that, through the sales of hand-crafted beaded jewelry, helps teach Ugandan women business skills so they can support their families. Matoke, also known as plantains or green bananas, are eaten daily in Uganda. They are often wrapped in their own leaves and steamed.

    4 medium tomatoes
    1 medium onion, finely chopped
    1 teaspoon cumin seeds
1/2 teaspoon mustard seeds
    1 tablespoon canola oil
    2 garlic cloves, minced
    3 to 4 red chili peppers, seeded and finely chopped
    2 teaspoons grated fresh gingerroot
1-1/2 teaspoons ground cumin
1-1/2 teaspoons ground coriander
    1 teaspoon salt
1/2 teaspoon ground turmeric
    4 yellow plantains, cut into 1/2-inch slices
    2 cups water
1/2 cup finely ground peanuts
    1 teaspoon minced fresh cilantro

In a large saucepan, bring 8 cups water to a boil. Add tomatoes; cover and boil for 30 seconds. Drain and immediately place tomatoes in ice water. Drain and pat dry. Peel and chop tomatoes; set aside.

In a large skillet, saute the onion, cumin seeds and mustard seeds in oil until the onion is tender. Add the garlic; cook 1 minute longer. Stir in the peppers, ginger, ground cumin, coriander, salt, turmeric and tomatoes. Bring to a boil. Reduce the heat; simmer, uncovered, for 5-7 minutes or until mixture is slightly thickened.

Add plantains and water. Bring to a boil. Reduce heat; simmer, uncovered, for 20 minutes or until plantains are tender, stirring occasionally. Stir in the peanuts. Sprinkle with cilantro. YIELD: 9 servings.

EDITOR'S NOTE: Wear disposable gloves when cutting hot peppers; the oils can burn skin. Avoid touching your face.

WHAT ARE PLANTAINS?
Plantains are a type of banana that are referred to as a "cooking banana." They are very popular in Latin American countries, have a mild flavor and are used in the United States similarly to how a potato would be.

GREEN ONION TARTAR SAUCE

ROGER SLIVON ❖ GENESEE DEPOT, WISCONSIN

Here's a traditional sauce worth making from scratch. It makes the meal feel very special, and guests are always impressed. You might never buy the bottled stuff again.

1/2 cup mayonnaise
    2 green onions, finely chopped
    1 whole dill pickle, finely chopped
    2 tablespoons sour cream
    1 teaspoon minced fresh parsley
    1 teaspoon cider vinegar
1/2 teaspoon sugar
1/4 teaspoon dried tarragon
1/8 teaspoon pepper

In a small bowl, combine all ingredients. Refrigerate until serving. YIELD: 3/4 cup.

GRUYERE POTATO BAKE

CECELIA SMITH ❖ SIERRA VISTA, ARIZONA

My friend shared this recipe with me, and after I discovered what Gruyere cheese was, this easy, delicious dish became a frequent request from my boys. It's so simple—only three ingredients plus salt and pepper to taste!

2 medium potatoes, thinly sliced
1/2 cup shredded Gruyere or Swiss cheese
Dash salt
Dash pepper
2 tablespoons chicken broth

In a greased 1-1/2-qt. baking dish, layer half of the potatoes, cheese, salt and pepper. Repeat layers. Drizzle broth over top.
  Bake, uncovered, at 350° for 35-40 minutes or until potatoes are tender. YIELD: 2 servings.

LEMON & ROSEMARY STEAK RUB

BEEF BOARD AND FEDERATION OF STATE BEEF COUNCILS

This is a great rub for any cut of beef. The lemon and rosemary really highlight the beef flavor.

1-1/2 teaspoons grated lemon peel
1 teaspoon dried rosemary, crushed
1/4 teaspoon dried thyme
1/4 teaspoon coarsely ground pepper
2 large garlic cloves, minced

Combine all ingredients. Rub over beef. YIELD: enough to season 2 lbs. of beef.

MASHED POTATOES 'N' BRUSSELS SPROUTS

RAYMONDE HEBERT BERNIER ❖ SAINT-HYACINTHE, QUEBEC

Tired of eating the same old mashed white potatoes? Try this tasty recipe. These potatoes are fluffy and delicious.

3 pounds potatoes (about 9 medium), peeled and quartered
2 cups fresh or frozen Brussels sprouts
2 garlic cloves, peeled
1/2 cup half-and-half cream
2 tablespoons butter
2 teaspoons chicken bouillon granules
1 teaspoon salt
1/4 teaspoon dried basil
1/8 teaspoon pepper

Place the potatoes in a large saucepan and cover with water. Bring to a boil. Reduce heat; cover and cook for 15-20 minutes or until tender.
  Meanwhile, place 1/2 in. of water and Brussels sprouts in a small saucepan; bring to a boil. Reduce heat; cover and cook for 5 minutes. Add garlic; cook 3-5 minutes longer or until tender.
  Drain potatoes, sprouts and garlic; cool slightly. Place in a food processor; cover and process for 1-2 minutes. Add the remaining ingredients; cover and process just until blended. Transfer to a serving bowl. YIELD: 6-8 servings.

LEMON BRUSSELS SPROUTS

MARY ANN DELL ✤ PHOENIXVILLE, PENNSYLVANIA

The younger the Brussels sprouts, the more delicate the flavor is in this recipe. This is a great side dish that's colorful when garnished with lemon curls and a little thinly sliced sweet onion.

    1/2 pound fresh Brussels sprouts
      2 tablespoons chopped onion
  4-1/2 teaspoons water
      1 teaspoon olive oil
      1 teaspoon lemon juice
    1/2 teaspoon grated lemon peel
    1/8 teaspoon pepper
  Dash salt

Cut an "X" in the core of each Brussels sprout. In a small microwave-safe bowl, combine the Brussels sprouts, onion, water and oil. Cover and microwave on high for 5-7 minutes or until crisp-tender, stirring once. Add the remaining ingredients; toss to coat. YIELD: 2 servings.

ASPARAGUS WITH BLUE CHEESE

ELNA EDGAR ✤ INNISFAIL, ALBERTA

This simple, elegant side would be ideal for a special dinner. Blue cheese adds a tangy richness to healthy steamed asparagus, and the bright green spears are sure signs of spring.

      1 pound fresh asparagus, trimmed
    1/4 cup crumbled blue cheese
      2 tablespoons minced fresh chives
      4 teaspoons olive oil
      2 teaspoons red wine vinegar
    1/8 teaspoon white pepper

Place asparagus in a steamer basket; place in a large saucepan over 1 in. of water. Bring to a boil; cover and steam for 4-5 minutes or until crisp-tender.

In a small bowl, combine the cheese, chives, oil, vinegar and pepper. Transfer the asparagus to an ungreased 15-in. x 10-in. x 1-in. baking pan; top with cheese mixture. Bake, uncovered, at 375° for 4-5 minutes or until cheese just begins to melt. YIELD: 4 servings.

BAKED POTATO SLICES

GEORGE & GRACE BARNES ✤ CLERMONT, FLORIDA

My husband has become a gourmet cook and this recipe is a part of his favorite meal. It is easy to assemble and delicious with its simple ingredients.

      2 medium russet potatoes
      1 tablespoon olive oil
  1-1/2 teaspoons salt-free seasoning blend
    1/4 teaspoon salt

Cut potatoes into 1/4-in. slices. Place in a large bowl; drizzle with oil. Sprinkle with seasoning blend and salt; toss to coat.

Arrange potatoes in a single layer in an ungreased 15-in. x 10-in. x 1-in. baking pan. Bake at 450° for 20-25 minutes or until golden brown, turning once. YIELD: 2 servings.

BACON AND GARLIC GREEN BEANS

SHANNON REYNOSO ❖ BAKERSFIELD, CALIFORNIA

Adding white wine, lemon juice and garlic gives a little kick to green beans. It was enough to turn our old, traditional holiday side into a year-round favorite.

    6 thick-sliced bacon strips, chopped
    1 small onion, thinly sliced
    6 tablespoons butter
    1 tablespoon olive oil
    3 garlic cloves, minced
1/4 cup white wine *or* chicken broth
    9 cups frozen French-style green beans, thawed
1/2 teaspoon salt
1/2 teaspoon garlic powder
1/4 teaspoon pepper
    2 to 3 tablespoons lemon juice

In a large skillet, cook bacon over medium heat until crisp. Remove to paper towels with a slotted spoon; drain. In the same skillet, saute onion in butter and oil until tender. Add garlic; cook 1 minute longer. Stir in wine; bring to a boil. Simmer, uncovered, for 5-8 minutes or until liquid is reduced by half.

Add the green beans, salt, garlic powder and pepper; heat through. Stir in lemon juice and bacon. YIELD: 8 servings.

COOKING WITH WINE

The general rule for cooking with wine is to use wine that you would also drink. For a recipe that calls for white wine, Sauvignon Blanc is a good dry white. A Chardonnay may also work, but may add more acidity to the dish.

WINTER VEGETABLE GRATIN

RACHEL DUEKER ❖ GERVAIS, OREGON

This creamy side dish gives you all the rich flavors you crave in a cold-weather meal. Use a mandolin cutter on the root vegetables to speed up preparation.

1 small onion, chopped
1 tablespoon butter
1 garlic clove, minced
1-1/2 cups heavy whipping cream
1/2 cup sour cream
4-1/2 teaspoons minced fresh rosemary *or* 1-1/2 teaspoons dried rosemary, crushed
1 tablespoon minced fresh basil *or* 1 teaspoon dried basil
1/2 teaspoon salt
1/2 teaspoon pepper
1/2 teaspoon ground cumin
3 medium Yukon Gold potatoes, peeled and thinly sliced
2 medium turnips, peeled and thinly sliced
1 medium sweet potato, peeled and thinly sliced

In a small skillet, saute onion in butter until tender. Add garlic; cook 1 minute longer. Stir in the cream, sour cream, rosemary, basil, salt, pepper and cumin. Bring to a gentle boil. Remove from the heat; cool for 10 minutes.

Layer half of the potatoes, turnips and sweet potato in a greased 8-in. square baking dish; pour half of the sauce over the top. Repeat layers.

Cover and bake at 350° for 45 minutes. Uncover; bake 10-15 minutes longer or until bubbly and potatoes are tender. Let stand for 10 minutes before serving. YIELD: 6 servings.

GLAZED CARROTS AND GREEN BEANS

SUSAN KAKUK ❖ PLYMOUTH, MINNESOTA

This simple dish is always a big hit, even with people who aren't vegetable lovers. I've substituted frozen green beans for fresh, omitting the blanching process, and the dish still tastes great.

6 cups water
1/2 pound fresh baby carrots
1/2 pound fresh green beans, trimmed
1/2 cup chicken broth
1 tablespoon butter
1 teaspoon sugar
Salt and pepper to taste

In a large saucepan, bring water to a boil. Add carrots; cover and cook for 1 minute. Add beans; cover and cook 2 minutes longer. Drain and immediately place the vegetables in ice water. Drain and pat dry.

Place the vegetables in a large skillet; add broth and butter. Bring to a boil; cook, uncovered, for 2-3 minutes or until liquid is reduced to about 2 teaspoons. Add the sugar, salt and pepper; cook and stir for 1 minute. YIELD: 6 servings.

VEGETABLE RIBBONS

PATTY SINGSTOCK ❖ RACINE, WISCONSIN

Simple elegance best describes this fresh-tasting farm dish. It's a great way to use the late summer harvest.

    3 medium carrots, peeled
    2 medium zucchini
    2 tablespoons butter
  3/4 cup reduced-sodium chicken broth
    2 tablespoons minced fresh parsley, *divided*

Using a vegetable peeler, cut the vegetables lengthwise into very thin strips.

In a large skillet over medium heat, melt butter. Add broth. Bring to a boil; cook until liquid is reduced to 1/3 cup. Add the vegetable strips and 1 tablespoon parsley; cook and stir for 2 minutes or just until crisp-tender. Sprinkle with remaining parsley. Serve with a slotted spoon. YIELD: 4 servings.

GERMAN NOODLE BAKE

KATHLEEN MEINEKE ❖ COLOGNE, NEW JERSEY

This is a recipe I serve each year for my holiday open house because everyone looks for it. Store-bought noodles can be substituted, but I prefer homemade noodles...and so does everyone else.

    1 cup all-purpose flour
  1/2 teaspoon salt
    2 eggs, lightly beaten
    2 quarts water
  CHEESE SAUCE
    3 tablespoons butter
    3 tablespoons all-purpose flour
  1/2 teaspoon salt
  1/2 teaspoon paprika
1-1/2 cups milk
    8 ounces Swiss cheese, diced
    2 eggs, well beaten

In a small bowl, combine flour and salt. Make a well in the center; add eggs. Stir together, forming a dough.

Turn dough onto a floured surface; knead for 5-6 minutes. Divide dough in half. Roll each portion into a 12-in. x 9-in. rectangle. Dust both sides of dough with flour; roll up, jelly-roll style. Cut into 1/4-in. slices. Unroll noodles on paper towels; let dry for up to 2 hours.

In a Dutch oven, bring water to a rapid boil. Add noodles; cook for 7-9 minutes or until tender.

Meanwhile, in a small saucepan, melt butter. Stir in the flour, salt and paprika until smooth; gradually add milk. Bring to a boil; cook and stir for 2 minutes or until thickened. Remove from the heat; stir in cheese until melted. Stir in eggs.

Drain noodles; transfer to a greased 11-in. x 7-in. baking dish. Top with cheese sauce. Cover and bake at 350° for 20 minutes. Uncover; bake 10-15 minutes longer or until bubbly. YIELD: 8 servings.

PLUM APPLE BUTTER

NANCY MICHEL ❖ LAKELAND, FLORIDA

Use the season's freshest fruits to create your own spread for breads and crackers. This creamy, fruity butter is perfect for a warm summer day.

  3 medium fresh plums, pitted and quartered
  2 medium tart apples, peeled and quartered
  1/4 cup water
  3/4 cup sugar
  1/4 to 1/2 teaspoon ground cinnamon
  1/4 teaspoon ground nutmeg
Dash ground allspice

Place the plums, apples and water in a large saucepan. Bring to a boil. Reduce heat; cover and simmer for 12-15 minutes or until tender. Cool slightly.

Place in a blender; cover and process until pureed. Return all to the saucepan. Add sugar and spices; return to a boil. Reduce heat; simmer, uncovered, for 15-20 minutes or until thickened, stirring frequently.

Cool to room temperature. Cover and store in the refrigerator for up to 3 weeks. YIELD: 1-1/4 cups.

EASY LEMON-BLUEBERRY JAM

JOYCE ROBBINS ❖ OLD HICKORY, TENNESSEE

After one taste of this delightfully sweet and simple jam, people will find it hard to believe that you didn't spend many long hours in a hot kitchen. Of course, you don't have to let them in on your "secret!"

  4 cups fresh blueberries
  2 cups sugar
  1 package (3 ounces) lemon gelatin

In a large saucepan, slightly crush 2 cups of blueberries. Add remaining berries and sugar, mix well. Bring to a boil, stirring constantly. Remove from the heat; stir in gelatin until dissolved. Pour hot jam into jars or containers. Cover and cool. Refrigerate. YIELD: 4 half-pints.

BEST CHILLED BEETS

DOTTIE EISIMINGER ❖ PALM CITY, FLORIDA

I didn't like beets until my mother made these. People have told me how much they like them. The ingredients may sound a bit unusual, but they really taste good together.

  3 cans (16 ounces *each*) sliced beets
  2 tablespoons cornstarch
  1 cup vinegar
  1/2 teaspoon salt
  3 tablespoons canola oil
  3 tablespoons ketchup
  1 teaspoon vanilla extract
  25 whole cloves, tied in a cheesecloth bag

Drain the beets, reserving 1-1/2 cups of juice in a large saucepan. Add cornstarch to juice and mix well. Add beets and remaining ingredients; bring to a boil. Reduce heat and simmer until the sauce is slightly thickened, stirring often. Remove the spice bag. Cover and refrigerate overnight. YIELD: 10-12 servings.

POTATO-STUFFED TOMATOES

TASTE OF HOME TEST KITCHEN

Even veggie-fearing kids will eat these up. Be sure not to bake the tomatoes much longer than 10 minutes or they might soften and fall apart.

2 small tomatoes
1/8 teaspoon salt
1/2 cup mashed potatoes (with added milk and butter)
1 tablespoon minced fresh parsley
2 tablespoons shredded Parmesan cheese, *divided*
1 tablespoon chopped green onion

Cut a thin slice off the top of each tomato. Scoop out pulp, leaving a 1/4-in. shell. Sprinkle salt on the insides of tomatoes; invert onto paper towels and let drain for 10 minutes.

Combine potatoes, parsley, 1 tablespoon cheese and onion. Spoon into tomatoes. Sprinkle with remaining cheese.

Place in a small baking dish coated with cooking spray. Bake at 400° for 10 minutes or until heated through. YIELD: 2 servings.

QUICK CRAN-APPLE RELISH

TAFFY HILL ❖ LOUISVILLE, KENTUCKY

This is a festive and colorful side dish that beautifully complements roasted chicken or poultry, since it adds a little zing. Also, I often put it in the microwave for 15 minutes for a zesty sauce.

7 oranges
10 unpeeled sweet apples
1 pound fresh *or* frozen cranberries
1/2 cup honey *or* sugar
Pinch salt

Peel six of the oranges; remove seeds and quarter. Quarter unpeeled orange and remove seeds. Place all orange sections in a blender or food processor and process until smooth. Remove to a large bowl.

In another bowl, chop apples and cranberries; add to oranges. Stir in honey and salt. Refrigerate several hours before serving. YIELD: 2 quarts.

BREADS, ROLLS & MORE

The irresistible aroma of fresh-baked breads, rolls, muffins, coffee cakes and more is what this chapter is all about. These homespun recipes will appeal to seasoned and novice bakers alike.

HOMEMADE BREAD

REV. WILLIS PIEPENBRINK ❖ OSHKOSH, WISCONSIN

Saturday in the Piepenbrink household was always baking day. My dad's mother would double the recipe twice and make 8 loaves to last a week!

    1 package (2 ounces) compressed yeast cake, crumbled
    1 teaspoon sugar
    2 cups warm water (80° to 90°), *divided*
  1/3 cup butter, softened
    1 tablespoon salt
6-1/2 cups all-purpose flour
Melted butter

In a 4-qt. bowl, dissolve yeast and sugar in 1/2 cup water. Let stand 5 minutes. Add the butter, salt, remaining water and 3 cups flour. Beat until smooth. Stir in enough remaining flour to make a soft dough.

Turn onto a floured surface; knead until smooth and elastic, about 6-8 minutes. Place in a greased bowl, turning once to grease the top. Cover with plastic wrap and let rise in a warm place until doubled, about 1 hour.

Punch dough down. Divide into 2 parts. Shape into loaves. Place in greased 8-in. x 4-in. loaf pans. Cover and let rise until doubled, about 30 minutes.

HOMEMADE BREAD STORAGE

It's best to store bread at room temperature in a cool dry place for up to 2-3 days. Heat and humidity cause the bread to mold. Storing it in the refrigerator turns it stale quickly. To keep bread soft, store in an airtight plastic bag.

Carefully brush tops with melted butter. Bake at 400° or until golden brown, about 35-40 minutes. Remove from pans and cool on a wire rack. YIELD: 2 loaves (16 slices each).

POTATO BISCUITS

SUSAN PLANTE ❖ BENNINGTON, VERMONT

The mashed potatoes in this recipe make these biscuits extra tender and moist.

    1 cup all-purpose flour
1-1/2 teaspoons brown sugar
    1 teaspoon baking powder
  1/4 teaspoon baking soda
  1/4 teaspoon salt
  1/2 cup mashed potatoes (without added milk and butter)
  1/2 cup buttermilk
    1 tablespoon butter, melted
1-1/2 teaspoons honey

In a small bowl, combine the flour, brown sugar, baking powder, baking soda and salt. In another bowl, combine the potatoes, buttermilk, butter and honey; stir mixture into dry ingredients just until moistened.

Turn onto a lightly floured surface; knead 8-10 times. Pat or roll out to 1/2-in. thickness; cut with a floured 2-1/2-in. biscuit cutter. Place 1 in. apart on an ungreased baking sheet.

Bake at 425° for 8-12 minutes or until golden brown. Serve warm. YIELD: 6 biscuits.

ZESTY JALAPENO CORN MUFFINS

SHARI DORE ✤ PORT SEVEN, ONTARIO

Because they taste so wonderful, I make these tender corn muffins at least twice a month. The recipe saves time because it starts with a mix—the muffins come together fast. My husband and relatives love the flavor, which comes from lime, jalapenos and other ingredients.

- 2 packages (8-1/2 ounces *each*) corn bread/muffin mix
- 1/4 cup minced fresh cilantro
- 1 tablespoon grated lime peel
- 2 teaspoons ground cumin
- 2 eggs
- 2/3 cup buttermilk
- 4 ounces cream cheese, cubed
- 2 jalapeno peppers, seeded and minced
- 4 green onions, finely chopped

In a large bowl, combine the muffin mixes, fresh cilantro, grated lime peel and cumin. Whisk the eggs and buttermilk; stir into the dry ingredients just until moistened. Fold in the cream cheese, jalapeno peppers and green onions. Fill greased or paper-lined muffin cups three-fourths full.

Bake at 400° for 16-20 minutes or until a toothpick inserted into a muffin comes out clean. Cool for 5 minutes before removing from pan to a wire rack. Serve warm. YIELD: 1 dozen.

EDITOR'S NOTE: Wear disposable gloves when cutting hot peppers; the oils can burn skin. Avoid touching your face.

POPPY SEED BREAD

HEATHER FRESE ✤ ALBANY, MISSOURI

My neighbor gave me this recipe. We usually eat one loaf and then give the other away or freeze it for later.

- 3 cups all-purpose flour
- 2-1/4 cups sugar
- 3 teaspoons baking powder
- 1-1/2 teaspoons salt
- 3 eggs
- 1-1/2 cups milk
- 1 cup canola oil
- 1 tablespoon plus 1-1/2 teaspoons poppy seeds
- 1-1/2 teaspoons *each* butter flavoring, almond extract and vanilla extract

GLAZE
- 3/4 cup confectioners' sugar
- 1/4 cup orange juice
- 1/2 teaspoon *each* butter flavoring, almond extract and vanilla extract

In a large bowl, combine flour, sugar, baking powder and salt. In a small bowl, whisk eggs, milk, oil, poppy seeds, butter flavoring and extracts. Stir into dry ingredients just until moistened.

Transfer to two greased 9-in. x 5-in. loaf pans. Bake at 350° for 55-60 minutes or until a toothpick inserted near the center comes out clean. Cool for 10 minutes before removing from pans to wire racks. Combine glaze ingredients; drizzle over warm loaves. YIELD: 2 loaves (16 slices each).

CRANBERRY ORANGE WALNUT BREAD

ELAINE KREMENAK ❖ GRANTS PASS, OREGON

Homemade cranberry bread is almost a natural occurrence in Oregon, a state famous for its cranberries. Each fall my husband and I go out and scrounge around picking up walnuts for this delicious bread. A lady was presenting this masterpiece at a food fair when I had the nerve to ask her for the recipe. She obliged, and it's been a steady item at our household ever since. I freeze the berries and have a ready supply all year long.

        2 cups all-purpose flour
        1 cup sugar
    1-1/2 teaspoons baking powder
        1 teaspoon baking soda
        1/2 teaspoon salt
        1 egg
        1/2 cup orange juice
    Grated peel of 1 orange
        2 tablespoons butter, melted
        2 tablespoons hot water
        1 cup fresh *or* frozen cranberries
        1 cup coarsely chopped walnuts

In a large bowl, combine the dry ingredients. In another bowl, beat egg. Add orange juice, peel, butter and hot water. Add to flour mixture, stirring just until moistened. Gently fold in cranberries and walnuts.

Spoon into a greased 9-in. x 5-in. loaf pan. Bake at 325° for 60 minutes or until a toothpick inserted near the center comes out clean. Cool for 10 minutes before removing from pan to a wire rack. YIELD: 1 loaf (16 servings).

MOM'S BROWN BREAD

PATRICIA WOOLNER ❖ ZION, ILLINOIS

For years I looked for the perfect brown bread recipe—one that tasted just like the bread we enjoyed as children. My searching paid off when I found this recipe. Now it isn't a holiday celebration without Mom's Brown Bread!

        1 cup water
    1-1/4 cups raisins
        3 tablespoons butter
    1-3/4 cups all-purpose flour
        1 cup sugar
        2 eggs, lightly beaten
    1-1/2 teaspoons baking soda
        1 teaspoon vanilla extract
        1/2 teaspoon salt

In a small saucepan, bring the water to a boil. Add the raisins, and butter; remove from the heat. In a large bowl, combine the flour, sugar, eggs, baking soda, vanilla and salt; stir into the raisin mixture.

Grease three 16-oz. vegetable or fruit cans. Divide batter between cans and place on a baking sheet. Bake at 350° for 35-40 minutes or until breads test done. Let stand 5 minutes before removing from cans. If necessary, remove bottom of cans and push breads through. Cool on a wire rack. YIELD: 3 loaves.

IF COOKING FOR TWO: Breads may be frozen to enjoy in months to come.

ROSE ROLLS

MARY WOLFE ❖ LACRETE, ALBERTA

These eye-catching cherry-filled rolls make any breakfast or coffee break special. They freeze very well...just thaw and reheat a few minutes before serving.

1 cup cubed peeled potatoes
1 cup water
1 package (1/4 ounce) active dry yeast
1 cup warm milk (110° to 115°)
1/2 cup sugar
1/2 cup butter, softened
2 teaspoons salt
1 egg
5-1/4 to 5-3/4 cups all-purpose flour
1 cup cherry pie filling
Vanilla Glaze

In a large saucepan, bring potatoes and water to a boil. Reduce heat; cover and simmer for 15-20 minutes or until tender. Drain potatoes, reserving 1/2 cup cooking liquid; cool liquid to 110°-115°. Mash potatoes; set aside to cool to 110°-115°.

In a large bowl, dissolve yeast in warm milk. Add the mashed potatoes, cooking liquid, sugar, butter, salt, egg and 1-1/2 cups flour; beat until smooth. Stir in enough remaining flour to form a soft dough. Do not knead. Cover and let rise in a warm place until doubled, about 1 hour.

Punch dough down. Turn onto a lightly floured surface; divide into 24 pieces. Gently roll each into a 12-in. rope. Holding one end of rope, loosely wrap dough, forming a coil. Tuck end under; pinch to seal. Place 2 in. apart on greased baking sheets. Cover and let rise until doubled, about 30 minutes.

With thumb, make a 1-in. indentation in center of each coil. Fill with cherry pie filling. Bake at 400° for 12-15 minutes or until golden brown. Remove from pans to wire racks to cool. Drizzle with Vanilla Glaze. YIELD: 2 dozen.

VANILLA GLAZE

TASTE OF HOME TEST KITCHEN

This easy glaze comes together quickly and adds just the right touch of sweetness to the Rose Rolls. This glaze also tastes wonderful drizzled over fruit turnovers.

1 cup confectioners' sugar
1/4 teaspoon vanilla extract
1 to 2 tablespoons milk

Combine confectioners' sugar, vanilla and enough milk to achieve desired consistency. YIELD: 1/2 cup.

In a large bowl, dissolve the yeast in warm water. Add the cheeses, milk, sugar, butter, salt and 3 cups flour. Beat on medium speed for 3 minutes. Stir in enough remaining flour to form a firm dough.

Do not knead. Cover and let rise in a warm place until doubled, about 1-1/2 hours.

Stir dough down; transfer to two greased 9-in. x 5-in. loaf pans. Cover and let rise until doubled, about 30 minutes.

In a small bowl, combine egg white and water. In another bowl, combine topping ingredients. Brush loaves with egg white mixture; sprinkle with topping. Bake at 375° for 25-30 minutes or until golden brown. Remove from pans to wire racks to cool. **YIELD: 2 loaves (16 slices each).**

GRANDMA'S CINNAMON ROLLS

DELLA TALBERT ❖ HOWARD, COLORADO

The sweet secret to these rolls is the decadent brown sugar sauce they're baked in. I serve them as dinner rolls or a special breakfast treat.

DOUGH
- 1 package (1/4 ounce) active dry yeast
- 1/4 cup sugar, *divided*
- 1 cup warm water (110° to 115°), *divided*
- 2 tablespoons butter, softened
- 1 egg
- 1 teaspoon salt
- 3-1/4 to 3-3/4 cups all-purpose flour

TOPPING
- 1 cup heavy whipping cream
- 1 cup packed brown sugar

FILLING
- 1/2 cup sugar
- 2 teaspoons ground cinnamon
- 1/2 cup butter, softened

🎖 CHEDDAR CHEESE BATTER BREAD

JEANNE KEMPER ❖ BAGDAD, KENTUCKY

As a dairy farmer, I like to promote our products. This cheesy, golden loaf—a winner at our state fair—tastes great fresh from the oven or cooled and sliced.

- 2 packages (1/4 ounce *each*) active dry yeast
- 3/4 cup warm water (110° to 115°)
- 3 cups (12 ounces) shredded cheddar cheese
- 3/4 cup shredded Parmesan cheese
- 2 cups warm 2% milk (110° to 115°)
- 3 tablespoons sugar
- 1 tablespoon butter, melted
- 2 teaspoons salt
- 6 to 6-1/2 cups all-purpose flour
- 1 egg white, beaten
- 1 tablespoon water

TOPPING
- 1/2 cup finely shredded cheddar cheese
- 1 garlic clove, minced
- 1/2 teaspoon sesame seeds
- 1/2 teaspoon poppy seeds
- 1/2 teaspoon paprika
- 1/4 teaspoon celery seed

In a large bowl, dissolve yeast and 1/2 teaspoon sugar in 1/4 cup warm water. Let stand for 5 minutes. Add the remaining sugar and water, butter, egg, salt and 1-1/2 cups of flour; beat until smooth. Stir in enough remaining flour to form a soft dough.

Turn onto a lightly floured surface; knead until smooth and elastic, about 6-8 minutes. Place in a greased bowl, turning once to grease top. Cover and let rise in a warm place until doubled, about 1 hour.

Meanwhile, combine topping ingredients; pour into a greased 13-in. x 9-in. baking pan; set aside. Combine filling ingredients; set aside.

Punch dough down and turn onto a lightly floured surface. Roll into a 15-in. x 8-in. rectangle; spread filling over dough. Roll up from the long side. Seal seam. Slice into 15 rolls; place with cut side down over topping. Cover and let rise until nearly doubled, about 30-45 minutes.

Bake at 375° for 25 minutes or until golden brown. Cool 3 minutes; invert pan onto a serving plate. YIELD: 15 rolls.

CINNAMON CHERRY ROLLS

NANCY ZIMMERMAN
CAPE MAY COURT HOUSE, NEW JERSEY

These pretty pastries are elegant and your guests will think you fussed. They are so quick and easy to prepare with refrigerated crescent rolls and maraschino cherries.

  1/4 cup packed brown sugar
    1 teaspoon ground cinnamon
    1 tube (8 ounces) refrigerated crescent rolls
    2 tablespoons butter, melted, *divided*
    1 jar (10 ounces) maraschino cherries, drained and chopped
  3/4 cup confectioners' sugar
    4 to 5 teaspoons milk

In a small bowl, combine brown sugar and cinnamon; set aside. Unroll crescent dough and separate into triangles. Brush with 1 tablespoon butter. Sprinkle with 1-1/2 teaspoons brown sugar mixture; top with cherries.

Roll up from the wide end. Place point side down on a greased baking sheet; curve ends slightly. Brush with remaining butter; sprinkle with remaining brown sugar mixture.

Bake at 375° for 12-15 minutes or until golden brown. In a small bowl, combine confectioners' sugar and enough milk to achieve drizzling consistency; drizzle over the warm rolls. YIELD: 8 rolls.

BUTTERY APPLE BISCUITS

ATHENA RUSSELL ❖ FLORENCE, SOUTH CAROLINA

What better way to start the day than with warm biscuits filled with apple and the homey sweetness of molasses? Make a double batch and freeze half for a sensible snack.

    1 cup self-rising flour
1-1/2 teaspoons sugar

Pinch salt
    3 tablespoons cold butter
    1 egg, lightly beaten
    2 tablespoons fat-free milk
    1 tablespoon molasses
  1/2 cup chopped peeled tart apple

In a small bowl, combine the flour, sugar and salt. Cut in butter until mixture resembles coarse crumbs. Combine the egg, milk and molasses; stir into flour mixture just until moistened. Stir in apple. Turn onto a lightly floured surface; knead 8-10 times.

Pat or roll out to 1/2-in. thickness; cut with a floured 2-1/2-in. biscuit cutter. Place 2 in. apart on a baking sheet coated with cooking spray. Bake at 425° for 6-8 minutes or until golden brown. Serve warm. YIELD: 6 biscuits.

EDITOR'S NOTE: As a substitute for 1 cup of self-rising flour, place 1-1/2 teaspoons baking powder and 1/2 teaspoon salt in a measuring cup. Add all-purpose flour to measure 1 cup.

MAKING BISCUITS

For a tender biscuit, don't overmix or overknead the dough. With trimmings, handle dough as little as possible. Use as little extra flour as needed. Overworking the dough or using too much flour results in a tough, dry product.

CHOCOLATE CHIP BANANA BREAD

JENNIFER FISHER ❖ AUSTIN, TEXAS

Here's a healthier version of a classic bread that cuts back on fat and offers something extra—chocolate chips! I can't think of a yummier way to use up ripe bananas.

    2 tablespoons butter, softened
1-1/2 cups sugar
    2 eggs
1-1/4 cups mashed ripe bananas (about 3 medium)
  1/2 cup fat-free sour cream
  1/4 cup unsweetened applesauce
    1 teaspoon vanilla extract
    3 cups all-purpose flour
    2 teaspoons baking soda
  3/4 teaspoon salt
    2 cups (12 ounces) semisweet chocolate chips

In a large bowl, beat butter and sugar until crumbly, about 2 minutes. Add eggs; mix well. Beat in the bananas, sour cream, applesauce and vanilla. Combine the flour, baking soda and salt; add to butter mixture just until moistened. Fold in chips. Transfer to two 9-in. x 5-in. loaf pans coated with cooking spray.

Bake at 350° for 40-45 minutes or until a toothpick inserted near center comes out clean. Cool for 10 minutes before removing from pans to wire racks. YIELD: 2 loaves (16 slices each).

POTATO ROLLS

BEATRICE MCGRATH ❖ NORRIDGEWOCK, MAINE

What better time to shape rolls into cloverleafs than for the celebration of St. Patrick's Day? I found this recipe in a magazine 40 years ago. These rolls are well received at fellowship dinners and are also popular at home. They are the lightest and tastiest rolls I make.

    1 package (1/4 ounce) active dry yeast
  1/4 cup warm water (110° to 115°)
    1 cup warm 2% milk (110° to 115°)
  1/4 cup shortening
  1/2 cup warm mashed potatoes
    1 egg
  1/4 cup sugar
1-1/4 teaspoons salt
    4 cups all-purpose flour

In a large bowl, dissolve yeast in water. Add the milk, shortening, potatoes, egg, sugar, salt and 2 cups flour. Beat until smooth. Add enough remaining flour to form a soft dough.

Turn onto a floured surface; knead until smooth and elastic, about 6-8 minutes. Place in a greased bowl, turning once to grease top. Cover and let rise in a warm place until doubled, about 1 hour.

Punch dough down and divide in half. Divide each half into 36 pieces; shape into balls. Place three balls each into greased muffin cups. Cover and let rise in a warm place until doubled, about 30 minutes.

Bake at 400° for 12-15 minutes or until golden. Remove to wire racks. Serve warm. YIELD: 2 dozen.

BLUEBERRY MUFFINS

KATRINA SHANER ❖ STRONGHURST, ILLINOIS

For a wonderful addition to your brunch menu, try these delicious muffins. The applesauce adds another layer of flavor that is difficult to detect—your guests will be asking, "What makes these muffins so delicious?"

    3 cups Quick Muffin Mix
    2 tablespoons brown sugar
    1 teaspoon ground cinnamon
    1 cup milk
    2 eggs
 1/4 cup applesauce
    1 teaspoon vanilla extract
1-1/4 cups fresh or frozen blueberries

In a large bowl, combine the Quick Muffin Mix, brown sugar and cinnamon. In another bowl, beat the milk, eggs, applesauce and vanilla. Stir into the dry ingredients just until moistened. Fold in the blueberries.

Fill greased or paper-lined muffin cups two-thirds full. Bake at 425° for 15-18 minutes or until a toothpick inserted in the muffin comes out clean. Cool in pan 10 minutes before removing to a wire rack. YIELD: about 1 dozen.

QUICK MUFFIN MIX

KATRINA SHANER ❖ STRONGHURST, ILLINOIS

This is the perfect dry ingredient start to any muffins. You can add your favorite mix-ins, such as dried and fresh fruit, nuts and chocolate bits, for a tasty breakfast muffin.

2-1/2 cups all-purpose flour
2-1/2 cups whole wheat flour
    1 cup wheat bran cereal
    1 cup quick-cooking oats
1-1/2 cups sugar
    2 tablespoons baking powder
    2 teaspoons salt

Combine all ingredients in a large airtight container. Store at room temperature until ready to use. Stir well before measuring for the muffin recipe. YIELD: about 6 cups.

Heavenly Coffee Cakes

Tender, moist, full-flavored coffee cakes like those found here aren't just for breakfast. They're so good, you'll be snacking on them all day long!

BLACKBERRY WHOLE WHEAT COFFEE CAKE

CAROL FORCUM ❖ MARION, ILLINOIS

This low-guilt coffee cake is high in luscious blackberry flavor. Wonderfully moist and tender, it's also good made with fresh or frozen blueberries or raspberries.

1-1/2 cups all-purpose flour
1-1/3 cups packed brown sugar
    1 cup whole wheat flour
    2 teaspoons baking powder
1/2 teaspoon baking soda
Dash salt
    1 egg
    1 cup buttermilk
1/3 cup canola oil
1/3 cup unsweetened applesauce
    2 teaspoons vanilla extract
    2 cups fresh *or* frozen blackberries

In a large bowl, combine the first six ingredients. In a small bowl, combine the egg, buttermilk, oil, applesauce and vanilla. Stir into dry ingredients just until moistened. Fold in blackberries.

Transfer to a 13-in. x 9-in. baking pan coated with cooking spray. Bake at 375° for 35-40 minutes or until a toothpick inserted near the center comes out clean. Cool on a wire rack. YIELD: 20 servings.

GRAHAM-STREUSEL COFFEE CAKE

BONITA HELLMICH ❖ GREENSBURG, INDIANA

With three children and 500 acres of farm, my husband and I are busy to say the least! But we like to get our day off to a good start with a hearty breakfast that often includes this easy-to-prepare yet moist and delicious coffee cake.

STREUSEL
1-1/2 cups graham cracker crumbs
    1 cup packed brown sugar
3/4 cup chopped pecans
2/3 cup butter, melted
    2 teaspoons ground cinnamon
CAKE
    1 package (18-1/4 ounces) white cake mix with pudding
    3 eggs, lightly beaten
    1 cup water
1/4 cup canola oil

In a large bowl, combine streusel ingredients; set aside. In another large bowl, combine the cake mix, eggs, water and oil. Beat on low speed until mixed; beat on medium speed for 2 minutes. Pour half into a greased 13-in. x 9-in. baking pan. Sprinkle with half of the streusel. Carefully spread remaining batter over streusel. Top with remaining streusel.

Bake at 350° for 35-40 minutes or until a toothpick inserted in the cake comes out clean. YIELD: 12-16 servings.

GLAZED APRICOT COFFEE CAKE

MARY ALICE RAMM ❖ MULESHOE, TEXAS

My family just loves apricots, so whenever I get a chance, I try to make this coffee cake. Your family and friends will be impressed with its pretty appearance and great taste.

    1 package (1/4 ounce) active dry yeast
1/4 cup warm water (110° to 115°)
3/4 cup warm milk (110° to 115°)
    1 egg
1/2 cup butter, softened
    4 to 4-1/2 cups all-purpose flour
1/2 cup sugar
1/2 teaspoon salt
APRICOT FILLING
   12 ounces dried apricots
3/4 cup water

CRANBERRY BANANA COFFEE CAKE

GLORIA FRIESEN ❖ CASPER, WYOMING

I make this moist cake for Christmas morning every year. It tastes like banana bread but has a sweet golden topping with a nutty crunch.

1/2 cup butter, softened
1/2 cup sugar
2 eggs
1 teaspoon vanilla extract
2 cups all-purpose flour
2 teaspoons baking powder
1 teaspoon ground cinnamon
1/4 teaspoon salt
1/4 teaspoon ground allspice
2 medium ripe bananas, mashed (about 3/4 cup)
1 cup whole-berry cranberry sauce

TOPPING
1/2 cup packed brown sugar
1/2 cup chopped pecans
2 tablespoons all-purpose flour
2 tablespoons butter, melted

In a large bowl, cream butter and sugar until light and fluffy. Beat in eggs and vanilla. Combine the dry ingredients; add to the creamed mixture alternately with bananas, beating well after each addition. Spread into a greased 13-in. x 9-in. baking pan. Top with cranberry sauce.

In a small bowl, combine the brown sugar, pecans and flour; stir in butter. Sprinkle over cranberries. Bake at 350° for 45-50 minutes or until a toothpick inserted near the center comes out clean. Cool in pan on a wire rack. YIELD: 12-15 servings.

3/4 cup sugar
1/4 teaspoon ground cinnamon

GLAZE
1/2 cup confectioners' sugar
1/2 teaspoon butter, softened
1/2 teaspoon vanilla extract
1 to 2 teaspoons milk

In a large bowl, dissolve yeast in warm water. Add warm milk, egg and butter; mix. Add 2-1/2 cups flour, sugar and salt; beat until smooth. Add enough remaining flour to form a soft dough.

Turn onto floured surface; knead until smooth and elastic, about 6-8 minutes. Place in a greased bowl, turning once to grease top. Cover and let rise in a warm place until doubled, about 1 hour.

For filling, combine apricots and water in a small saucepan. Cover and simmer for 30 minutes. Cool 10 minutes. Pour into a blender; process at high speed until smooth. Stir in sugar and cinnamon; set aside.

Punch dough down. Divide in half and roll each half into a 15-in. x 12-in. rectangle. Place on a greased baking sheet. Spread half of the filling in a 15-in. x 4-in. strip down center of dough. With a sharp knife, cut dough on each side of apricot filling into 1-in.-wide strips. Fold strips alternately across filling to give braided effect. Repeat with remaining dough and filling. Cover and let rise until doubled, about 30 minutes.

Bake at 375° for 20 minutes or until golden brown. Cool on wire racks for 15 minutes. Meanwhile, in small bowl, combine the confectioners' sugar, butter, vanilla and enough milk to achieve desired consistency; drizzle over warm coffee cakes. Serve warm or allow to cool completely. YIELD: 2 coffee cakes.

1/2 teaspoon salt
1 egg
2/3 cup 2% milk
1/2 cup butter, melted
1/2 cup butter pecan *or* maple syrup
1/4 cup sour cream
1/2 teaspoon vanilla extract

TOPPING
3 tablespoons all-purpose flour
3 tablespoons sugar
1/2 teaspoon ground cinnamon
2 tablespoons cold butter
2 tablespoons chopped pecans

In a large bowl, combine the flour, brown sugar, baking powder and salt. In another bowl, combine the egg, milk, butter, syrup, sour cream and vanilla. Stir into dry ingredients just until moistened. Fill greased or paper-lined muffin cups three-fourths full.

For topping, combine the flour, sugar and cinnamon; cut in butter until crumbly. Stir in pecans. Sprinkle over tops.

Bake at 400° for 18-22 minutes or until a toothpick inserted in the muffin comes out clean. Cool for 5 minutes before removing from pan to a wire rack. Serve warm. YIELD: 1 dozen.

EASY ORANGE ROLLS

PEGGY KRAEMER ❖ THIEF RIVER, MINNESOTA

Life on a dairy farm is busy, so I need breakfast recipes that are simple yet delicious. This was probably one of the first recipes my teenage daughter made herself.

1 cup sugar
1/2 cup butter, cubed
1/4 cup orange juice
2 tablespoons grated orange peel
3 tubes (10 ounces *each*) refrigerated biscuits

In a small saucepan, combine the sugar, butter, orange juice and peel. Heat until sugar is dissolved and butter is melted. Pour into a greased 10-in. fluted tube pan.

Place 12 biscuits on their sides in a ring around the outer edge, overlapping slightly. Arrange remaining biscuits in same manner, creating two more rings.

Bake at 350° for 25-30 minutes or until golden brown. Immediately turn upside down onto serving platter. Serve warm. YIELD: 12-16 servings.

BUTTER PECAN MUFFINS

JUDY REAGAN ❖ HANNIBAL, MISSOURI

Our youngest son lives in Georgia, where we gather the fresh pecans we use for these smooth, buttery muffins.

2 cups all-purpose flour
1/2 cup packed brown sugar
2 teaspoons baking powder

MOIST CORN BREAD

CHRISTINE MAZZARELLA ❖ BROCKPORT, NEW YORK

This recipe is perfect when you want to make an easy "dump and mix" corn bread.

1 egg, lightly beaten
1-1/2 cups fresh *or* frozen corn, thawed
1 can (8-1/4 ounces) cream-style corn
1 package (8-1/2 ounces) corn bread/muffin mix
1 cup (8 ounces) fat-free plain yogurt
1/4 cup reduced-calorie stick margarine, melted

In a large bowl, combine all the ingredients. Pour into an 8-in. square baking dish coated with cooking spray.

Bake at 350° for 35-40 minutes or until edges are lightly browned and a toothpick inserted near the center comes out clean. Let stand for 10 minutes before cutting. Serve warm. YIELD: 9 servings.

MAKING CORN BREAD

To avoid overmixing, stir the batter by hand just until moistened. Lumps in the batter are normal and desired. If you like a more crusty corn bread, use a dark pan or skillet instead of one with a light finish.

APPLE CIDER CINNAMON ROLLS

KIM FORNI ❖ CLAREMONT, NEW HAMPSHIRE

Feeling creative, I put an apple spin on a traditional cinnamon roll recipe. The results were yummy! A panful is perfect for a weekend morning in autumn.

3-1/4 cups all-purpose flour
1/4 cup sugar
1 package (1/4 ounce) quick-rise yeast
1/2 teaspoon salt
3/4 cup 2% milk
1/4 cup apple cider *or* juice
1/4 cup plus 1/3 cup butter, softened, *divided*
1 egg
2 cups finely chopped peeled tart apples
1-1/4 cups packed brown sugar
3/4 cup finely chopped walnuts
3 teaspoons ground cinnamon

APPLE CIDER CREAM CHEESE FROSTING
2 cups apple cider *or* juice
1 cinnamon stick (3 inches)
1 package (8 ounces) cream cheese, softened
1/4 cup butter, softened
1 cup confectioners' sugar

In a large bowl, combine 2-1/4 cups flour, sugar, yeast and salt. In a small saucepan, heat the milk, cider and 1/4 cup butter to 120°-130°. Add to dry ingredients; beat just until moistened. Add egg; beat until smooth. Stir in enough remaining flour to form a soft dough (dough will be sticky).

Turn onto a floured surface; knead until smooth and elastic, about 6-8 minutes. Cover and let rest for 10 minutes. Roll into a 15-in. x 10-in. rectangle. Spread remaining butter to within 1/2 in. of edges. Combine the apples, brown sugar, walnuts and cinnamon; sprinkle over butter.

Roll up jelly-roll style, starting with a long side; pinch the seam to seal. Cut into 12 slices. Place cut side down in a greased 13-in. x 9-in. baking dish. Cover and let rolls rise in a warm place for 30 minutes.

Bake at 325° for 30-35 minutes or until golden brown. For frosting, place cider and cinnamon stick in a small saucepan. Bring to a boil; cook until liquid is reduced to 1/4 cup, about 20 minutes. Discard cinnamon stick; cool cider.

In a large bowl, beat cream cheese and butter until fluffy. Add confectioners' sugar and reduced cider; beat until smooth. Spread over warm rolls. YIELD: 1 dozen.

GLAZED CRANBERRY SWEET POTATO BREAD

SWEET POTATO FESTIVAL COMMITTEE
VARDAMAN, MISSISSIPPI

The Sweet Potato Festival Committee of Vardaman, Mississippi shared this recipe, which stars their crop. Slices of the moist bread topped with an orange glaze make a sweet snack to enjoy anytime.

3-1/2 cups all-purpose flour
1-2/3 cups sugar
  2 teaspoons baking soda
  2 teaspoons pumpkin pie spice
  1 teaspoon baking powder
3/4 teaspoon salt
  4 eggs, lightly beaten
  2 cups mashed cooked sweet potatoes
  1 can (14 ounces) whole-berry cranberry sauce
2/3 cup canola oil
3/4 cup chopped pecans

GLAZE
  1 cup confectioners' sugar
1/4 cup orange juice concentrate
1/8 teaspoon ground allspice

In a large bowl, combine the flour, sugar, baking soda, pie spice, baking powder and salt. In another large bowl, combine the eggs, sweet potatoes, cranberry sauce and oil. Stir into dry ingredients just until moistened. Fold in pecans.

Pour into two greased 9-in. x 5-in. loaf pans. Bake at 350° for 55-60 minutes or until a toothpick inserted near the center comes out clean. Cool for 10 minutes before removing from pans to wire racks to cool completely. In a small bowl, combine the glaze ingredients until smooth; drizzle over cooled loaves. YIELD: 2 loaves (16 servings each).

SOURDOUGH STARTER

DELILA GEORGE ❖ JUNCTION CITY, OREGON

Some 25 years ago, I received a bread recipe and some starter from a good friend who is now a neighbor. I use this sourdough starter to make many loaves of bread.

1 package (1/4 ounce) active dry yeast
2 cups warm water (110° to 115°)
2 cups all-purpose flour

In a 4-qt. nonmetallic bowl, dissolve the yeast in the warm water; let stand for 5 minutes. Add the flour and stir until smooth. Cover the bowl loosely with a clean towel. Let stand in a warm place (80°-90°) to ferment for 48 hours; stir several times daily. The mixture will become bubbly and rise, and it will have a "yeasty" sour aroma. A transparent yellow liquid will form on top.

Use this starter for your favorite sourdough recipes. The starter will keep in the refrigerator for up to 2 weeks. Use and replenish at least every 2 weeks. Replenish with equal amounts of flour and water to restore the volume; stir. YIELD: about 3 cups.

SOURDOUGH ENGLISH MUFFINS

JEAN GRAF-JOYCE ❖ ALBANY, OREGON

You have to make the Sourdough Starter first before you can make this recipe, but it's worth it. The starter really adds depth of flavor. This recipe was a winner in a local newspaper contest years ago and has become a family favorite. The muffins are fun to make on a griddle and delicious to eat.

2-3/4 to 3 cups all-purpose flour
    1 cup water
1/2 cup Sourdough Starter
1/3 cup instant nonfat dry milk powder
    1 tablespoon sugar
3/4 teaspoon salt
1/4 cup cornmeal, *divided*
Butter, jam or honey

In a large bowl, combine 2 cups flour, water and Sourdough Starter. Cover and let stand overnight.

Combine the milk powder, sugar, salt and 1/2 cup flour. Add to sour dough mixture; mix well. Turn onto a floured surface; knead until smooth and no longer sticky, about 2-3 minutes, adding more flour if needed.

Roll to 1/2-in. thickness. Cut with a 3-in. round cookie cutter. Grease baking sheets and sprinkle with 2 tablespoons cornmeal. Place muffins 2 in. apart on prepared baking sheets. Sprinkle remaining cornmeal over muffin tops. Cover and let rise in a warm place until doubled, about 45 minutes.

In a lightly greased griddle or electric skillet, cook muffins at 275° for 10 minutes. Turn and cook 10-15 minutes longer or until golden brown. Split with a sharp knife or a fork and toast if desired. Serve with butter, jam or honey. YIELD: 1 dozen.

ICEBOX BUTTERHORNS

JUDY CLARK ❖ ELKHART, INDIANA

If you'd like a roll that melts in your mouth, try these. They smell absolutely heavenly as they bake to a golden brown. People will be impressed when these rolls land on the table.

2 packages (1/4 ounce each) active dry yeast
1/4 cup warm water (110° to 115°)
2 cups warm milk (110° to 115°)
1/2 cup sugar
1 egg, lightly beaten
1 teaspoon salt
6-1/2 cups all-purpose flour
3/4 cup butter, melted
Additional melted butter

In a large bowl, dissolve yeast in water. Add the milk, sugar, egg, salt and 3 cups flour; beat until smooth. Beat in butter and remaining flour (dough will be slightly sticky). Do not knead. Place in a greased bowl. Cover and refrigerate overnight.

Punch down dough and divide in half. On a floured surface, roll each half into a 12-in. circle. Cut each circle into pie-shaped wedges. Beginning at the wide end, roll up each wedge. Place rolls, point side down, 2 in. apart on greased baking sheets. Cover and let rise in a warm place until doubled, about 1 hour.

Bake at 350° for 15-20 minutes or until golden brown. Immediately brush tops with melted butter. Remove from pans to wire racks to cool. Yield: 2 dozen.

PROOFING YEAST

Dissolve one package of yeast and 1 teaspoon sugar in 1/4 cup warm water (110° to 115°). Let stand for 5 to 10 minutes. If the mixture foams up, the yeast is active and the mixture can be used. If it does not foam, the yeast should be discarded.

COOKIES, BARS & CANDIES

Satisfying your sweet tooth has never been so delectable. These goodies are popular at potlucks, in bake sales or as special treats at home. Your family and friends will vote you the best baker on the block!

ALMOND RUSKS

LUCILLE DUNN ❖ ALMA CENTER, WISCONSIN

I grew up in a Scandinavian community and enjoyed many Swedish treats as a child. This is one recipe I've kept through the years, and it's become a favorite snack for my nieces and nephews. It is crunchy yet not too sweet...a delicious treat to take along on any outing!

    3 eggs, lightly beaten
    1 cup sugar
    1 cup canola oil
3-1/2 cups all-purpose flour
    1 cup finely chopped almonds
1-1/2 teaspoons baking powder
    1 teaspoon salt

In a large bowl, whisk the eggs, sugar and oil. Combine flour, almonds, baking powder and salt; gradually add to sugar mixture until well combined. Chill until firm.

Divide dough into three pieces. Roll each piece into an 8-in. x 2-in. rectangle; place on a greased baking sheet.

Bake at 350° for 15-20 minutes or until firm to the touch. Cool on a wire rack for 15 minutes. Reduce heat to 300°.

Carefully cut each rectangle into 1/2-in. slices. Place slices cut side down on baking sheets. Bake for 8-10 minutes. Remove to wire racks to cool. YIELD: 4 dozen.

IF COOKING FOR TWO: Extra cookies keep well when stored in airtight containers.

SOUR CREAM APPLE SQUARES

NANCY WIT ❖ FREMONT, NEBRASKA

Mom and I formulated this recipe back in the '50s after visiting a friend's farm where they made the most delicious sour cream ever. Our first try was perfect, and these apple squares soon became a favorite to serve at social functions. Years ago, we made six pans of these squares when a young Johnny Carson presented his magic show at our card club!

    2 cups all-purpose flour
    2 cups packed brown sugar
1/2 cup butter, softened
    1 cup chopped nuts
    2 teaspoons ground cinnamon
    1 teaspoon baking soda
1/2 teaspoon salt
    1 cup (8 ounces) sour cream
    1 teaspoon vanilla extract
    1 egg, beaten
    2 cups chopped peeled tart apples
Whipped cream, optional

In a large bowl, combine the flour, brown sugar and butter; beat at low speed until crumbly. Stir in nuts. Press about 2-3/4 cups into an ungreased 13-in. x 9-in. baking pan.

To the remaining crumb mixture, add the cinnamon, baking soda, salt, sour cream, vanilla and egg. Beat until thoroughly combined. Stir in apples. Spoon evenly over crust. Bake at 350° for 35-40 minutes or until a toothpick inserted near the center comes out clean. Cool on a wire rack. Cut into squares. Garnish with whipped cream if desired. YIELD: 12-15 servings.

PFEFFERNUESSE

N.R. URIE ❖ PUEBLO, CALIFORNIA

These spicy cookies are a tradition with the Dutch, Danish and German cultures. The word is translated as "pepper nuts" because of the cookies' flavor and ingredients.

1/2 cup butter, softened
3/4 cup sugar
3/4 cup packed brown sugar
1 egg
1/2 cup heavy whipping cream
1/3 cup corn syrup
2 tablespoons honey
1 teaspoon anise extract
1/2 teaspoon vanilla extract
4 cups all-purpose flour
1/2 teaspoon *each* salt, baking soda and cream of tartar
1/2 teaspoon *each* ground cinnamon, cloves and nutmeg
1/4 teaspoon ground allspice
1/4 teaspoon pepper

In a large bowl, cream butter and sugars until light and fluffy. Beat in the egg, cream, corn syrup, honey and extracts. Combine the dry ingredients; gradually add to the creamed mixture and mix well. Cover and refrigerate overnight.

Roll dough into 1-in. balls. Place 2 in. apart on greased baking sheets. Bake at 400° for 10-11 minutes or until golden brown. Cool on wire racks. YIELD: 5-1/2 dozen.

CHOCOLATE-BERRY BARS

GRACE LAIRD ❖ BARKER, TEXAS

I created this recipe by accident when I wanted to make Rice Krispie bars with dried fruit. All I had in my cupboard were dried cranberries and chocolate chips, so I tossed them in.

5-1/2 cups crisp rice cereal
1/2 cup semisweet chocolate chips
1/2 cup dried cranberries
1/4 cup toasted wheat germ
1 package (10-1/2 ounces) miniature marshmallows
2 teaspoons canola oil
2 teaspoons milk

In a large bowl, combine the cereal, chocolate chips, cranberries and wheat germ; set aside.

In a large microwave-safe bowl, combine the marshmallows, oil and milk. Microwave, uncovered, on high for 45 seconds; stir. Microwave 30-45 seconds longer or until marshmallows are puffed and melted; stir until smooth.

Pour over cereal mixture; stir until chips are melted. Spread into a lightly greased 13-in. x 9-in. pan. Cut into bars. YIELD: about 1-1/2 dozen.

EDITOR'S NOTE: This recipe was tested in a 1,100-watt microwave.

PEANUT BUTTER FINGERS

MARGIE LOWRY ❖ MCCAMMON, IDAHO

Always a hit with the teenagers in our house, these rich bars are sure to please the peanut butter lovers in your family. They're great for serving at holiday time.

3/4 cup butter, softened
3/4 cup creamy peanut butter
3/4 cup sugar
3/4 cup packed brown sugar
2 eggs
1-1/2 teaspoons vanilla extract
1-1/2 cups all-purpose flour
1-1/2 cups quick-cooking oats
3/4 teaspoon baking soda
1/2 teaspoon salt
1 cup (6 ounces) semisweet chocolate chips

GLAZE
3/4 cup creamy peanut butter
1 cup confectioners' sugar
4 to 6 tablespoons milk
1 cup chopped peanuts

In a large bowl, cream the butter, peanut butter and sugars until light and fluffy. Add eggs, one at a time, beating well after each addition. Beat in vanilla. Combine the flour, oats, baking soda and salt; add to creamed mixture and mix well. Pour into a greased 15-in. x 10-in. x 1-in. baking pan.

Bake at 325° for 18-20 minutes or until a toothpick inserted near the center comes out clean. Immediately sprinkle with chocolate chips. Allow chips to soften for a few minutes, then spread over bars.

For glaze, in a small bowl, beat peanut butter and confectioners' sugar until smooth. Add enough milk to achieve spreading consistency. Carefully spread over warm bars; sprinkle with peanuts. Cool before cutting into bars. YIELD: 5 dozen.

EDITOR'S NOTE: Reduced-fat peanut butter is not recommended for this recipe.

CHOCOLATE CASHEW CLUSTERS

VIRGINIA SAUER ❖ WANTAGH, NEW YORK

People are crazy about these cashews coated in toffee and three kinds of chocolate. They make gift-giving sweet and simple for me!

  16 ounces white baking chocolate, chopped
   7 ounces milk chocolate, chopped
   7 ounces bittersweet chocolate, chopped
   4 cups salted cashews
 3/4 cup milk chocolate English toffee bits

In a large heavy saucepan over low heat, cook and stir the chocolates until melted. Remove from the heat; stir in cashews and toffee bits. Drop by tablespoonfuls onto waxed paper. Refrigerate for 10-15 minutes or until set. Store in an airtight container. YIELD: 3 pounds.

PUMPKIN WHOOPIE PIES

THE FEDERATED CHURCH OF MARLBOROUGH
MARLBOROUGH, NEW HAMPSHIRE

Folks line up for these plump, yummy cookies oozing with a very creamy filling. Volunteers make them for the Keene Pumpkin Festival.

      3 cups all-purpose flour
  1-1/2 cups sugar
      2 teaspoons baking powder
      2 teaspoons baking soda
  1-1/2 teaspoons ground cinnamon
      1 teaspoon ground nutmeg
      1 teaspoon ground cloves

  1/2 teaspoon salt
    5 eggs
    1 can (15 ounces) solid-pack pumpkin
  1/2 cup water
  1/2 cup canola oil
    1 teaspoon vanilla extract

CREAM CHEESE FILLING
    4 ounces cream cheese, softened
  1/4 cup butter, softened
    2 cups confectioners' sugar
    1 teaspoon vanilla extract

In a large bowl, combine the flour, sugar, baking powder, baking soda, cinnamon, nutmeg, cloves and salt. In another bowl, whisk the eggs, pumpkin, water, oil and vanilla. Stir into dry ingredients just until moistened.

Drop batter by 2 tablespoonfuls 2 in. apart onto greased baking sheets. Bake at 350° for 8-10 minutes. Remove cookies to wire racks to cool completely.

In a small bowl, beat the filling ingredients until smooth. Spread over the bottom of half of the cookies; top with remaining cookies. Store in the refrigerator. YIELD: 2 dozen.

MOCHA ALMOND FUDGE

JEANETTE PATTON ❖ DAYTON, OHIO

I probably found this recipe in a magazine, and it has to date back to the '60s. I find the dessert to be very easy, with good texture and flavor. Friends with whom I share this treat think so, too.

    1 teaspoon butter
    1 cup semisweet chocolate chips
  1/3 cup sweetened condensed milk
    1 tablespoon instant coffee granules
Dash salt
  1/4 cup chopped almonds, toasted
  1/4 teaspoon almond extract

Line a 9-in. x 5-in. loaf pan with foil and grease the foil with butter; set aside.

In a large microwave-safe bowl, combine the chocolate chips, milk, coffee granules and salt. Microwave, uncovered, on high for 1 minute; stir. Microwave at additional 15-second intervals, stirring until smooth. Stir in almonds and extract. Spread into prepared pan. Refrigerate for 1 hour or until firm.

Using foil, lift fudge out of pan. Gently peel off foil; cut fudge into 1-in. squares. Store in an airtight container in the refrigerator. YIELD: about 1/2 pound.

CARAMEL CASHEW BROWNIES

MARILYN MILLER ❖ FORT WASHINGTON, PENNSYLVANIA

These ooey-gooey brownies are bursting with chocolate chips, gobs of caramel and plenty of cashews.

  3/4 cup butter, softened
1-1/2 cups packed brown sugar
    3 eggs
    3 ounces unsweetened chocolate, melted and cooled
    3 teaspoons vanilla extract
1-1/4 cups all-purpose flour
    1/4 teaspoon salt
1-1/2 cups 60% cacao bittersweet chocolate baking chips
    1 cup chopped cashews

TOPPING
   16 caramels
    3 tablespoons 2% milk

In a large bowl, cream the butter and sugar until light and fluffy. Add the eggs, one at a time, beating well after each addition. Beat in the chocolate and vanilla. Combine the flour and salt; gradually beat into creamed mixture just until moistened. Stir in the chocolate chips.

Pour into two greased 9-in. square baking pans. Sprinkle with cashews. Bake at 325° for 20-25 minutes or until a toothpick inserted near the center comes out with moist crumbs (do not overbake). Cool on wire racks.

In a small saucepan, combine caramels and milk. Cook and stir over medium-low heat until caramels are melted. Drizzle over brownies. YIELD: about 2-1/2 dozen.

CHERRY WALNUT BALLS

SUZANNE MCKINLEY ❖ LYONS, GEORGIA

This old-fashioned holiday candy brightens up cookie plates and has become one of my signature confections, requested by family and friends. I made this up by combining two recipes.

    1 egg, lightly beaten
1/2 cup sugar
1/2 cup finely chopped walnuts
1/2 cup chopped dates
1/4 cup flaked coconut
1/4 teaspoon almond extract
1/4 teaspoon vanilla extract
Dash salt
    18 candied cherries
Confectioners' sugar

In a large bowl, combine the egg, sugar, walnuts, dates, coconut, extracts and salt. Transfer to a greased 8-in. square baking dish. Bake at 350° for 25 minutes, stirring every 8 minutes. Remove from the oven; stir well. Cool.

Shape about 1 tablespoon of the walnut mixture around each candied cherry, forming a ball. Sprinkle with confectioners' sugar. Store in an airtight container at room temperature. YIELD: 1-1/2 dozen.

ORIGINAL BROWN BUTTER REFRIGERATOR COOKIES

IONE DIEKFUSS ❖ MUSKEGO, WISCONSIN

These tasty, crispy cookies won *Country Woman's* first-ever recipe contest, back in December 1970. They're quick and easy to prepare. The Test Kitchen made a batch recently, and the staff agreed they're as tasty today as they were then and are great for dunking in milk or coffee.

    1 cup butter, cubed
    2 cups packed brown sugar
    2 eggs
    3 cups all-purpose flour
    1 teaspoon cream of tartar
    1 teaspoon baking soda
1/4 teaspoon salt
    1 cup finely chopped pecans

Heat butter in a large saucepan over medium heat until golden brown, about 7-9 minutes (do not burn). Remove from the heat; stir in brown sugar until blended.

Transfer to a large bowl; whisk in eggs one at a time. Combine the flour, cream of tartar, baking soda and salt; gradually add to butter mixture and mix well. Stir in pecans.

Shape into four 8-in. rolls; wrap each in plastic wrap. Refrigerate for 8 hours or overnight.

Cut into 1/4-in. slices. Place 2 in. apart on ungreased baking sheets. Bake at 375° for 5-7 minutes or just until set. Cool for 1 minute before removing from pans to wire racks. YIELD: About 10-1/2 dozen.

MAPLE OATMEAL COOKIES

CECILE BRANON ❖ FAIRFIELD, VERMONT

No other food product is more closely tied to Vermont than maple syrup. So when I want to give someone a traditional taste of my home state, I bring out a warm batch of these chewy cookies.

3/4 cup butter, softened
1/2 cup sugar
    1 egg
    1 cup maple syrup
    1 teaspoon vanilla extract
    3 cups quick-cooking oats
1-1/4 cups all-purpose flour
    1 teaspoon baking soda
1/2 teaspoon salt
1/2 cup chopped pecans
1/2 cup raisins

In a large bowl, cream butter and sugar until light and fluffy. Beat in the egg, syrup and vanilla. Combine the oats, flour, baking soda and salt; gradually add to creamed mixture and mix well. Stir in pecans and raisins.

Drop by tablespoonfuls 2 in. apart onto greased baking sheets. Bake at 350° for 10-12 minutes or until lightly browned. Cool for 2 minutes before removing from pans to wire racks. YIELD: 5-1/2 dozen.

BIRCH PRETZEL LOGS

MARY BIEBL ✦ ST. PAUL, MINNESOTA

At the root of this treat is plenty of penny-wise practicality. I first started making the "logs" after I saw some chocolate-dipped pretzels at a shop. They sure were appealing—but the price was outrageous. So I came up with my own version. Nowadays, I often tie bundles of plastic-wrapped "logs" with ribbons to give out at Christmas, or I'll set a stack out on a pretty plate for a party.

    1 pound white candy coating, coarsely chopped
    1 package (10 ounces) pretzel rods
1/2 cup semisweet chocolate chips
    1 small heavy-duty resealable plastic bag

In a microwave, melt candy coating; stir until smooth. Pour into an ungreased 8-in. square pan or a tall glass. Roll or dip pretzels in coating, leaving 1 in. of space on the end you are holding; allow excess to drip off. Place on waxed paper-lined baking sheets; let stand until set.

In a microwave, melt chocolate chips; stir until smooth. Pour into a small resealable plastic bag. Carefully cut a very small hole in the bottom corner of the bag. Pipe stripe markings across the pretzel rods to resemble birch trees. Allow to set. Store in an airtight container. YIELD: about 2 dozen.

NAPOLEON CREMES

GLORIA JESSWEIN ✦ NILES, MICHIGAN

For the annual Christmas open house we host, I set out a buffet with lots of food and candies like these lovely layered treats. They're so creamy...and with a green pistachio layer of pudding peeking out, they're very merry.

    1 cup butter, softened, *divided*
1/4 cup sugar
1/4 cup baking cocoa
    1 teaspoon vanilla extract
    1 egg, lightly beaten
    2 cups finely crushed graham cracker crumbs
      (about 32 squares)
    1 cup flaked coconut
    3 tablespoons milk
    1 package (3.4 ounces) instant pistachio *or* lemon pudding
      mix
    2 cups confectioners' sugar

TOPPING
    1 cup (6 ounces) semisweet chocolate chips
    3 tablespoons butter

In a large heavy saucepan, combine 1/2 cup butter, sugar, cocoa and vanilla; cook and stir until butter is melted. Stir a small amount of hot mixture into egg; return all to the pan, stirring constantly. Cook and stir until mixture thickens, about 5 minutes. Stir in the graham cracker crumbs and coconut. Press into a greased 9-in. square pan.

In a small bowl, beat remaining butter until smooth. Add milk, pudding mix and confectioners' sugar; beat until fluffy. Spread over crust. Refrigerate until firm, 1-1/2 to 2 hours.

In a microwave, melt chocolate chips and butter; stir until smooth. Cool. Spread over pudding layer. Chill until set. Cut into bars. YIELD: 4 dozen.

KIDS' SUSHI

LORRI REINHARDT ❖ BIG BEND, WISCONSIN

I've taken these fun, mock sushi rolls to picnics and parties and served them at home with an Asian dinner. Kids always enjoy the bite-sized treats.

10 Fruit Roll-Ups
10 pieces multicolored licorice
4 cups miniature marshmallows
1/4 cup butter, cubed
5 cups crisp rice cereal

Unroll the Fruit Roll-Ups, leaving paper attached. Cut licorice lengthwise into thin strips; set aside. In a large microwave-safe bowl, combine marshmallows and butter. Microwave, uncovered, on high for 2 minutes or until melted, stirring once a minute. Add cereal; stir to coat.

Place about 1/2 cup cereal mixture on the edge of each roll-up; place the licorice in the center of the mixture. Roll up sushi rolls to about 1-inch diameter. Discard the paper. Trim edges of rolls; cut each into four pieces. Store in an airtight container. YIELD: 40 pieces.
EDITOR'S NOTE: This recipe was tested in a 1,100-watt microwave.

THE SKINNY ON MARSHMALLOWS
To keep marshmallows from turning hard, store them in the freezer. When thawed, they're like fresh. To separate sticky marshmallows, place a spoonful of powdered sugar in the bag and shake it well.

COCONUT-LEMON CHEESECAKE DESSERT

LESLIE DICKSON ❖ BUFFALO, WYOMING

This refreshing sweet treat was a huge hit when I brought it to our ladies fellowship meeting at church. Everyone loved the buttery coconut crust, lemony filling and rich sour cream topping.

1-1/2 cups all-purpose flour
1 cup flaked coconut, toasted
3/4 cup butter, softened
1/2 cup confectioners' sugar
FILLING
1 package (8 ounces) cream cheese, softened
2/3 cup sugar
2 eggs, lightly beaten
1/3 cup lemon juice
1 tablespoon grated lemon peel
TOPPING
1-1/2 cups sour cream
1/3 cup sugar
1/2 teaspoon vanilla extract
1-1/2 cups flaked coconut, toasted

Place the flour, coconut, butter and confectioners' sugar in a food processor; cover and process until combined. Press into an ungreased 13-in. x 9-in. baking dish. Bake at 350° for 15-20 minutes or until lightly browned.

In a small bowl, beat cream cheese and sugar until light and fluffy. Beat in the eggs, lemon juice and peel just until combined. Pour over crust. Bake for 18-20 minutes or until edges are lightly browned and filling is set.

Combine the sour cream, sugar and vanilla; spread over filling. Sprinkle with the coconut. Bake 10 minutes longer. Cool on a wire rack. Refrigerate for at least 4 hours before cutting. YIELD: 15 servings.

CUTOUT WEDDING COOKIES

GRACE VAN TIMMEREN ❖ GRAND RAPIDS, MICHIGAN

The dessert table shapes up sweetly when we make these crisp, almond-flavored cookies for family weddings. Hearts, lips, doves, bells and other love-themed cutters work well.

3/4 cup butter, softened
1 cup sugar
2 eggs
1 teaspoon almond extract
2-1/2 cups all-purpose flour
1 teaspoon baking powder
1 teaspoon salt

FROSTING
1/2 cup butter, softened
4-1/2 cups confectioners' sugar
1-1/2 teaspoons vanilla extract
5 to 6 tablespoons 2% milk

Paste food coloring of your choice
Edible glitter and colored sugar
Sprinkles, optional

In a large bowl, cream butter and sugar until light and fluffy. Beat in eggs and extract. Combine the flour, baking powder and salt; gradually add to creamed mixture and mix well. Cover and refrigerate for 1 hour or until easy to handle.

On a well-floured surface, roll dough to 1/4-in. thickness. Cut with floured 2-1/2-in. to 4-in. love-themed cookie cutters. Place 2 in. apart on greased baking sheets. Bake at 400° for 6-8 minutes or until set. Remove to wire racks to cool completely.

For frosting, in a large bowl, beat butter until light and fluffy. Beat in the confectioners' sugar, vanilla and enough milk to achieve desired consistency. Tint frosting as desired; frost cookies. Combine equal amounts of edible glitter and colored sugar; sprinkle over cookies. Decorate some cookies with sprinkles if desired. YIELD: about 4 dozen.

EDITOR'S NOTE: Edible glitter is available from Wilton Industries. Call 800-794-5866 or visit *www.wilton.com.*

PLANTATION BARS

JEANETTE PEDERSON ❖ MONICO, WISCONSIN

Instead of the typical melted marshmallows, this clever recipe calls for melted vanilla chips. With crisp rice cereal, peanut butter and nuts, these bars taste almost like candy.

2 packages (10 to 12 ounces *each*) vanilla *or* white chips
1 cup peanut butter
7 cups crisp rice cereal
1 cup salted peanuts
2 cups confectioners' sugar
2 tablespoons plus 2 teaspoons water
4-1/2 teaspoons meringue powder
1/4 teaspoon cream of tartar
Red and blue food coloring
Red, blue and white sprinkles

In a large microwave-safe bowl, combine the vanilla chips and peanut butter. Microwave, uncovered, at 50% power for 1-1/2 to 3-1/2 minutes or until melted; stir until smooth. Stir in cereal and peanuts. Press into a greased 13-in. x 9-in. pan. Let stand at room temperature until firm, about 30 minutes.

Divide the pan of bars in half. On one half, cut out stars using a greased 2-1/2-in. star-shaped cookie cutter. Cut remaining half into 3-1/4-in. x 1-1/4-in. bars for stripes.

In a small bowl, combine the confectioners' sugar, water, meringue powder and cream of tartar; beat on low speed just until combined. Beat on high for 4-5 minutes or until stiff peaks form. Divide frosting among three bowls. Tint one red and one blue and leave remaining frosting white. Decorate cutouts with frosting and sprinkles. YIELD: 1-1/2 dozen.

EDITOR'S NOTE: This recipe was tested in a 1,100-watt microwave. Meringue powder is available from Wilton Industries. Call 1-800-794-5866 or visit *www.wilton.com*.

CHAMPIONSHIP CHOCOLATE CHIP BARS

CHERYL COSTELLO ❖ FESTUS, MISSOURI

As the name suggests, you'll earn rave reviews next time these bars make an appearance on your table. Don't forget to have copies of the recipe on hand!

1-1/2 cups all-purpose flour
1/2 cup packed brown sugar
1/2 cup cold butter, cubed
2 cups (12 ounces) semisweet chocolate chips, *divided*
1 can (14 ounces) sweetened condensed milk
1 egg
1 teaspoon vanilla extract
1 cup chopped walnuts

In a large bowl, combine flour and brown sugar; cut in butter until crumbly. Stir in 1/2 cup chocolate chips. Press firmly into a greased 13-in. x 9-in. baking pan. Bake at 350° for 15 minutes.

Meanwhile, combine the milk, egg, vanilla, walnuts and remaining chips. Spread evenly over hot crust. Bake for 20-25 minutes or until light golden brown. Cool on a wire rack. Cut into bars. YIELD: about 2-1/2 dozen.

GRANDMA'S SUGAR COOKIES

ANN DEHASS AND LEE ANN MILLER ❖ WILMOT, OHIO

Whenever company came to our house, my mother would bring out a batch of her sugar cookies. To this day, our whole family holds this recipe dear.

1/2 cup butter, softened
1 cup plus 2 teaspoons sugar, *divided*
1 egg
1 teaspoon vanilla extract
2-2/3 cups all-purpose flour
1 teaspoon baking powder
1/2 teaspoon baking soda
1/2 teaspoon salt
1/4 teaspoon ground nutmeg
1/2 cup sour cream
27 to 30 raisins

In a large bowl, cream butter and 1 cup sugar until light and fluffy. Beat in egg and vanilla. Combine the flour, baking powder, baking soda, salt and nutmeg; add to creamed mixture alternately with sour cream, beating well after each addition. Cover and refrigerate for 1-2 hours or until easy to handle.

On a lightly floured surface, roll dough to 1/4-in. thickness. Cut with a floured 2-1/2-in. round cookie cutter. Place 2 in. apart on lightly greased baking sheets. Sprinkle with remaining sugar. Place a raisin in the center of each cookie.

Bake at 375° for 10-12 minutes or until set and bottoms are lightly browned. Cool for 1 minute before removing to wire racks. YIELD: about 2 dozen.

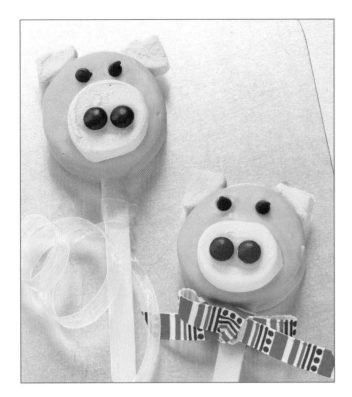

PIGGY POPS

LORRI REINHARDT ❖ BIG BEND, WISCONSIN

Anyone with a sweet tooth will go hog wild for these candy-coated pigs. My mother-in-law and I made the cute cookie pops for a bake sale.

16 large pink and/or white marshmallows
 1 tablespoon sugar
 2 packages (10 to 12 ounces each) white baking chips
 2 tablespoons shortening
 3 to 4 drops red food coloring, optional
32 double-stuffed Oreo cookies
32 Popsicle sticks or craft sticks
64 miniature semisweet chocolate chips (about 1 tablespoon)
64 M&M's miniature baking bits (about 2 tablespoons)

Cut marshmallows into thirds horizontally; cut the center portion of each into four wedges for ears. Roll cut sides of ears in sugar to prevent sticking together. Set ears and remaining portions aside.

In a microwave, melt baking chips and shortening; stir until smooth. Stir in food coloring if desired.

Twist apart sandwich cookies. Dip the end of a Popsicle stick into melted baking chip mixture and place on a cookie half; replace cookie top. Repeat. Place pops on waxed paper-lined baking sheets; refrigerate for 10 minutes or until set.

Reheat baking chip mixture if necessary; dip a pop in mixture and allow excess to drip off. Return to waxed paper-lined baking sheet. While wet, position a marshmallow slice on the cookie for a snout. Add ears on top edge of cookie; hold for a few seconds or until set. Add chocolate chip eyes. Place two baking bits on snout, securing with a dab of baking chip mixture. Repeat. Let stand until set. YIELD: 32 pops.

BERLINER KRANZ COOKIES

EDIE DESPAIN ❖ LOGAN, UTAH

These traditional wreath-shaped cookies make a great Christmas gift and a pretty presentation on a buffet table. So get ready for the compliments. My mother handed down the recipe to me.

    4 hard-cooked eggs
    1 cup butter-flavored shortening
    1 cup sugar
    4 uncooked egg yolks
1/2 teaspoon almond extract
3-3/4 cups all-purpose flour
1/4 teaspoon salt
1/2 cup half-and-half cream
    1 egg white, lightly beaten
Red and green sugar
Red-hot candies

Cut hard-cooked eggs in half lengthwise. Remove yolks; discard whites or save for another use. Press yolks through a potato ricer or strainer into a small bowl.

In a large bowl, cream shortening and sugar until light and fluffy. Beat in the uncooked egg yolks, hard-cooked egg yolks and extract. Combine flour and salt; add to the creamed mixture alternately with cream, beating well after each addition. Refrigerate for 1 hour or until easy to handle.

On a lightly floured surface, roll out the dough to 1/8-in. thickness; cut with a floured 2-1/2-in. doughnut cutter. Reroll scraps if desired.

Place 1 in. apart on ungreased baking sheets; brush with egg white. Sprinkle as desired with colored sugar. Bake at 350° for 6 minutes; carefully decorate as desired with candies. Bake 4-8 minutes longer or until edges are lightly browned. Remove to wire racks to cool. YIELD: 4 dozen.

DAZZLING DESSERTS

Life is short! Eat dessert first! Overflowing with scrumptious sweets, such as impressive cakes, homespun pies, creamy puddings, frosty desserts and much more, this chapter is sure to be one you'll turn to time and again!

For topping, place the sugar, lemon juice, flour, cinnamon and nutmeg in Dutch oven; mix well. Add apples. Bring to a boil; cover and simmer 15 minutes or just until apples are tender.

Gently stir as needed. Remove from heat; carefully stir in pecans. Cool to room temperature. Set aside 3 tablespoons of topping; refrigerate the rest until serving time.

For filling, combine cream cheese, eggs, sugar and vanilla in a large bowl; mix until well blended. Add reserved topping; mix well. Pour into crust. Bake at 350° for 50 minutes. Turn oven off, but leave cheesecake in oven with door ajar for another 1 hour. Cool to room temperature; chill at least 4 hours. Just before serving, top with apple topping. YIELD: 12 servings.

YOGURT ICE POPS

DENISE PATTERSON ✤ BAINBRIDGE, OHIO

These fun, refreshing peach pops get smooth, creamy goodness from yogurt. Any fruit can be substituted in the recipe. We've even used bananas. Yum!

   1 envelope unflavored gelatin
   1 cup cold water
 1/2 cup sugar
1-1/2 cups (12 ounces) peach yogurt
   2 cups sliced peeled fresh or frozen peaches
   1 medium ripe banana, quartered
  16 Popsicle molds or paper cups (3 ounces each) and Popsicle sticks

In a small saucepan, sprinkle gelatin over cold water; let stand for 1-2 minutes. Stir in sugar. Cook and stir over low heat until gelatin and sugar are dissolved.

Transfer to a blender; add the yogurt, peaches and banana. Cover and process until smooth. Fill each mold or cup with 1/4 cup peach mixture; top with holders or insert sticks into cups. Freeze. YIELD: 16 pops.

APPLE PECAN CHEESECAKE

BARBARA MARTIN THOMPSON
POLLOCK PINES, CALIFORNIA

This dessert is an original treat that I gladly developed after experimenting and combining parts of several other recipes. After a little bit of trial and error, I can claim this recipe as one of my very own!

CRUST
1-1/2 cups graham cracker crumbs
 1/2 cup sugar
 1/3 cup butter, melted

TOPPING
 1/2 cup sugar
 1/2 cup lemon juice
   1 tablespoon all-purpose flour
 1/2 teaspoon ground cinnamon
Dash ground nutmeg
   6 medium Granny Smith or tart apples, peeled and thinly sliced
 1/2 cup chopped pecans

FILLING
   3 packages (8 ounces each) cream cheese, softened
   3 eggs
 3/4 cup sugar
1-1/2 teaspoon vanilla extract

Combine crust ingredients; press into bottom and 1-1/2 in. up sides of a 9-in. springform pan. Refrigerate.

CHOCOLATE SHEET CAKE

BARBARA WALSH ❖ MURDOCK, NEBRASKA

Here's a great dessert to serve a big family or to bring to the potluck or church supper. The tender, moist cake and chocolaty frosting is every sweet tooth's dream come true.

    1/2 cup butter, softened
      2 cups sugar
      2 eggs
      3 teaspoons vanilla extract
      2 cups all-purpose flour
      1 teaspoon baking soda
    1/2 teaspoon salt
      1 cup water
    1/2 cup 2% milk
      2 ounces unsweetened chocolate, melted and cooled

FROSTING
      1 cup sugar
    1/2 cup 2% milk
    1/2 cup butter, cubed
      2 tablespoons baking cocoa

In a large bowl, cream butter and sugar until crumbly. Add the eggs, one at a time, beating well after each addition. Beat in vanilla. Combine the flour, baking soda and salt; add to creamed mixture alternately with the water and milk. Beat in chocolate until combined.

Pour into a greased 15-in. x 10-in. x 1-in. baking pan. Bake at 325° for 25-30 minutes or until a toothpick inserted near the center comes out clean. Cool on a wire rack.

For frosting, in a small saucepan, combine the sugar, milk, butter and cocoa. Bring to a boil; cook and stir for 1 minute. Remove from the heat. Transfer to a bowl; stir occasionally until completely cooled. Beat until smooth; spread over cake. YIELD: 24 servings.

BROILED BANANA CRISP

DOROTHY SANDER ❖ FAIRFAX, MINNESOTA

For a quick dessert, try this wonderful banana recipe. The oats and brown sugar add a wonderful sweetness and crunch to this crisp.

      2 small firm bananas
      1 tablespoon lemon juice
      2 tablespoons quick-cooking oats
      2 tablespoons brown sugar
  4-1/2 teaspoons all-purpose flour
    1/4 teaspoon ground cinnamon
    1/8 teaspoon ground nutmeg
      2 tablespoons cold butter
Vanilla ice cream, optional

Peel the bananas; first cut in half lengthwise, then widthwise. Place the bananas in a greased 9-in. square dish. Sprinkle with lemon juice.

Combine the oats, brown sugar, flour, cinnamon and nutmeg. Cut in butter until mixture resembles coarse crumbs. Sprinkle over bananas.

Broil 4-6 in. from the heat for 3-4 minutes or until bubbly. Serve with ice cream if desired. YIELD: 2 servings.

CHEWY DATE TORTE

SAXON WHITE ❖ BOISE, IDAHO

Mother used to make this dessert only once each year, for Christmas dinner. When I was a child, this torte seemed like the very best food in the world, and it was so difficult to wait a whole year for it. When I grew up and became a mother, I decided to change that—today, I make Chewy Date Torte not only at Christmas, but at Thanksgiving and other special occasions as well. For variety, I sometimes add a cup of chopped apples to the recipe.

  2 eggs
  1 cup sugar
  1/4 cup all-purpose flour
  1 teaspoon baking powder
  1/4 teaspoon salt
  2 tablespoons milk
  2 tablespoons butter, melted
  1 teaspoon vanilla extract
  1 package (8 ounces) pitted dates, chopped
  1 cup chopped walnuts
Whipped cream
Additional chopped nuts, optional

In a large bowl, beat eggs. Gradually add sugar, beating until thoroughly combined. Combine the flour, baking powder and salt; stir into bowl. Add milk, butter and vanilla; stir just until combined. Stir in dates and nuts.

Pour into a greased 9-in. square baking pan. Bake at 350° for 30 minutes or until the torte tests done. Cool. Cut into squares; top with whipped cream and additional nuts if desired. YIELD: 9 servings.

PINEAPPLE CREAM PIE

ELAINE SALONEK ❖ WAVERLY, MINNESOTA

My mother-in-law's pineapple pie was a favorite with the threshing crew. A nice, big slice of it made the harvest work more enjoyable. Now, I make Theresa's trademark pie in remembrance of her.

Pastry for single-crust pie (9 inches)

CREAM LAYER
  1/2 cup sugar
  2 tablespoons cornstarch
  1/2 teaspoon salt
  2 cups 2% milk
  3 egg yolks, lightly beaten
  2 tablespoons butter
  1 teaspoon vanilla extract

PINEAPPLE LAYER
  1/3 cup sugar
  2 tablespoons cornstarch
  1/4 cup water
  1 can (20 ounces) crushed pineapple, undrained
  2 tablespoons butter

MERINGUE
  3 egg whites
  1/2 teaspoon vanilla extract
  1/4 teaspoon cream of tartar
  6 tablespoons sugar

Line a 9-in. deep-dish pie plate with pastry; trim and flute edges. Line unpricked pastry with a double thickness of heavy-duty foil. Bake at 450° for 8 minutes. Remove foil; bake 5-7 minutes longer or until lightly browned. Cool on a wire rack.

In a small saucepan, combine the sugar, cornstarch and salt. Stir in milk until smooth. Cook and stir over medium-high heat until thickened and bubbly. Reduce heat to low; cook and stir 2 minutes longer. Remove from the heat. Stir a small amount of hot mixture into egg yolks; return all to the pan, stirring constantly. Bring to a gentle boil; cook and stir for 2 minutes. Remove from the heat; stir in butter and vanilla. Transfer to prepared pastry.

For pineapple layer, in a small saucepan, combine sugar and cornstarch. Stir in water until smooth. Add pineapple. Bring to a boil over medium-high heat; cook and stir for 2 minutes or until thickened. Remove from the heat; stir in butter. Gently spread over cream mixture.

For meringue, in a large bowl, beat the egg whites, vanilla and cream of tartar on medium speed until soft peaks form. Gradually beat in sugar, 1 tablespoon at a time, on high until stiff peaks form. Spread over hot filling, sealing edges to crust.

Bake at 350° for 15 minutes or until golden brown. Cool on a wire rack for 1 hour; refrigerate for 1-2 hours before serving. YIELD: 8 servings.

DATE PECAN PIE

MARIE DELFFS ❖ NORMANDY, TENNESSEE

At our house, we call this "oh-so-good pie." It's rather like a traditional Southern pecan pie without being overly sweet.

Pastry for single-crust pie (9 inches)
  1/2 cup butter, cubed
    1 cup sugar
2-1/2 teaspoons vinegar
    1 teaspoon ground cinnamon
  1/2 teaspoon ground nutmeg
    4 eggs, lightly beaten
    1 cup finely chopped dates
  1/2 cup chopped pecans
    1 cup heavy whipping cream, whipped

Line a 9-in. pie plate with pastry; trim and flute edges. Line pastry shell with a double thickness of heavy-duty foil. Bake at 450° for 8 minutes. Remove foil; bake 5 minutes longer. Cool on a wire rack.

In a small saucepan, melt butter. Remove from the heat; whisk in the sugar, vinegar, cinnamon and nutmeg. Stir in the eggs, dates and pecans. Pour into crust.

Bake at 375° for 35-40 minutes or until set. Cool on a wire rack. Serve with the whipped cream. Refrigerate the leftovers. YIELD: 6-8 servings.

BROWN RICE PUDDING

LORIE MINER ❖ KAMAS, UTAH

Brown rice gives this creamy pudding a deep, nutty flavor, while lemon and mango make it subtly sweet and refreshing. It's a healthy snack or dessert any time of the year.

1-1/4 cups water
  1/2 cup uncooked brown rice
    3 teaspoons grated lemon peel, *divided*
  1/4 teaspoon salt
    3 cups 2% milk
    3 tablespoons brown sugar
    1 teaspoon vanilla extract
Optional toppings: fresh mango, ground cinnamon and
    flaked coconut

In a large saucepan, combine the water, rice, 1-1/2 teaspoons lemon peel and salt. Bring to a boil. Reduce heat; cover and simmer for 30-45 minutes or until tender.

Stir in milk and brown sugar. Cook, uncovered, for 40-50 minutes or until desired consistency, stirring occasionally. Remove from the heat; stir in vanilla and remaining lemon peel. Chill if desired.

Spoon into dessert dishes. Add toppings as desired. YIELD: 4 servings.

FRUITCAKE PIE

DORIS HEATH ❖ FRANKLIN, NORTH CAROLINA

This recipe came from a friend who knows how much we love fruitcake. The pie has similar flavors, but it's more manageable to make than a large batch of fruitcake. I usually serve it with whipped cream. It's excellent with ice cream, too.

Pastry for single-crust pie (9 inches)
   1 cup pecan halves, *divided*
  3/4 cup red candied cherries, *divided*
  1/2 cup chopped dates
  1/4 cup chopped candied pineapple
   6 tablespoons butter, softened
  1/2 cup packed brown sugar
   3 eggs, lightly beaten
  1/2 cup light corn syrup
  1/4 teaspoon *each* ground cloves, ginger and nutmeg

Line a 9-in. pie plate with pastry; set aside. Chop 1/2 cup pecans; set remaining pecan halves aside. Chop 1/2 cup cherries; halve remaining cherries and set aside. Combine the dates, pineapple and chopped pecans and cherries; sprinkle over crust.

In a small bowl, cream butter and brown sugar until light and fluffy. Beat in the eggs, corn syrup, cloves, ginger and nutmeg. Pour over fruit mixture. Top with the reserved pecan and cherry halves.

Bake at 350° for 35-40 minutes or until set. Cool on a wire rack. Refrigerate leftovers. YIELD: 8 servings.

PEANUT BUTTER 'N' BANANA PUDDING

TRACI RODARTE ❖ GAS CITY, INDIANA

When my grandmother cooked at a small country school, she earned the reputation of good cook. This recipe was given to her when she was a young mother, and it has been a family favorite for years. The bananas pair well with the creamy homemade pudding, and the roasted peanuts add a nice crunch.

3/4 cup packed brown sugar
  1 tablespoon cornstarch
  1 cup 2% milk
  1 egg, beaten
  1 tablespoon peanut butter
1/2 teaspoon butter
1/2 teaspoon vanilla extract
  1 medium banana, sliced
  1 tablespoon chopped dry roasted peanuts

In a small saucepan, combine the brown sugar, cornstarch and milk until smooth. Cook and stir over medium-high heat until thickened and bubbly. Reduce heat to low; cook and stir 2 minutes longer.

Remove from the heat. Stir a small amount of hot filling into egg; return all to the pan, stirring constantly. Bring to a gentle boil; cook and stir 2 minutes longer. Remove from the heat. Stir in the peanut butter, butter and vanilla. Cool for 15 minutes, stirring occasionally.

Transfer to dessert dishes. Refrigerate if desired. Just before serving, top with banana slices and peanuts. YIELD: 2 servings.

 # TRIPLE-LAYER LEMON CAKE

CONNIE JURJEVICH ✤ ATMORE, ALABAMA

A smooth and silky citrus filling separates the three layers of my lemon cake. It's a homemade favorite that friends and family never tire of. Serve it after a special spring or summer meal.

  2 cups sugar
3/4 cup canola oil
  4 eggs, *separated*
  1 teaspoon vanilla extract
  3 cups all-purpose flour
  3 teaspoons baking powder
1/4 teaspoon salt
  1 cup 2% milk

FILLING
3/4 cup sugar
  2 tablespoons cornstarch
1/8 teaspoon salt
1/2 cup water
  1 egg, lightly beaten
1/3 cup lemon juice
1-1/2 teaspoons grated lemon peel
  1 tablespoon butter, softened

FROSTING
  1 cup butter, softened
  6 cups confectioners' sugar
  2 tablespoons lemon juice
  1 teaspoon grated lemon peel
  4 to 6 tablespoons heavy whipping cream

In a large bowl, beat sugar and oil. Beat in egg yolks and vanilla. Combine dry ingredients; add to sugar mixture alternately with milk, beating well after each addition. In a large bowl, beat egg whites until stiff peaks form; fold into batter.

Pour into three greased and waxed paper-lined 9-in. round baking pans. Bake at 350° for 20-25 minutes or until a toothpick comes out clean. Cool for 10 minutes; remove to wire racks to cool.

For filling, in a large saucepan, combine sugar, cornstarch and salt. Stir in water until smooth. Cook and stir over medium-high heat until thickened and bubbly. Reduce heat; cook and stir 2 minutes longer. Remove from heat. Stir a small amount of hot filling into egg; return all to the pan, stirring constantly. Bring to a gentle boil; cook and stir 2 minutes longer. Remove from the heat. Gently stir in lemon juice, peel and butter. Cool to room temperature without stirring. Cover and refrigerate.

In a large bowl, combine the butter, confectioners' sugar, lemon juice, peel and enough cream to achieve desired spreading consistency. Spread filling between cake layers. Frost top and sides of cake. Store in the refrigerator. YIELD: 12-14 servings.

Dessert in a Glass

There's something elegant and extra special when guests can enjoy a smooth, creamy mousse, pudding or parfait in their own serving dish. These recipes are impressive yet easy.

MAPLE SYRUP CREAM

JANICE COURNOYER ❖ LORETTE, MANITOBA

This was a favorite dessert of my French ancestors from Quebec. The mousse is very creamy, smooth and light with a rich maple flavor. It's pretty with a garnish of thin butter cookies or fresh berries.

    1 tablespoon unflavored gelatin
    1/4 cup cold water
    1/2 cup milk
    2/3 cup maple syrup
    1/8 teaspoon salt
    2 cups heavy whipping cream
Additional maple syrup

In a small bowl, sprinkle gelatin over cold water; let stand for 1 minute. In a small saucepan, bring the milk to a gentle boil; stir in the gelatin mixture until dissolved. Remove from the heat; stir in the syrup and salt. Cover and refrigerate for 45 minutes or until partially set.

In a large bowl, beat the heavy cream until stiff peaks form; fold into the gelatin mixture. Spoon into eight individual serving dishes. Cover and refrigerate for at least 4 hours or until set. Just before serving, drizzle with the additional maple syrup. YIELD: 8 servings.

OLD FASHIONED COFFEE PUDDING

CEAL LANGER ❖ GLENDALE, WISCONSIN

This pudding was handed down from my husband's great-grandmother. To give an idea of how old this recipe is, it was translated from her German script found in an old ledger when she'd collected favorite recipes from her friends. It's a bona fide and delicious "antique." The only modern touch that I've added to it is the option of using decaffeinated coffee.

    1/4 cup sugar
    4 tablespoons all-purpose flour
Pinch salt
    2 cups cold strong coffee
    2 egg yolks, lightly beaten
    1 teaspoon vanilla extract
    1/2 cup heavy whipping cream, whipped until stiff
Additional whipped cream, optional
Shaved bittersweet chocolate, optional

In a large saucepan, combine the sugar, flour and salt. Stir in coffee until smooth. Cook and stir over medium-high heat until thickened and bubbly. Reduce heat to low; cook and stir 2 minutes longer.

Remove from the heat. Stir a small amount of hot filling into egg yolks; return all to the pan, stirring constantly. Bring to a gentle boil; cook and stir 2 minutes longer. Remove from the heat. Stir in vanilla. Cool. Fold in whipping cream. Chill. Garnish with additional whipped cream and chocolate if desired. YIELD: 4 servings.

AMARETTO PEACH PARFAITS

CONNIE MCDOWELL ❖ GREENWOOD, DELAWARE

This beautiful peach dessert makes the kind of impression a cook dreams about. Making the meringues a day ahead speeds up the prep time considerably.

> 4 egg whites
> 1/2 teaspoon cream of tartar
> 1 cup sugar

PARFAITS
> 5 cups sliced peeled fresh *or* frozen peaches, thawed
> 1/4 cup sugar
> 1 tablespoon plus 1/4 cup amaretto, *divided*
> 1/2 cup cream cheese, softened
> 1 cup confectioners' sugar
> 2 cups heavy whipping cream
> Optional toppings: toasted flaked coconut *and/or* sliced almonds

In a large bowl, beat egg whites and cream of tartar on medium speed until soft peaks form. Gradually add sugar, 1 tablespoon at a time, beating on high until stiff glossy peaks form and sugar is dissolved.

Drop by heaping tablespoonfuls 2 in. apart onto parchment paper-lined baking sheets. Bake at 250° for 32-38 minutes or until firm to the touch. Turn oven off; leave meringues in oven for 1 hour. Remove from the oven and cool on baking sheets.

In a large bowl, combine the peaches, sugar and 1 tablespoon amaretto. Cover and refrigerate for at least 30 minutes. In another bowl, beat cream cheese and confectioners' sugar until smooth. Beat in cream and remaining amaretto until thickened.

Crumble two-thirds of the cookies; place 2 tablespoons crushed cookies in each of six dessert dishes. Layer with half of the peaches, amaretto cream and remaining crushed cookies; repeat layers. Garnish with coconut and/or almonds if desired. Store leftover cookies in an airtight container. YIELD: 6 servings plus about 1 dozen leftover cookies.

LEMON VELVET DESSERT

MARIA BARNET ❖ ELKINS PARK, PENNSYLVANIA

The first time I whipped up this light and lemony mousse, everyone oohed and aahed. No one believed me when I told them how simple it was to make, because it tastes like I slaved over it all day. It truly comes together, however, with only six ingredients. It's a delight in the summer, but fits with meals any time of the year.

> 1 package (8 ounces) cream cheese, softened
> 1/2 cup lemon curd
> 1 envelope unflavored gelatin
> 1/2 cup water
> 1 cup heavy whipping cream, whipped
> 1 teaspoon grated lemon peel

In a small bowl, beat the cream cheese and lemon curd until smooth; set aside.

In a small saucepan, sprinkle gelatin over water; let stand for 1 minute. Cook and stir over low heat until gelatin is completely dissolved, about 2 minutes.

Beat the unflavored gelatin into the cream cheese mixture. Fold in the whipped cream and grated lemon peel. Pour into eight dessert cups. Cover and refrigerate for 1 hour or until firm. YIELD: 8 servings.

BROWN SUGAR ANGEL FOOD CAKE

JANET EVERETT ❖ WINFIELD, IOWA

Brown sugar makes this moist, tender angel food cake deliciously different. Chunks of chopped toffee give its fluffy frosting some flavorful snap. The cake is lovely with a hot cup of coffee.

1-1/2 cups egg whites (about 10)
1-3/4 cups packed brown sugar, *divided*
    1 cup cake flour
1-1/2 teaspoons cream of tartar
1-1/2 teaspoons vanilla extract
    1/2 teaspoon salt

TOFFEE/TOPPING
    1 teaspoon plus 1 cup butter, *divided*
1-1/2 cups chopped pecans
1-1/2 cups packed brown sugar
    1 cup (6 ounces) semisweet chocolate chips
    1 carton (12 ounces) frozen whipped topping, thawed

Place egg whites in a large bowl; let stand at room temperature for 30 minutes. Sift 1 cup brown sugar and flour together twice; set aside.

Add the cream of tartar, vanilla and salt to egg whites; beat on medium speed until soft peaks form. Gradually add remaining brown sugar, about 2 tablespoons at a time, beating on high until stiff glossy peaks form and sugar is dissolved. Gradually fold in flour mixture, about 1/2 cup at a time.

Gently spoon into an ungreased 10-in. tube pan. Cut through batter with a knife to remove air pockets. Bake on the lowest oven rack at 350° for 25-30 minutes or until lightly browned and entire top appears dry. Immediately invert pan; cool completely, about 1 hour.

Run a knife around side and center tube of pan. Remove cake to a serving plate.

For toffee, line a 13-in. x 9-in. baking pan with foil; grease the foil with 1 teaspoon butter. Sprinkle pecans into prepared pan; set aside.

In a small heavy saucepan over medium-low heat, bring brown sugar and remaining butter to a boil, stirring constantly. Cover and cook for 2 minutes. Cook and stir with a clean spoon until a candy thermometer reads 300° (hard-crack stage). Immediately pour into prepared pan. Sprinkle with chips; spread with a knife when melted. Refrigerate for about 1 hour or until set.

Frost cake with whipped topping. Finely chop half of the toffee; press onto cake. Serve with remaining toffee if desired. Store leftover toffee in an airtight container. YIELD: 16 servings.

EDITOR'S NOTE: We recommend that you test your candy thermometer before each use by bringing water to a boil; the thermometer should read 212°. Adjust your recipe temperature up or down based on your test.

WALNUT-APPLE SNACK CAKE

BARBARA ZAVERSON ❖ HUDSON, NEW HAMPSHIRE

Hungry for harvesttime? This tasty cake puts the season's best in the spotlight. Featuring apples, walnuts, spices and toffee bits for sweetness, it will satisfy you to the core.

2/3 cup butter, softened
1-3/4 cups packed brown sugar
    2 eggs
    1 teaspoon vanilla extract
    2 cups all-purpose flour
    2 teaspoons baking powder
    1/2 teaspoon ground cinnamon
    1/4 teaspoon salt
    1/4 teaspoon ground nutmeg

1-1/4 cups chopped peeled tart apples
1/3 cup English toffee bits *or* almond brickle chips
1/3 cup chopped walnuts
Vanilla ice cream, optional

In a large bowl, cream butter and brown sugar until light and fluffy. Add eggs, one at a time, beating well after each addition. Beat in vanilla. Combine the flour, baking powder, cinnamon, salt and nutmeg; gradually add to creamed mixture and mix well. Fold in the apples, toffee bits and walnuts.

Transfer to a greased 13-in. x 9-in. baking dish. Bake at 350° for 20-25 minutes or until a toothpick inserted near the center comes out clean. Cool on a wire rack. Cut into squares. Serve with ice cream if desired. YIELD: 18 servings.

ICEBOX CAKE

CINDY HAWKINS ❖ NEW YORK, NEW YORK

You don't have to bake to serve a wonderful dessert! This "cake" is made from chocolate wafers and whipping cream. It is so delicious.

2 cups heavy whipping cream
2 tablespoons confectioners' sugar
1 teaspoon vanilla extract
1 package (9 ounces) chocolate wafers
Chocolate curls, optional

In a large bowl, beat cream until soft peaks form. Add sugar and vanilla; beat until stiff. Spread heaping teaspoonfuls on the cookies. Make six stacks of cookies; turn stacks on edge and place on a serving platter, forming a 14-in.-long cake.

Frost top and sides with remaining whipped cream. Garnish with chocolate curls if desired. Refrigerate for 4-6 hours before serving. YIELD: 10-12 servings.

LEMON COCONUT CUPCAKES

DEBRA HENDERSON ❖ BOONEVILLE, ARKANSAS

Lemon plus coconut equals big smiles in this cupcake equation. The zesty gems are a hit with my family, friends and neighbors. The sour cream in the cake batter makes the cupcakes super moist.

3/4 cup butter, softened
1 cup sugar
3 eggs
3 teaspoons grated lemon peel
1/2 teaspoon vanilla extract
1-1/2 cups all-purpose flour
1/2 teaspoon baking powder
1/2 teaspoon baking soda
1/4 teaspoon salt
1/2 cup sour cream
1/2 cup flaked coconut

LEMON COCONUT FROSTING
4 ounces cream cheese, softened
2 tablespoons butter, softened
1 teaspoon grated lemon peel
1/4 teaspoon vanilla extract
1/4 teaspoon lemon juice
1-1/4 cups confectioners' sugar
3/4 cup flaked coconut, *divided*
Shredded lemon peel, optional

In a large bowl, cream butter and sugar until light and fluffy. Add eggs, one at a time, beating well after each addition. Beat in lemon peel and vanilla. Combine the flour, baking powder, baking soda and salt; add to creamed mixture alternately with sour cream. Beat just until combined. Fold in coconut.

Fill paper-lined muffin cups three-fourths full. Bake at 350° for 18-22 minutes or until a toothpick inserted near the center comes out clean. Cool for 10 minutes before removing from pans to wire racks to cool completely.

In a small bowl, beat the cream cheese, butter, grated lemon peel, vanilla and lemon juice until fluffy. Gradually beat in confectioners' sugar until smooth; stir in 1/4 cup coconut. Frost cupcakes; sprinkle with remaining coconut. Garnish with shredded lemon peel if desired. YIELD: 15 cupcakes.

FROSTING CUPCAKES QUICKLY

To quickly frost cupcakes, place frosting in a bowl. The frosting should be a soft, spreadable consistency. If too stiff, add milk a teaspoon at a time until desired consistency. Dip top of cupcake into frosting, twist slightly and lift up.

FRESH STRAWBERRY DESSERT

BETTY OUTLAW ❖ EVANSVILLE, INDIANA

Each year, my husband reminds me of the approaching strawberry season by putting in an early request for this dessert. One of my own original recipes, it's eye-catching, yet holds up well in travel.

CRUST
1-1/2 cups all-purpose flour
3/4 cup chopped pecans
1/2 cup cold butter, cubed

FILLING
1 cup butter, softened
1 package (8 ounces) cream cheese, softened
2 cups confectioners' sugar
1 teaspoon vanilla extract
2 quarts fresh strawberries, halved

GLAZE
1 cup sugar
3 tablespoons cornstarch
1 cup water
3 tablespoons strawberry gelatin
2 teaspoons lemon juice
Whipped cream

In a small bowl, combine flour and nuts. Cut in butter until mixture resembles coarse crumbs. Press into a greased 13-in. x 9-in. baking dish. Bake at 300° for 25-30 minutes or until set; cool completely on a wire rack.

For filling, in a small bowl, cream the butter, cream cheese, confectioners' sugar and vanilla until light and fluffy. Spread over crust; cover and chill.

For glaze, 2-3 hours before serving, combine sugar and cornstarch in a small saucepan. Stir in water until smooth. Bring to a boil; cook and stir for 1-2 minutes or until thickened and bubbly. Remove from the heat; stir in gelatin until dissolved. Stir in lemon juice. Cool to lukewarm, stirring occasionally.

PEARS AND CRANBERRIES POACHED IN WINE

EVA AMUSO ❖ CHESHIRE, MASSACHUSETTS

This recipe is proof that an elegant dessert doesn't have to take tons of work. The oven does the cooking for the simple yet impressive dinner finale.

6 medium pears
2 cups fresh *or* frozen cranberries, thawed
1-1/2 cups white wine *or* white grape juice
1/2 cup sugar
1/2 cup cranberry juice
2 tablespoons butter
2 teaspoons grated lemon peel
Creme fraiche *or* whipped cream

Peel, core and halve the pears. Place cut side up in a greased 13-in. x 9-in. baking dish; sprinkle with cranberries. In a small saucepan, combine the wine, sugar, cranberry juice, butter and lemon peel. Cook and stir over medium heat until sugar is dissolved; spoon over pears.

Cover and bake at 375° for 30-35 minutes or until pears are tender, basting occasionally. Serve with creme fraiche. YIELD: 12 servings.

Meanwhile, arrange strawberries over filling. Spoon glaze over berries. Chill until serving. Garnish with whipped cream. YIELD: 12-15 servings.

RUSTIC PEACH TART WITH RASPBERRY DRIZZLE

TERESA RALSTON ❖ NEW ALBANY, OHIO

Sweet peaches and tangy raspberry sauce make for a heavenly combination in this yummy tart. Everyone loves the crunchy, brown sugar crumb topping.

Pastry for single-crust pie (9 inches)
2-1/2 cups sliced peeled fresh *or* frozen peaches
   1/3 cup packed brown sugar
   2 tablespoons all-purpose flour
   1/4 teaspoon ground cinnamon

TOPPING
   1/2 cup all-purpose flour
   1/3 cup packed brown sugar
   1/4 cup cold butter, cubed

RASPBERRY DRIZZLE
   1/4 cup water
   1 cup fresh *or* frozen raspberries, thawed
   2 tablespoons sugar
Fresh mint leaves, optional

Roll pastry into a 14-in. circle; place on a parchment paper-lined baking sheet. Set aside.

In a large bowl, combine the peaches, brown sugar, flour and cinnamon; spoon over pastry to within 2 in. of edges. Fold up edges of pastry over filling, leaving center uncovered. For topping, combine flour and brown sugar; cut in butter until mixture resembles coarse crumbs. Sprinkle over filling.

Bake at 400° for 20-25 minutes or until crust is golden brown and filling is bubbly. Using the parchment paper, slide tart onto a wire rack to cool.

For raspberry drizzle, place the water, raspberries and sugar in a blender; cover and process until pureed. Strain raspberry mixture, reserving juice; discard seeds. Serve with tart. Garnish with mint if desired. YIELD: 8 servings (1/2 cup drizzle).

PEELING FRESH PEACHES

Place peaches in a large pot of boiling water for 10-20 seconds or until the skin splits. Remove with a slotted spoon. Transfer to an ice water bath to cool the peaches and stop the cooking process. Use a paring knife to peel the skin.

Cool Cravings

*Frosty desserts seem to taste best during the warm and sunny months,
but no one could refuse these deliciously sweet and icy creations any time of the year.*

 ## RHUBARB ICE CREAM

DENISE LINNETT ✦ PICTON, ONTARIO

I sampled a scoop of this unique flavor at an ice cream shop and knew I had to try making my own. So I raided my garden for rhubarb and added lemon and ginger. Yummy!

- 3 cups sliced fresh *or* frozen rhubarb
- 2 cups sugar
- 1 cup milk
- 1 cup heavy whipping cream
- 2 teaspoons lemon juice
- 1 teaspoon minced fresh gingerroot

Place rhubarb in an ungreased 13-in. x 9-in. baking dish. Sprinkle with sugar; toss to coat. Cover and bake at 375° for 30-40 minutes or until tender, stirring occasionally.

Cool slightly. Process rhubarb in batches in a food processor; transfer to a bowl. Cover and refrigerate until chilled.

In a large bowl, combine the milk, cream, lemon juice and ginger; stir in rhubarb.

Fill cylinder of ice cream freezer two-thirds full; freeze according to manufacturer's directions. Transfer to a freezer container; freeze for 2-4 hours before serving. YIELD: 1 quart.

MANGO ICE CREAM

GABRIELLE BERRYER ✦ HOMESTEAD, FLORIDA

For a deliciously fruity treat on a hot summer day, try this delicious ice cream. Mango is a wonderful tropical fruit that everyone should try!

- 3 to 4 medium mangoes, peeled
- 1 tablespoon lime juice
- 1 envelope unflavored gelatin
- 4-1/2 teaspoons cold water
- 1 can (5 ounces) evaporated milk
- 2/3 cup sweetened condensed milk
- Dash salt

Cut mangoes into chunks; puree in a food processor. Strain and discard fibers. Place 2 cups puree in a small bowl; add lime juice (refrigerate any remaining puree for another use).

In a small microwave-safe bowl, sprinkle gelatin over cold water; let stand for 1 minute. Microwave on high for 20 seconds; stir. Let stand until gelatin is completely dissolved.

Gradually add puree to gelatin mixture. In a large bowl, combine evaporated milk and condensed milk; stir in mango mixture and salt. Refrigerate for several hours or overnight.

Fill cylinder of ice cream freezer two-thirds full; freeze according to manufacturer's directions. Transfer to a freezer container; freeze for 2-4 hours. Remove from the freezer 15-20 minutes before serving. YIELD: 1 quart.

PEACH ICE

CARMA BLOSSER ✦ LIVERMORE, COLORADO

If the fresh peach is delicious, this recipe is even tastier! It's a very light dessert for those counting calories, and it's truly a cinch to prepare.

- 1/3 cup warm water (120° to 130°)
- 2 tablespoons sugar
- 1 small peach, peeled
- 2 teaspoons lemon juice

Combine water and sugar until sugar is dissolved. Place the peach, lemon juice and sugar mixture in a blender. Cover and process for 1 minute or until blended. Transfer to freezer container; cover and freeze for 3 hours or until almost firm.

Transfer to blender. Cover and process for 30-40 seconds or until slushy. Return to container; cover and freeze overnight.

Remove from the freezer just before serving. Using a fork, scrape into two dessert dishes. YIELD: 2 servings.

🎗 CRANBERRY BUTTERMILK SHERBET

LISA SPEER ✤ PALM BEACH, FLORIDA

Light, refreshing cranberry sherbet is a great change of pace from rich, filling holiday food. It's also popular on hot, summer days. The buttermilk adds a nice tang.

1 cup fresh *or* frozen cranberries
1/4 cup packed brown sugar
1/4 cup orange juice
1/2 teaspoon grated lemon peel
1/2 teaspoon grated orange peel
1 cinnamon stick (3 inches)
2 cups buttermilk
1 cup sugar
1 cup light corn syrup
1/4 cup lemon juice
Dash salt

In a small saucepan, combine the first six ingredients; cook over medium heat until the berries pop, about 15 minutes. Discard cinnamon. Mash cranberry mixture; chill.

In a large bowl, combine the buttermilk, sugar, corn syrup, lemon juice and salt; add cranberry mixture. Fill the cylinder of ice cream freezer two-thirds full; freeze according to the manufacturer's directions. Transfer to a freezer container; freeze for 2-4 hours before serving. YIELD: about 1 quart.

PEACH ICE CREAM

FLORINE BRUNS ✤ FREDERICKSBURG, TEXAS

Peaches are a pleasure eaten plain. But when blended into ice cream, they are incredible. Lighter than commercial brands, this cool concoction is a natural family pleaser.

4 medium peaches, peeled and sliced *or* 1 package (16 ounces) frozen unsweetened sliced peaches, thawed
1-1/4 cups sugar, *divided*
1-1/2 teaspoons unflavored gelatin
2 tablespoons cold water
4 cups half-and-half cream
1 egg, lightly beaten
1 teaspoon vanilla extract
1/2 teaspoon almond extract

In a food processor, combine peaches and 3/4 cup sugar; cover and process until pureed. Set aside. In a small microwave-safe bowl, sprinkle gelatin over cold water; let stand for 1 minute. Microwave on high for 20 seconds; stir. Let stand until gelatin is completely dissolved.

Meanwhile, in a large saucepan, heat cream to 175°; stir in remaining sugar until dissolved. Whisk a small amount of hot mixture into egg. Return all to pan, whisking constantly. Cook and stir over low heat until mixture reaches at least 160° and coats the back of a metal spoon. Remove from heat; stir in the peach puree, gelatin mixture and extracts until blended. Cool quickly by placing pan in a bowl of ice water; stir for 2 minutes.

Press waxed paper onto surface of custard. Refrigerate for several hours or overnight.

Fill cylinder of ice cream freezer two-thirds full; freeze according to manufacturer's directions. Refrigerate remaining mixture until ready to freeze. When ice cream is frozen, transfer to a freezer container; freeze for 2-4 hours before serving. YIELD: 2-1/2 quarts.

RHUBARB CHEESE PIE

STACEY MEYER ❖ PLYMOUTH, WISCONSIN

This tangy rhubarb pie is topped with a luscious cream cheese layer.

Pastry for single-crust pie (9 inches)
4-1/2 teaspoons all-purpose flour
    1 tablespoon cornstarch
    1 cup sugar, *divided*
    1/2 cup water
    3 cups sliced fresh *or* frozen rhubarb
    1 teaspoon vanilla extract, *divided*
  12 ounces cream cheese, softened
    2 eggs, lightly beaten
    1 egg yolk

Line a 9-in. pie plate with pastry; flute edges. Line unpricked pastry shell with a double thickness of heavy-duty foil. Bake at 450° for 8 minutes. Remove foil; bake 5 minutes longer. Cool on a wire rack.

In a small saucepan, combine the flour, cornstarch and 1/2 cup sugar. Add water and rhubarb; stir until blended. Bring to a boil; cook and stir for 2 minutes or until thickened. Remove from the heat; stir in 1/2 teaspoon vanilla. Transfer to prepared pastry.

In a small bowl, beat the cream cheese and remaining sugar and vanilla until smooth. Add eggs and egg yolk; beat on low speed just until combined. Spread over top of pie.

Cover edges with foil. Bake at 325° for 25-30 minutes or until set. Cool on a wire rack for 1 hour. Cover and refrigerate for at least 4 hours before serving. YIELD: 8 servings.

EDITOR'S NOTE: If using frozen rhubarb, measure rhubarb while still frozen, then thaw completely. Drain in a colander, but do not press liquid out.

PINEAPPLE CHIFFON PIE

CAROLYN REDMON ❖ SANGER, TEXAS

This pie's light, creamy filling and refreshing pineapple flavor could very well make this old favorite a new classic in your recipe box. Best of all, it comes together with just a handful of ingredients!

1-1/2 cups crushed vanilla wafers (about 45 wafers)
    1 cup sugar
    1/3 cup butter, melted
    1 package (3 ounces) lemon gelatin
1-1/2 cups unsweetened pineapple juice
    1 egg, lightly beaten
1-3/4 cups heavy whipping cream, whipped

Combine the vanilla wafer crumbs, sugar and butter; press onto the bottom and up the sides of an ungreased 9-in. pie plate. Bake the pie crust at 375° for 8-10 minutes or until lightly browned. Cool on a wire rack.

In a small saucepan, combine the gelatin, pineapple juice and egg. Cook and stir over low heat until mixture is slightly thickened and a thermometer reads 160° (do not boil), about 10 minutes. Remove from the heat; transfer to a bowl. Cover and refrigerate for 30 minutes, stirring occasionally.

Fold whipped cream into filling. Spread evenly into crust. Refrigerate for 4 hours or until set. YIELD: 8 servings.

TOFFEE-MOCHA CREAM CAKE

JULIE YODER ❖ HUTCHINSON, KANSAS

Guests' eyes will sparkle when they catch a glimpse of this rich, beautiful layer cake. The dessert serves 12, so it's ideal for a party or special occasion.

    1 cup butter, softened
    2 cups sugar
    2 eggs
1-1/2 teaspoons vanilla extract
2-2/3 cups all-purpose flour
    3/4 cup baking cocoa
    2 teaspoons baking soda
    1/4 teaspoon salt
    1 cup buttermilk
    2 teaspoons instant coffee granules
    1 cup boiling water
FILLING
    1/2 teaspoon instant coffee granules
    1 teaspoon hot water
    2 cups heavy whipping cream
    1 tablespoon brown sugar
    1 package (8 ounces) milk chocolate English toffee bits

In a large bowl, cream the butter and sugar until light and fluffy. Add the eggs, one at a time, beating well after each addition. Beat in the vanilla.

1 cup (6 ounces) semisweet chocolate chips
1/2 cup sugar
2-1/4 cups 2% milk, *divided*
1 teaspoon vanilla extract
1 cup heavy whipping cream

CREAM
1 cup heavy whipping cream
2 tablespoons confectioners' sugar
1 teaspoon vanilla extract
2 drops red food coloring, optional

Drain strawberries, reserving syrup. Refrigerate strawberries. Add enough cold water to syrup to measure 3/4 cup. Sprinkle gelatin over syrup mixture; let stand for 1 minute.

In a large saucepan, combine the chocolate chips, sugar and 1/2 cup milk. Cook and stir over low heat until the chips are melted. Add gelatin mixture; cook and stir 1 minute longer or until gelatin is dissolved.

Remove from the heat; stir in the vanilla and the remaining milk. Pour into a large bowl. Refrigerate until partially set, about 40 minutes.

In a small bowl, beat cream until soft peaks form; fold into chocolate mixture. Transfer to a 6-cup ring mold coated with cooking spray. Refrigerate until firm, about 2 hours.

For cream, place reserved strawberries in a food processor; cover and process until pureed. In a small bowl, beat cream until it begins to thicken. Add the confectioners' sugar, vanilla and food coloring if desired; beat until soft peaks form. Fold in strawberry puree.

To serve, unmold Bavarian onto a serving plate. Spoon strawberry cream into center and over top of ring. YIELD: 10 servings.

Combine the flour, cocoa, baking soda and salt; add to the creamed mixture alternately with buttermilk, beating well after each addition. In a small bowl, dissolve coffee granules in boiling water; stir into batter.

Pour into three greased and floured 9-in. round baking pans. Bake at 350° for 15-20 minutes or until a toothpick inserted near the center comes out clean. Cool for 10 minutes before removing from pans to wire racks to cool completely.

For filling, in a large bowl, dissolve coffee granules in hot water. Add cream and brown sugar; beat until stiff peaks form.

Place bottom cake layer on a serving plate. Spread with 1-1/3 cups filling; sprinkle with 1/2 cup toffee bits. Repeat layers twice. Store in the refrigerator. YIELD: 12 servings.

CHOCOLATE BAVARIAN WITH STRAWBERRY CREAM

RACHEL FANKELL ✦ GRAYSON, KENTUCKY

Strawberries are my favorite fruit, so I'm always looking for new ways to use them. This elegant, fancy-looking dessert is an easy way to impress guests.

1 package (10 ounces) frozen sweetened sliced strawberries, thawed
2 envelopes unflavored gelatin

🎗 APPLE UPSIDE-DOWN CAKE

LINDA WETSCH ❖ MANDAN, NORTH DAKOTA

Topped with walnuts and caramelized tart apple slices, this cake is both easy and dazzling. It never fails to make tasters say, "Wow!"

      1/3 cup butter, melted
        1 cup packed brown sugar
        3 medium tart apples, peeled and sliced
      1/2 cup chopped walnuts
CAKE
        3 tablespoons butter, softened
      3/4 cup sugar
        2 eggs
        1 cup all-purpose flour
      3/4 teaspoon baking powder
      1/2 teaspoon baking soda
      1/4 teaspoon salt
      1/4 teaspoon ground cinnamon
      1/2 cup buttermilk
        3 tablespoons sour cream
        1 teaspoon apple brandy *or* rum, optional

Pour butter into an ungreased 9-in. round baking pan; sprinkle with 1/2 cup brown sugar. Arrange apples in a single layer over brown sugar; layer with walnuts and remaining brown sugar.

In a large bowl, cream butter and sugar until light and fluffy. Add eggs, one at a time, beating well after each addition. Combine the flour, baking powder, baking soda, salt and cinnamon; add to the creamed mixture alternately with buttermilk and sour cream, beating well after each addition. Beat in brandy if desired.

Spoon batter over brown sugar layer. Bake at 350° for 30-35 minutes or until a toothpick inserted near the center comes out clean. Cool for 10 minutes before inverting onto a serving plate. Serve warm. YIELD: 8 servings.

LEMON DELIGHT DESSERT

PAM HOLLOWAY ❖ BAKER, FLORIDA

This sunny yellow dessert, a recipe originally from my husband's aunt, is always requested for special occasions in our family, and it's so easy to make. Count yourself lucky if there's a piece left over—it tastes even better the next day!

        2 cups all-purpose flour
  1-1/2 cups chopped pecans
      1/4 teaspoon salt
        1 cup butter, melted
        1 package (8 ounces) cream cheese, softened
  3-3/4 cups confectioners' sugar
        1 carton (16 ounces) frozen whipped topping, thawed
        1 can (15-3/4 ounces) lemon pie filling

In a small bowl, combine the flour, pecans and salt. Stir in butter. Press into an ungreased 13-in. x 9-in. baking dish. Bake at 350° for 20-25 minutes or until golden brown. Cool on a wire rack.

In a large bowl, beat cream cheese and confectioners' sugar until smooth. Fold in whipped topping. Spread over crust. Top with pie filling. Store in the refrigerator. YIELD: 15 servings.

CHERRY SUPREME DESSERT

SHERRI KEIM ❖ GRAND JUNCTION, COLORADO

Marshmallows and a tart cherry topping lend flavor and eye appeal to this popular dessert. Better yet, it's easy enough for kids to make!

      3/4 cup crisp rice cereal
      1/4 cup chopped walnuts
        2 tablespoons brown sugar
        2 tablespoons butter, melted
        4 cups miniature marshmallows

1 cup heavy whipping cream, whipped
1 can (21 ounces) cherry pie filling

In a small bowl, combine the cereal, walnuts, brown sugar and butter. Press into a greased 8-in. square dish. Fold marshmallows into whipped cream; spread over the cereal mixture. Top with the pie filling. Cover and refrigerate for at least 2 hours. YIELD: 9 servings.

 APPLE KOLACHES

ANN JOHNSON ✤ EVANSVILLE, INDIANA

A fellow home economist shared this recipe for a sweet, fruit-filled pastry. My son, who isn't a dessert fan, was disappointed when he came home to find his dad had polished off the last kolache in the batch.

1 cup butter, softened
1 package (8 ounces) cream cheese, softened
2 cups all-purpose flour

1-1/2 cups finely chopped peeled apples
1/4 teaspoon ground cinnamon

ICING
1 cup confectioners' sugar
4-1/2 teaspoons 2% milk
1/2 teaspoon vanilla extract

In a large bowl, beat butter and cream cheese until light and fluffy. Gradually add flour and mix well. Divide dough into two portions; cover and refrigerate for 2 hours or until easy to handle.

In a small bowl, combine apples and cinnamon. On a lightly floured surface, roll one portion of dough into a 15-in. x 9-in. rectangle; cut into 3-in. squares. Place a teaspoonful of apple mixture in the center of each square. Overlap two opposite corners of dough over filling; pinch tightly to seal.

Place 2 in. apart on ungreased baking sheets. Repeat with remaining dough and apple mixture. Bake at 400° for 10-12 minutes or until bottoms are lightly browned. Cool for 1 minute before removing from pans to wire racks. Combine the icing ingredients; drizzle over warm kolaches. YIELD: 2-1/2 dozen.

COOKING FOR TWO

For dishes that have smaller yields but are big on taste, turn to these must-try recipes. They are the perfect size for one- or two-person households but deliever all of flavor you'd expect from a country kitchen!

CHOCOLATE PEANUT COOKIES

CLARA COULSON MINNEY
WASHINGTON COURT HOUSE, OHIO

When I make chocolate chip cookies, I bake this variation, which is chock-full of other flavors. The cookies are crisp on the outside, and moist and tender in the middle.

1/4 cup butter, softened
1/4 cup peanut butter
1/4 cup packed brown sugar
2 tablespoons sugar
2 tablespoons beaten egg
2 tablespoons 2% milk
1/2 teaspoon vanilla extract
1 cup all-purpose flour
1/2 teaspoon baking soda
1/8 teaspoon salt
1/3 cup honey-roasted peanuts
1/3 cup semisweet chocolate chips
1/3 cup coarsely chopped miniature peanut butter cups

In a large bowl, cream the butter, peanut butter and sugars until light and fluffy. Beat in the egg, milk and vanilla. Combine the flour, baking soda and salt; gradually add to creamed mixture and mix well. Stir in the peanuts, chocolate chips and peanut butter cups.

Drop by tablespoonfuls 2 in. apart onto ungreased baking sheets. Bake at 350° for 10-12 minutes or until golden brown. Remove to wire racks. Store in an airtight container. YIELD: about 2 dozen.

RASPBERRY-LEMON SPRITZER

MARGIE WILLIAMS ✤ MOUNT JULIET, TENNESSEE

This is my favorite summer refreshment. It isn't too sweet, and the color is spectacular.

1/2 cup fresh *or* frozen raspberries, thawed
1/3 cup sugar
2-1/2 cups club soda, chilled
1/4 cup lemon juice
Ice cubes
2 lemon slices

Place the raspberries and sugar in a food processor; cover and process until pureed. Strain the fruit mixture, reserving the juice and discarding the seeds.

In a small pitcher, combine the club soda, lemon juice and raspberry juice. Serve in tall glasses over ice. Garnish with lemon slices. YIELD: 2 servings.

SUMMERTIME STRAWBERRY SALAD

CYNTHIA HALL-SWAN ✤ WATERTOWN, NEW YORK

I created this recipe a few years ago, when I tried a variation of a fruit dip as a dressing. It works well with the fresh taste of strawberries in season.

2 ounces cream cheese, softened
2 tablespoons marshmallow creme
1/4 teaspoon vanilla extract
1 tablespoon orange juice
1-1/4 cups halved fresh strawberries
1/4 cup *each* green grapes, seedless red grapes and fresh blueberries

In a small bowl, combine the cream cheese, marshmallow creme and vanilla; beat until smooth. Gradually add the orange juice. In a small serving bowl, combine the fruit. Drizzle with dressing; toss gently to coat. YIELD: 2 servings.

ITALIAN CHICKEN SALAD SANDWICHES

GIOVANNA KRANENBERG ❖ MAHNOMEN, MINNESOTA

We really love this recipe. The Italian pickled vegetables give it a distinctive taste. I sometimes serve it on a bed of lettuce or as an appetizer on crackers.

2/3 cup shredded cooked chicken breast
3 tablespoons shredded carrot
3 tablespoons finely chopped celery
2 tablespoons mild giardiniera, chopped
2 teaspoons finely chopped onion
1 small garlic clove, minced
1/4 cup fat-free mayonnaise

Dash pepper
4 slices sourdough bread
2 lettuce leaves

In a small bowl, combine the first six ingredients. Add mayonnaise and pepper; toss to coat. Spoon 1/2 cup salad onto two bread slices; top with lettuce and remaining bread. YIELD: 2 servings.

EASY CHICKEN BROTH
If cooking chicken for the sandwiches, save the water in which the chicken is cooked. Strain the water, pour into ice cube trays and freeze. When frozen, transfer to freezer bags and use them in recipes that call for chicken broth.

HOT TOMATO DRINK

MARTHA VAN HORN ❖ BETHEL PARK, PENNSYLVANIA

This recipe came from a friend at least 25 years ago. It is simple to make and keeps well in the refrigerator. It is a big hit with men and women as well as children.

2 cups tomato juice
1 cup water
1/4 cup sugar
2 tablespoons lemon juice
1/2 teaspoon ground cinnamon
1/4 teaspoon salt
1/8 teaspoon celery salt
1/8 teaspoon paprika
6 whole cloves

In a large saucepan, combine the first eight ingredients. Place cloves on a double thickness of cheesecloth; bring up corners of cloth and tie with string to form a bag.

Add spice bag to saucepan; bring to a boil. Reduce heat; cover and simmer for 10 minutes. Discard the spice bag. Stir before serving. YIELD: 3 servings.

CALIFORNIA EGG BAKE

EDIE FARM ❖ FARMINGTON, NEW MEXICO

I love breakfast, and I'm always looking for new egg dishes to serve my husband and myself. This recipe fills the bill for something easy to make.

3 eggs, lightly beaten
1/4 cup sour cream
1/4 teaspoon salt

1 medium tomato, chopped
1 green onion, sliced
1/4 cup shredded cheddar cheese

In a small bowl, whisk the eggs, sour cream and salt; stir in the tomato, onion and cheese. Pour into a greased 2-cup baking dish.

Bake, uncovered, at 350° for 25-30 minutes or until a knife inserted in the center comes out clean. YIELD: 2 servings.

BACON CHEESEBURGERS FOR 2

DEBORAH BIGGS ❖ OMAHA, NEBRASKA

For my change-of-pace burgers, popular toppings are cooked inside the patties. That way, you get a burst of cheese and bacon flavors in every bite.

5 slices ready-to-serve fully cooked bacon
1/3 cup crumbled Gorgonzola cheese
2 teaspoons balsamic vinegar
1/4 teaspoon salt
1/4 teaspoon pepper
1/2 pound lean ground beef (90% lean)
2 hamburger buns, split
2 slices tomato
1/3 cup fresh baby spinach

Heat bacon according to package directions for crisp bacon; cool. Finely crumble into a large bowl; add the cheese, vinegar, salt and pepper. Crumble beef over mixture and mix well. Shape into two patties.

Grill burgers, covered, over medium heat or broil 4 in. from the heat for 4-5 minutes on each side or until a thermometer reads 160° and juices run clear. Serve on buns with tomato and spinach. YIELD: 2 servings.

ZUCCHINI FRIES FOR 2

SARAH GOTTSCHALK ❖ RICHMOND, INDIANA

I often make these fun fries for my husband and myself, especially when our garden is full of zucchini.

- 2 small zucchini
- 1 egg white
- 1/4 cup all-purpose flour
- 3 tablespoons cornmeal
- 1/2 teaspoon *each* salt, garlic powder, chili powder, paprika and pepper
- Cooking spray
- Marinara or spaghetti sauce, warmed

Cut zucchini into 3-in. x 1/2-in. x 1/2-in. pieces. In a shallow bowl, whisk egg white. In another shallow bowl, combine the flour, cornmeal and seasonings. Dip zucchini in egg white, then roll in flour mixture.

Place zucchini on a baking sheet coated with cooking spray; spray with additional cooking spray. Bake at 425° for 18-22 minutes or until golden brown, turning once. Serve with the marinara sauce. YIELD: 2 servings.

MIXED BERRY SUNDAES FOR 2

EDIE DESPAIN ❖ LOGAN, UTAH

Before serving these yogurt sundaes, get ready for requests for seconds. We enjoy them for breakfast. What an easy way to get our fruit and calcium.

- 1/4 cup halved fresh strawberries
- 1/4 cup *each* fresh raspberries, blueberries and blackberries
- 3 teaspoons honey, *divided*
- 1/2 cup fat-free plain Greek yogurt
- 2 tablespoons pomegranate juice
- 2 tablespoons chopped walnuts, toasted

In a small bowl, combine berries and 1 teaspoon honey; spoon berries into two dessert dishes.

Combine the Greek yogurt, pomegranate juice and remaining honey; spoon over the berries. Sprinkle with toasted walnuts. YIELD: 2 servings.

EDITOR'S NOTE: If Greek yogurt is not available in your area, line a strainer with a coffee filter and place over a bowl. Place 1 cup fat-free yogurt in prepared strainer; refrigerate overnight. Discard liquid from bowl; proceed as directed.

THAI STEAK SALAD

RADELLE KNAPPENBERGER ❖ OVIEDO, FLORIDA

Thai food is popular in our household, so my husband and I developed this fresh, fuss-free alternative to a meat-and-potatoes dinner. The spicy-sweet dressing is incredible!

    1 tablespoon lime juice
    1 tablespoon reduced-sodium soy sauce
    1 tablespoon honey
    1 teaspoon balsamic vinegar
    1/4 teaspoon hot pepper sauce
    1 small garlic clove, minced
Dash salt
    2 tablespoons olive oil, *divided*
    1 boneless beef top loin steak (8 ounces)
    4 cups torn romaine
    2 tablespoons salted peanuts
    2 tablespoons fresh basil leaves, chopped

For the dressing, in a small bowl, combine the lime juice, soy sauce, honey, vinegar, pepper sauce, garlic and salt. Whisk in 1 tablespoon oil; set aside.

In a large skillet over medium heat, cook steak in remaining oil for 6-8 minutes on each side or until meat reaches desired doneness (for medium-rare, a thermometer should read 145°; medium, 160°; well-done, 170°). Remove from the pan and let stand for 5 minutes.

Divide romaine between two plates. Slice beef; arrange over romaine. Sprinkle with peanuts and basil; drizzle with dressing. YIELD: 2 servings.

EDITOR'S NOTE: Top loin steak may be labeled as strip steak, Kansas City steak, New York strip steak, ambassador steak or boneless club steak in your region.

🎗 PEPPERED FILETS WITH CHERRY PORT SAUCE FOR 2

BARBARA LENTO ❖ HOUSTON, PENNSYLVANIA

I like to serve my peppery beef steaks with a light, vegetable side dish. Creative cooks can substitute dried cranberries for the cherries and feta for blue cheese.

    2 beef tenderloin steaks (8 ounces *each*)
    2 teaspoons coarsely ground pepper
    1 cup dry red wine
    1/2 cup chopped red onion
    1/3 cup golden raisins
    1/3 cup dried cherries
    2 tablespoons sugar
1-1/2 teaspoons cornstarch
    1/4 teaspoon ground mustard
Dash salt
    2 teaspoons cold water
    1/4 cup crumbled blue cheese

Sprinkle steaks with pepper. Grill, covered, over medium heat or broil 4 in. from the heat for 6-8 minutes on each side or until meat reaches desired doneness (for medium-rare, a thermometer should read 145°; medium, 160°; well-done, 170°).

Meanwhile, in a small saucepan, combine the wine, onion, raisins, cherries and sugar. Bring to a boil; cook until liquid is reduced by half.

Combine the cornstarch, mustard, salt and water until smooth. Gradually stir into the pan. Bring to a boil; cook and stir for 2 minutes or until thickened. Serve sauce with steaks; sprinkle with cheese. YIELD: 2 servings.

STEAK AU POIVRE FOR 2

CRYSTAL BRUNS ❖ ILIFF, COLORADO

With the punch of peppercorns and a smooth beefy sauce, this steak is delicious. You'll love the hint of sweetness the bittersweet chocolate adds to the savory meat.

    2 beef tenderloin steaks (5 ounces *each*)
    2 tablespoons olive oil, *divided*
    1 tablespoon whole white *or* black peppercorns, crushed
1/4 teaspoon salt
    1 tablespoon finely chopped shallot
1/4 cup port wine
    1 tablespoon balsamic vinegar
1/4 cup condensed beef consomme, undiluted
    1 teaspoon minced fresh rosemary *or* 1/4 teaspoon dried rosemary, crushed
1/2 ounce bittersweet chocolate, chopped

Brush steaks with 1 tablespoon oil; sprinkle with peppercorns and salt. In a small skillet over medium heat, cook steaks in 2 teaspoons oil for 4-5 minutes on each side or until meat reaches desired doneness (for medium-rare, a thermometer should read 145°; medium, 160°; well-done, 170°). Remove and keep warm.

In the same skillet, saute shallot in remaining oil until tender. Add wine and vinegar, stirring to loosen browned bits from pan. Bring to a boil; cook and stir for 2-3 minutes or until slightly thickened. Add beef consomme and rosemary. Bring to a boil. Add chocolate, stirring until melted and sauce is thickened. Serve sauce with steaks. YIELD: 2 servings.

A BIT ABOUT SHALLOTS
Shallots are part of the onion family and have a mild onion-garlic flavor. In place of 3 to 4 shallots, use 1 medium onion plus a pinch of garlic powder or (if you like the taste of garlic) 1 minced garlic clove.

APPLE-BACON MINI LOAVES

JAY DAVIS ❖ KNOXVILLE, TENNESSEE

I came up with this recipe for a tailgate party at a University of Tennessee football game. The school colors are orange and white, so the cheddar cheese was just the right touch.

    1 cup all-purpose flour
    2 tablespoons sugar
    1 teaspoon baking powder
1/4 teaspoon salt
    1 egg
1/2 cup 2% milk
    2 tablespoons butter, melted
    1 cup (4 ounces) shredded sharp cheddar cheese
1/3 cup crumbled cooked bacon
1/4 cup finely chopped apple

In a large bowl, combine the flour, sugar, baking powder and salt. In another bowl, whisk the egg, milk and butter. Stir into dry ingredients just until moistened. Fold in the cheese, bacon and chopped apple.

   Transfer to two greased 5-3/4-in. x 3-in. x 2-in. loaf pans. Bake at 350° for 25-30 minutes or until a toothpick inserted near the center comes out clean. Cool for 10 minutes before removing from pans to wire racks. YIELD: 2 mini loaves (6 slices each).

OLD-FASHIONED FUDGE CAKE

MARY SCHILLINGER ❖ WOODSTOCK, GEORGIA

This simple one-layer cake is moist, has a nice texture and cuts well. Plus, the frosting is fast and easy to make.

1/4 cup shortening
    1 cup sugar
    1 egg
    1 egg white

1/2 teaspoon vanilla extract
    1 cup plus 2 tablespoons all-purpose flour
4-1/2 teaspoons baking cocoa
1/2 teaspoon baking soda
1/2 teaspoon salt
1/4 cup 2% milk
1/2 cup boiling water
FROSTING
3/4 cup sugar
1/4 cup half-and-half cream
    2 tablespoons butter
1/3 cup miniature marshmallows
1/4 cup semisweet chocolate chips

In a large bowl, cream shortening and sugar until light and fluffy. Add egg, then egg white, beating well after each addition. Stir in vanilla. Combine the flour, cocoa, baking soda and salt; add to the creamed mixture alternately with milk, beating well after each addition. Stir in water until smooth. Pour into a greased and floured 6-in. round baking pan.

   Bake at 350° for 40-45 minutes or until a toothpick inserted near the center comes out clean. Cool for 10 minutes before removing from pan to a wire rack to cool completely.

   In a small saucepan over low heat, combine the sugar, cream and butter. Bring to a boil; cook and stir for 2 minutes. Remove from the heat; stir in marshmallows and chocolate chips until smooth. Spread frosting over top and sides of cake. YIELD: 6 servings.

SALAD GREENS WITH HONEY MUSTARD VINAIGRETTE

SABRINA SMITH ❖ SPENCER, WEST VIRGINIA

Goat cheese makes such a nice accent for this refreshing salad. The delicious dressing has the perfect balance of sweetness and acidity, and it clings well to the greens.

2 cups spring mix salad greens

1/4 cup crumbled goat cheese

2 slices red onion, separated into rings

DRESSING

4 teaspoons honey

1 tablespoon finely chopped shallot

1 tablespoon cider vinegar

1 tablespoon olive oil

1 tablespoon Dijon mustard

2 teaspoons lemon juice

1/8 teaspoon salt

1/8 teaspoon pepper

In a serving bowl, combine the salad greens, cheese and onion. In a small bowl, whisk the dressing ingredients. Pour over salad; toss to coat. YIELD: 2 servings.

CHICKEN WITH ARTICHOKES AND SHRIMP

REBECCA BAIRD ✤ SALT LAKE CITY, UTAH

Besides adding color to the dish, the shrimp complement the flavor of the chicken. The recipe has recently become one of our favorites.

1/4 cup all-purpose flour

1/4 teaspoon salt, optional

1/4 teaspoon pepper

2 boneless skinless chicken breast halves (4 ounces *each*)

2 teaspoons canola oil

8 uncooked medium shrimp, peeled and deveined

1 can (14 ounces) water-packed artichoke hearts, rinsed, drained and chopped

1 plum tomato, chopped

2 garlic cloves, minced

1/3 cup reduced-sodium chicken broth

1 tablespoon minced fresh basil

1 tablespoon minced fresh parsley

1 tablespoon butter

3 tablespoons shredded Parmesan cheese

In a large resealable plastic bag, combine the flour, salt if desired and pepper; add chicken and shake to coat.

In a large skillet, cook the chicken in oil over medium heat for 5-6 minutes on each side or until a thermometer reads 170°. Remove and keep warm.

Add the shrimp, artichokes, tomato and garlic to the skillet; cook for 4 minutes. Add the broth, basil, parsley and butter; heat through. Pour over chicken and sprinkle with cheese. YIELD: 2 servings.

CITRUS MELON SORBET

PATRICIA HANCOCK ❖ HAWTHORNE, NEW JERSEY

I serve this refreshing dish between courses or as a delicious dessert. When I was young, my mom used to make this in the summer.

3/4 cup sugar
1/4 cup orange juice
2 tablespoons lime juice
3 cups cubed honeydew
1 teaspoon grated lime peel
1 teaspoon grated lemon peel

In a small saucepan, bring the sugar and orange and lime juices to a boil. Cook and stir until sugar is dissolved; set aside to cool.

Place the honeydew in a food processor; add sugar syrup and lime and lemon peels. Cover and process for 1-2 minutes or until smooth.

Transfer to an 8-in. square baking dish. Freeze for 1 hour or until edges begin to firm; stir. Freeze 3 hours longer or until firm.

Just before serving, transfer to a food processor; cover and process for 1-2 minutes or until smooth. YIELD: 4 servings.

MIXED GREENS WITH CREAMY HONEY MUSTARD DRESSING

PHYLLIS SCHMALZ ❖ KANSAS CITY, KANSAS

The dressing for this salad is one of my favorites. It comes together easily, is a good balance of sweet and tart, and coats the greens well.

4 cups spring mix salad greens
1/4 cup julienned carrot
1/4 cup grape tomatoes
DRESSING
1/2 cup reduced-fat plain yogurt
2 tablespoons white wine vinegar
2 tablespoons Dijon mustard
2 tablespoons honey

In a serving bowl, combine the salad greens, carrot and grape tomatoes. In a small bowl, whisk the dressing ingredients. Drizzle over or serve with the salad. Refrigerate any leftover dressing. YIELD: 2 servings (3/4 cup dressing).

WHITE VINEGAR

Distilled white vinegar has a strong, sharp flavor and is most often used for pickling foods. White wine vinegar is milder than distilled white vinegar. For savory dishes, most people prefer white wine vinegar.

CHICKEN CORDON BLEU

BETTY PALMESINO ❖ PHOENIX, ARIZONA

This is a great, fast dinner for two, and the leftovers are just as tasty. It's easy to fix and makes an elegant entree.

    2 boneless skinless chicken breast halves (6 ounces *each*)
    2 slices deli ham
    2 slices Gruyere *or* Swiss cheese
    1/4 cup butter, melted
    1/2 cup dry bread crumbs
    1/2 teaspoon salt
    1/8 teaspoon paprika

Flatten chicken to 1/4-in. thickness; top each with ham and cheese. Roll up and tuck in ends; secure with toothpicks.

Place butter in a shallow bowl. In another shallow bowl, combine the bread crumbs, salt and paprika. Dip chicken in butter, then roll in crumb mixture.

Transfer to a greased 8-in. square baking dish. Bake at 350° for 40-45 minutes or until the chicken is no longer pink. Discard toothpicks. YIELD: 2 servings.

BROCCOLI-POTATO MASH

SARAH VASQUES ❖ MILFORD, NEW HAMPSHIRE

With a mild broccoli flavor, these fluffy mashed potatoes make a colorful side dish to accompany any entree. It truly is a delicious way to get green vegetables worked into your diet, and it's a great way to sneak veggies onto the dinner plate for those with finicky taste.

    1 large Yukon Gold potato, peeled and cubed
    1/3 cup fresh broccoli florets
    1/4 cup 2% milk
 1-1/2 teaspoons butter
    1/8 teaspoon salt
    1/8 teaspoon pepper

Place the peeled and cubed potato in a small saucepan and cover with water. Bring to a boil. Reduce the heat; cover and cook for 10-15 minutes or until tender, adding the broccoli during the last 4 minutes.

Drain potato and broccoli; mash with milk, butter, salt and pepper. YIELD: 2 servings.

BRAISED BEEF WITH MUSHROOMS

PAMELA BOERSMA ❖ CHINO, CALIFORNIA

This slow-cooked beef is so tender, it melts in your mouth. The flavorful ingredients, such as red wine, soup mix, Worcestershire and garlic, have time to season the meat until it has amazing flavor. It's a delicious entree that's the perfect size for a duo.

3/4 pound beef stew meat
1 tablespoon canola oil
1 small onion, sliced
1/3 cup dry red wine or beef broth
1 cup sliced fresh mushrooms
1 cup water
2 tablespoons onion soup mix
1-1/2 teaspoons Worcestershire sauce
1 garlic clove, minced
Dash pepper

In a large saucepan, brown the beef stew meat in the canola oil in batches. Remove the browned meat and set aside.

In the drippings, saute onion until tender. Add wine, stirring to loosen browned bits from pan. Bring to a boil. Return beef to the pan. Add the remaining ingredients. Reduce heat; cover and simmer for 1 to 1-1/2 hours or until meat is tender. YIELD: 2 servings.

CHEDDAR-TOPPED MASHED POTATOES

COLLEEN MEAKER ❖ CAMILLUS, NEW YORK

It may seem silly to make mashed potatoes for two people, but sometimes that's all you want, without any leftovers. These smooth and creamy mashed potatoes say "comfort food" all the way. The sour cream and butter make them wonderfully rich, and the cheddar cheese adds bright color and delightful flavor.

2 medium potatoes, peeled and cubed
1 tablespoon 2% milk
1 tablespoon sour cream
1 tablespoon butter
Dash each salt and pepper
1/4 cup shredded cheddar cheese

Place potatoes in a small saucepan and cover with water. Bring to a boil. Reduce heat; cover and cook for 8-12 minutes or until tender.

Drain the cooked potatoes; mash with the milk, sour cream, butter, salt and pepper. Transfer to a greased 2-cup baking dish. Sprinkle with the shredded cheese. Bake, uncovered, at 350° for 10-15 minutes or until heated through and cheese is melted. YIELD: 2 servings.

VEGETABLE SKILLET

FRANCES KYNOCH ❖ THUNDER BAY, ONTARIO

I found this recipe in a magazine years ago and make it all the time. It's one of the most simple, speedy and tasty skillet side dishes ever invented.

1 medium sweet red pepper, julienned
1 medium zucchini, julienned
1 tablespoon olive oil
1 garlic clove, minced
1/4 teaspoon salt
1/8 teaspoon pepper

In a small skillet, saute red pepper and zucchini in oil until tender. Add garlic; cook 1 minute longer. Stir in salt and pepper. YIELD: 2 servings.

APPLE PEAR CRISP

RON SLIVON ❖ SURPRISE, ARIZONA

The fruit is tender, and the crunchy topping isn't overly sweet. It's even more delicious with vanilla ice cream.

1 medium apple, peeled and chopped
1 medium ripe pear, peeled and chopped
1 tablespoon brown sugar
2 teaspoons all-purpose flour
1-1/2 teaspoons lemon juice
1/2 teaspoon apple pie spice
TOPPING
1 tablespoon all-purpose flour
1 tablespoon butter, melted
1 tablespoon brown sugar
1/4 teaspoon apple pie spice
1/3 cup old-fashioned oats
2 tablespoons chopped pecans

Combine the first six ingredients. Divide between two greased 8-oz. ramekins. Combine flour, butter, brown sugar and pie spice; stir in oats and pecans. Sprinkle over fruit mixture.

Bake at 375° for 18-22 minutes or until bubbly and golden brown. Serve warm. YIELD: 2 servings.

HOMEMADE APPLE PIE SPICE

If you don't have apple pie spice handy, here's how to make your own (by the teaspoon): Combine 1/2 teaspoon ground cinnamon, 1/4 teaspoon ground nutmeg, 1/8 teaspoon ground cardamom and 1/8 teaspoon ground allspice.

GINGERSNAP PEAR TRIFLES

TASTE OF HOME TEST KITCHEN

Crystallized ginger adds both sweetness and spice to this simple trifle. Layer in pears, crumbled cookies and whipped cream, and you have autumn comfort in a dish!

1/2 cup heavy whipping cream
1/4 cup lemon curd
1/2 cup crushed gingersnap cookies
1 cup chopped canned pears
2 tablespoons chopped crystallized ginger

In a small bowl, beat the cream until soft peaks form. Fold in the lemon curd.

Layer half of the crumbled cookies, pears and whipped cream in two dessert dishes. Repeat layers. Sprinkle with ginger. Serve immediately. YIELD: 2 servings.

ORANGE COCOA SANDIES

NELLA PARKER ✤ HERSEY, MICHIGAN

When I was growing up, I loved to help my mom cut out the appealing dessert recipes from newspapers and magazines. Then we would paste them all into a big book. This recipe is one of our favorites from the collection.

1/2 cup butter, softened
1/2 cup plus 2 tablespoons confectioners' sugar, *divided*
1/2 teaspoon orange extract
1 cup all-purpose flour
2 tablespoons baking cocoa
1/2 cup finely chopped pecans

In a large bowl, cream butter and 1/2 cup confectioners' sugar until light and fluffy; beat in extract. Combine flour and cocoa; gradually add to creamed mixture. Stir in pecans.

Roll into 1-in. balls. Place 1 in. apart on ungreased baking sheets. Bake at 350° for 12-14 minutes or until set. Cool for 1-2 minutes before removing to wire racks. Dust with remaining confectioner's sugar. YIELD: about 2 dozen.

CREAMED CORN WITH PEAS

TANA WHITTON ✤ LAS VEGAS, NEVADA

I created this recipe for Thanksgiving dinner one year. It's very much a comfort food. I love the blending of the sweetness of corn with the earthiness of mushrooms. When I want a special side, this is it.

1-1/3 cups frozen corn, thawed
1/3 cup sliced fresh mushrooms
4 teaspoons thinly sliced green onion
2 tablespoons plus 1-1/2 teaspoons butter
4 teaspoons all-purpose flour
1/2 cup chicken broth
1/3 cup heavy whipping cream
Dash *each* salt and pepper
1/3 cup frozen peas, thawed
2 tablespoons shredded Parmesan cheese

In a small skillet, saute the corn, mushrooms and onion in butter until the mushrooms are tender. Stir in the flour until blended;

gradually add the broth. Bring to a boil. Cook and stir for 1-2 minutes or until thickened. Remove from the heat. Add the heavy cream, salt and pepper; stir in the peas and Parmesan cheese. YIELD: 2 servings.

RED PEPPER MEAT LOAF

KERRY BARNETT-AMUNDSON ✤ OCEAN PARK, WASHINGTON

This recipe is a nice alternative to the usual beef meat loaf. It's plenty moist and so flavorful with the sweet red pepper. Leftovers are great for sandwiches the next day.

2 tablespoons beaten egg
1-1/2 teaspoons 2% milk
3/4 cup coarsely crumbled corn bread
1/4 cup finely chopped sweet red pepper
2 tablespoons finely chopped onion
Dash dried basil
1/2 pound ground pork
1/2 pound ground turkey
2 tablespoons barbecue sauce

In a small bowl, combine the beaten egg, milk, corn bread, sweet red pepper, onion and basil. Crumble the ground pork and turkey over the egg mixture and mix well. Shape into a loaf and place in a greased 8-in. square baking dish. Drizzle with the barbecue sauce.

Bake, uncovered, at 350° for 40-45 minutes or until a thermometer reads 165°. YIELD: 4 servings.

HOME-STYLE MASHED POTATOES

PAULA MONTIJO ✤ LEBANON, PENNSYLVANIA

For a hearty accompaniment to any meat entree, whip up these mashed potatoes—a sure pleaser!

1/2 pound cubed peeled potatoes
2 tablespoons beaten egg
1 tablespoon finely chopped onion
2-1/2 teaspoons 2% milk
2-1/2 teaspoons butter
1/4 teaspoon salt
Dash pepper
Dash celery seed
1 slice white bread, cubed and toasted

Place potatoes in a large saucepan; cover with water. Cover and bring to a boil. Cook for 10-15 minutes or until very tender; drain well.

Transfer to a small bowl. Add the egg, onion, milk, butter, salt, pepper and celery seed; beat on low speed until light and fluffy. Stir in bread cubes.

Transfer to a greased shallow 3-cup baking dish. Bake, uncovered, at 350° for 20-25 minutes or until a thermometer reads 160°. YIELD: 2 servings.

HOMEMADE MACADAMIA CRUSTED TILAPIA

KARIN BESSER ❖ DELTONA, FLORIDA

I ordered this entree at a restaurant on our first wedding anniversary. It was so wonderful, I couldn't wait to re-create the recipe at home. Every time I make it, my husband and I recall a very special evening.

1/4 cup all-purpose flour
1 egg, beaten
1/2 cup finely chopped macadamia nuts
1/4 cup dry bread crumbs
1/4 cup grated Parmesan cheese
1 teaspoon garlic powder
2 tilapia fillets (6 ounces *each*)
2 tablespoons canola oil
1/4 cup Thai peanut sauce

Place flour and egg in separate shallow bowls. In another shallow bowl, combine nuts, bread crumbs, cheese and garlic powder. Coat tilapia with flour, then dip in egg and coat with nut mixture.

In a large skillet, cook fillets in oil over medium heat for 5-6 minutes on each side or until fish flakes easily with a fork. Serve with peanut sauce. YIELD: 2 servings.

OVEN-FRIED PARMESAN POTATOES

JANE HARLOW ❖ PANAMA CITY, FLORIDA

I found this recipe in a newspaper and adjusted it somewhat by adding additional Parmesan cheese. This is a wonderful side dish, and since the potatoes are cooked with the skin on, they are nutritious as well as delicious.

2 medium potatoes, sliced
1 tablespoon canola oil
3 tablespoons grated Parmesan cheese
1/2 teaspoon garlic powder
1/2 teaspoon paprika
1/4 teaspoon salt
1/8 teaspoon pepper

Place potatoes in a large bowl. Drizzle with oil. Sprinkle with cheese, garlic powder, paprika, salt and pepper; toss to coat. Transfer to a greased 15-in. x 10-in. x 1-in. baking pan.

Bake, uncovered, at 450° for 25-30 minutes or until golden brown, stirring once. YIELD: 2 servings.

SWEETHEART SLAW

DEBBY MOUNTJOY ❖ HOUSTON, TEXAS

I named this salad "sweetheart slaw" because of the fruit and the fact that all the sweethearts in my life love it. It's a colorful refresher with a delicious blend of flavors.

1-1/2 cups shredded red cabbage
1/2 cup chopped peeled mango
1/3 cup chopped sweet red pepper
1/4 cup sliced fresh strawberries
3 tablespoons balsamic vinegar
4-1/2 teaspoons olive oil
4-1/2 teaspoons honey

In a serving bowl, combine the cabbage, mango, pepper and strawberries. In a small bowl, whisk the vinegar, oil and honey. Drizzle over cabbage mixture; toss to coat. Chill until serving. YIELD: 2 servings.

COCONUT-FILLED FUDGE CAKE

BETTY JO HARTLEY ❖ PRICE, UTAH

My sister shared this recipe with me, and it has become a
favorite for family birthdays. The yummy coconut center is
a pleasant surprise.

  1 package (3 ounces) cream cheese, softened
1/4 cup sugar
  2 tablespoons beaten egg
1/2 teaspoon vanilla extract
1/3 cup flaked coconut
1/3 cup semisweet chocolate chips

CAKE
2/3 cup sugar
1/3 cup canola oil
  2 tablespoons beaten egg
1/4 teaspoon vanilla extract
1/3 cup hot water
1/3 cup buttermilk
  1 cup all-purpose flour
1/4 cup baking cocoa
1/2 teaspoon baking powder
1/2 teaspoon baking soda
1/2 teaspoon salt
  3 tablespoons chopped pecans
Confectioners' sugar, optional

In a small bowl, beat the cream cheese, sugar, egg and vanilla
until smooth. Stir in coconut and chocolate chips; set aside.

In large bowl, beat the sugar, oil, egg and vanilla extract until
well blended. In a small bowl, combine the hot water and
buttermilk; set aside. Combine the flour, cocoa, baking powder,
baking soda and salt; add to the sugar mixture alternately with
the buttermilk mixture, beating well after each addition. Stir in
the chopped pecans.

Pour half of the batter into a greased and floured 8-in. fluted
tube pan. Spoon cream cheese mixture over batter to within 1/2
in. of edges; top with remaining batter.

Bake at 350° for 35-40 minutes or until a knife inserted near
the center comes out clean. Cool for 10 minutes before removing
from the pan to a wire rack to cool completely. Dust with the
confectioners' sugar if desired. YIELD: 6 servings.

FLORENTINE FRITTATA FOR TWO

ANGELA BUCHANAN ✤ LONGMONT, COLORADO

This easy recipe makes a delicious breakfast or weeknight dinner using on-hand ingredients. For a heartier dish, add some leftover chicken or shrimp.

      3 eggs
      3 egg whites
      2 tablespoons 2% milk
      2 tablespoons chopped pitted Greek olives
  1/4 teaspoon salt
  1/4 teaspoon pepper
  1/4 cup oil-packed sun-dried tomatoes
  1/2 teaspoon dried basil
  1/4 teaspoon dried rosemary, crushed
      3 cups fresh baby spinach, coarsely chopped
  1/2 cup crumbled feta cheese

In a small bowl, whisk the first six ingredients; set aside. Arrange tomatoes in an 8-in. ovenproof skillet; sprinkle with basil and rosemary. Heat the pan over medium heat. Pour egg mixture into the pan; top with spinach. Cover and cook for 3-5 minutes or until eggs begin to set.

Uncover skillet; sprinkle with cheese. Broil 3-4 in. from the heat for 3-5 minutes or until eggs are completely set. Let stand for 5 minutes before serving. YIELD: 2 servings.

GREEK SALAD PITAS

NICOLE FILIZETTI ✤ JACKSONVILLE, FLORIDA

Fresh Greek salad combines with a velvety smooth bean dip for this healthy meal-in-a-pocket. You can also serve the spread with crackers or as a dip with cut vegetables.

  3/4 cup canned garbanzo beans or chickpeas, rinsed and drained
      2 tablespoons lemon juice
      1 tablespoon sliced green olives with pimientos
      1 teaspoon olive oil
      1 garlic clove, minced
      1 cup fresh baby spinach
  1/4 cup chopped seeded peeled cucumber
  1/4 cup crumbled feta cheese
      2 tablespoons chopped marinated quartered artichoke hearts
      2 tablespoons sliced Greek olives
  1/4 teaspoon dried oregano
      2 whole wheat pita pocket halves

Place the first five ingredients in a food processor; cover and process until smooth. Set aside.

In a small bowl, combine the spinach, cucumber, cheese, artichokes, olives and oregano.

Spread the bean mixture into pita halves; add salad. Serve immediately. YIELD: 2 servings.

CHOCOLATE-ALMOND BANANA SPLITS

CANDACE MCMENAMIN ✤ LEXINGTON, SOUTH CAROLINA

When your kids just can't wait to dig into something sweet, put together these speedy banana splits. Experiment with various flavors of ice cream.

      2 milk chocolate candy bars with almonds (1.45 ounces each), chopped
      3 tablespoons heavy whipping cream
      2 medium bananas

1 cup chocolate ice cream
2 tablespoons chopped almonds, toasted

In a microwave, melt candy bars with cream. Stir until blended; keep warm.

Halve bananas lengthwise; arrange in two dessert dishes. Add ice cream; drizzle with warm chocolate sauce. Sprinkle with almonds. YIELD: 2 servings.

TOSSED SALAD WITH SIMPLE VINAIGRETTE

MARTHA ATWELL ❖ ALAMOGORDO, NEW MEXICO

This simple salad has a light, fresh flavor. Friends who eat it for the first time in my home ask for the recipe.

1-1/2 cups torn leaf lettuce
1/3 cup thinly sliced peeled cucumber
1/4 cup chopped seeded tomato
2 fresh basil leaves, thinly sliced
1 green onion, sliced
2 teaspoons rice vinegar
1-1/2 teaspoons olive oil
Dash *each* salt and pepper

Combine the lettuce, cucumber, tomato, basil and onion. In a small bowl, whisk the vinegar, oil, salt and pepper. Pour over salad; toss to coat. YIELD: 2 servings.

TRAIL MIX APPLE SALAD

MELISSA BOYLE ❖ DULUTH, MINNESOTA

I created this salad as a way to make use of the many wonderful apple varieties available in the fall. It's also a great way to add healthy nuts and seeds to your diet.

1 medium apple, coarsely chopped
3/4 teaspoon lemon juice
2 tablespoons chopped walnuts
1 tablespoon sunflower kernels
1 tablespoon dried cranberries
2 teaspoons honey
1 teaspoon flaxseed
1/8 teaspoon ground cinnamon

In a small bowl, combine the chopped apple and lemon juice. Add the walnuts, sunflower kernels, dried cranberries, honey, flaxseed and cinnamon; toss to coat. Chill until serving. YIELD: 2 servings.

MEALS IN MINUTES

Each recipe in this chapter is a hearty entree that's ready in just 30 minutes or less! Best of all, many of the easy dishes are robust enough to impress your guests and even steal the show at holiday get-togethers.

SALMON WITH PINEAPPLE SAUCE

KRISTINE TUPPER ❖ CENTRAL, ALASKA

We catch the key ingredient for this entree fresh from our local waters. I'm wild about 49th state cuisine—from berries to game and fish.

2 salmon fillets (6 ounces *each*)
1 teaspoon cornstarch
1/4 cup unsweetened pineapple juice
2 tablespoons reduced-sodium soy sauce
1 teaspoon water
1 tablespoon brown sugar
1/4 teaspoon ground ginger
Dash cayenne pepper
3/4 cup unsweetened pineapple tidbits

Place salmon in an ungreased 8-in. square baking dish. Bake, uncovered, at 350° for 20-25 minutes or until fish flakes easily with a fork.

In a small saucepan, combine the cornstarch, pineapple juice, soy sauce and water until smooth. Stir in the brown sugar, ginger and cayenne. Bring to a boil; cook and stir for 1-2 minutes or until thickened. Add pineapple; heat through. Serve with salmon. YIELD: 2 servings.

PASA DE SHUTO

MARTY MARTIN ❖ OGDEN, UTAH

My father, who had worked on the railroad, used to make this dish for special family occasions. After he passed away, our family discovered that no one else had the recipe! Then one of my school friends mentioned Pasa de Shuto and shared her recipe with me. I experimented with it until it tasted just the way my father made it.

1 pound bulk sausage
1 pound ground beef
6 cups chopped vegetables (carrots, onions, green peppers, fresh mushrooms and celery)
1 can (10-3/4 ounces) condensed tomato soup, undiluted
1 can (10-3/4 ounces) condensed cream of mushroom soup, undiluted
1 can (8 ounces) tomato sauce
2 teaspoons chili powder
1/2 teaspoon ground cloves
1/2 teaspoon ground cinnamon
1/2 teaspoon salt
1 package (12 ounces) thin spaghetti, broken into 1-inch lengths

In a large skillet, brown sausage and beef until no longer pink; drain. Add vegetables and saute just until crisp-tender. Stir in soups, tomato sauce and spices.

Meanwhile, cook the broken spaghetti according to package directions; drain. Add to skillet and stir gently to mix. YIELD: 10-12 servings.

PINEAPPLE CHICKEN

MARIAN PLATT ❖ SEQUIM, WASHINGTON

I've been making this flavorful recipe since a friend gave it to me 30 years ago.

In a small bowl, beat the butter, chili powder, mustard and cayenne until smooth. Refrigerate until serving.

Rub the steaks with pepper and sugar. Grill, covered, over medium heat for 5-6 minutes on each side or until meat reaches desired doneness (for medium-rare, a thermometer should read 145°; medium, 160°; well-done, 170°). Spoon chili butter over steak. YIELD: 2 servings.

BROILED FISH

ANN BERG ❖ CHESAPEAKE, VIRGINIA

My mother's secret in preparing this recipe was to butter the fish first before dusting it with flour. This technique seals in the moisture of the fish, making it succulent and absolutely delicious.

      4 orange roughy, red snapper, catfish *or* trout fillets
        (1-1/2 to 2 pounds)
      6 tablespoons butter, melted, *divided*
      1 tablespoon all-purpose flour
Paprika
Juice of 1 lemon
      1 tablespoon minced fresh parsley
      2 teaspoons Worcestershire sauce

Place fish on a broiler rack that has been coated with cooking spray. Drizzle 3 tablespoons butter over fillets; dust with flour and sprinkle with paprika.

Broil 5-6 in. from the heat for 5 minutes or until fish just begins to brown. Combine lemon juice, parsley, Worcestershire sauce and remaining butter; pour over fish. Broil 5 minutes longer or until fish flakes easily with a fork. YIELD: 4 servings.

      1/2 cup barbecue sauce
      1/2 cup orange juice
      1/4 cup packed brown sugar
      2 tablespoons canola oil
      2 tablespoons all-purpose flour
      1/4 teaspoon salt, optional
      4 cups cubed cooked chicken
      1 can (8 ounces) pineapple chunks, drained
      1 can (8 ounces) sliced water chestnuts, drained
    1-1/2 teaspoons ground ginger
Hot cooked rice

In a large saucepan, combine the first six ingredients until smooth. Bring to a boil; reduce heat and simmer for 2 minutes, stirring occasionally.

Add the chicken, pineapple, water chestnuts and ginger; cover and simmer for 10 minutes or until heated through. Serve with rice. YIELD: 4 servings.

RIBEYES WITH CHILI BUTTER

ALLAN STACKHOUSE JR. ❖ JENNINGS, LOUISIANA

A couple of spoonfuls of spicy butter made with chili powder and mustard give steak a delicious Southwestern slant.

      1/4 cup butter, softened
      1 teaspoon chili powder
      1/2 teaspoon Dijon mustard
Dash cayenne pepper
      2 beef ribeye steaks (8 ounces *each*)
      1/2 to 1 teaspoon coarsely ground pepper
      1/4 teaspoon sugar

PAN-FRIED VENISON STEAK

GAYLEEN GROTE ✣ BATTLEVIEW, NORTH DAKOTA

Growing up, this recipe was a family favorite when we had deer meat. I loved it, and now my children do too!

1 pound venison *or* beef tenderloin, cut into 1/2-inch slices
2 cups crushed saltines
2 eggs
3/4 cup milk
1 teaspoon salt
1/2 teaspoon pepper
5 tablespoons canola oil

Flatten venison to 1/4-in. thickness. Place saltines in a shallow bowl. In another shallow bowl, whisk the eggs, milk, salt and pepper. Coat venison with saltines, then dip in egg mixture and coat a second time with saltines.

In a large skillet over medium heat, cook venison in oil in batches for 2-3 minutes on each side or until meat reaches desired doneness (for medium-rare, a thermometer should read 145°; medium, 160°; well-done, 170°). YIELD: 4 servings.

QUICK SPAGHETTI CARBONARA

JANAAN CUNNINGHAM ✣ GREENDALE, WISCONSIN

This is a wonderful tomatoless spaghetti that still has plenty of dimension. The bacon has such a savory flavor it will make your family ask for seconds—and thirds.

1 package (8 ounces) spaghetti
1 garlic clove, minced

3 tablespoons butter
1 egg, lightly beaten
8 bacon strips, cooked and crumbled
1/4 cup grated Parmesan cheese

Cook spaghetti according to package directions. Meanwhile, in a large skillet, saute garlic in butter over medium heat for 1 minute. Reduce heat to low; add egg. Cook and stir until egg mixture coats a metal spoon and reaches 160° (mixture will look like a soft frothy egg).

Drain spaghetti and place in a bowl. Pour sauce over and sprinkle with bacon; toss gently to coat. Gently stir in cheese. YIELD: 4 servings.

BROCCOLI CHICKEN TORTELLINI

JUNE PARKER ✣ RENO, NEVADA

When I concocted this recipe years ago, I had just discovered fresh tortellini. I added the alfredo sauce and fresh broccoli and liked the way it tasted. I serve it with crusty French or sourdough bread.

1 cup refrigerated cheese tortellini
1 cup fresh broccoli florets
1 cup cubed cooked chicken
1 cup Alfredo sauce
Dash seasoned salt

Cook tortellini according to package directions, adding broccoli during the last 3 minutes of cooking. Drain. Stir in the chicken, Alfredo sauce and seasoned salt; cook and stir until heated through. YIELD: 2 servings.

SALMON WITH TARRAGON SAUCE

AGNES WARD ❖ STRATFORD, ONTARIO

Here's a fast and foolproof microwave method for tender salmon steaks covered with a distinctive Dijon and green onion sauce.

 4 salmon fillets (6 ounces *each*)
1/4 teaspoon salt
1/4 teaspoon white pepper
 2 tablespoons white wine *or* chicken broth
 1 tablespoon butter
 1 green onion, finely chopped
 1 tablespoon all-purpose flour
 1 teaspoon Dijon mustard
1/2 teaspoon dried tarragon
2/3 cup 2% milk

Place salmon in a greased 2-qt. microwave-safe dish; sprinkle with salt and pepper. Pour wine over top. Cover and microwave on high for 4-6 minutes or until fish flakes easily with a fork. Remove salmon and keep warm.

Add butter and onion to the pan juices; cover and microwave on high for 1 minute. Stir in the flour, mustard and tarragon until blended; gradually stir in milk. Cook, uncovered for 1-2 minutes or until thickened; stirring every 30 seconds. Serve with salmon. YIELD: 4 servings.

EDITOR'S NOTE: This recipe was tested in a 1,100-watt microwave.

PURCHASING FRESH FISH

When buying fresh fish fillets or steaks, look for firm flesh that has a moist look and that is springy to the touch. Don't purchase fish that looks dried out. Fresh fish should have a mild smell, not a strong odor.

One-Skillet Wonders

If cleaning up after a meal is what you dread most, then these recipes are for you. Each entree is cooked in a single skillet. An easy salad and a basket of rolls complete the meal!

HERBED SHRIMP SKILLET

RUTH BELLER ❖ SUN CITY, CALIFORNIA

I love corn, especially in this dish. During summer, when I can use fresh corn instead of frozen, it's even better. Either way, it comes together very quickly.

- 1 small onion, chopped
- 1 small green pepper, chopped
- 3 tablespoons butter
- 3 cups frozen corn
- 2 teaspoons sugar
- 1/2 teaspoon salt
- 1/2 teaspoon dried basil
- 1/2 teaspoon dried thyme
- 1/4 teaspoon pepper
- 3/4 pound uncooked medium shrimp, peeled and deveined

In a large skillet, saute onion and green pepper in butter for 2 minutes. Stir in the corn, sugar, salt, basil, thyme and pepper. Cover and cook over medium-low heat for 5-8 minutes or until corn is tender.

Add shrimp; cook and stir for 3-4 minutes or until shrimp turn pink. YIELD: 4 servings.

PAN-SEARED LAMB CHOPS

MATTHEW LAWRENCE ❖ VASHON, WASHINGTON

An aromatic trio of garlic, rosemary and mint enhances the flavor of these chops, along with the luxuriously flavorful sauce on top.

- 3 garlic cloves, minced
- 2 teaspoons minced fresh rosemary
- 1 teaspoon minced fresh mint
- 1/4 teaspoon salt
- 1/8 teaspoon pepper
- 4 lamb loin chops (4 ounces *each*)
- 1 tablespoon butter
- 1 tablespoon olive oil
- 1/4 cup white wine
- 1/4 cup heavy whipping cream

Combine the first five ingredients; rub over chops. In a large skillet over medium heat, cook chops in butter and oil for 6-8 minutes on each side or until meat reaches desired doneness (for medium-rare, a thermometer should read 145°; medium, 160°; well-done, 170°). Remove and keep warm.

Add wine to the same skillet, stirring to loosen browned bits from pan. Stir in cream; cook for 1-2 minutes or until slightly thickened. Serve with chops. YIELD: 2 servings.

SKILLET CASSOULET

BARBARA BRITTAIN ❖ SANTEE, CALIFORNIA

This is a classic dish that normally takes from a few hours to a couple of days to make, but I've made it simple and easy by preparing it in a skillet. Chock-full of flavor, the little spice from the smoked kielbasa makes a nice, hearty combo for a flavorful meal in one. Serve it with warm, crusty bread slathered in butter for a complete dinner.

1/4 pound smoked turkey kielbasa, cut into 1/2-inch slices
1/4 pound fully cooked boneless ham, cubed
2 medium carrots, sliced
1 celery rib, sliced
1/2 medium red onion, sliced
2 teaspoons canola oil
2 garlic cloves, minced
1 can (15 ounces) cannellini *or* white kidney beans, rinsed and drained
1 can (14-1/2 ounces) no-salt-added diced tomatoes, drained
3/4 teaspoon dried thyme
1/8 teaspoon pepper

In a large skillet, saute the turkey kielbasa, cooked ham, carrots, celery and red onion in canola oil until the sausage is browned and the vegetables are tender. Add the minced garlic and cook 1 minute longer.

Stir in the beans, diced tomatoes, thyme and pepper. Bring to a boil. Reduce the heat; simmer, uncovered, for 4-5 minutes or until heated through. YIELD: 3 servings.

TURKEY TENDERLOINS WITH RASPBERRY BBQ SAUCE

DEIRDRE DEE COX ❖ MILWAUKEE, WISCONSIN

Sweet and tangy raspberry sauce is a perfect complement to versatile turkey tenderloins. In fact, the sauce is so good, you'll be tempted to eat it with a spoon.

2 turkey breast tenderloins (5 ounces *each*)
1/8 teaspoon salt
1/8 teaspoon pepper
2 teaspoons olive oil
1 teaspoon cornstarch
1/4 cup cranberry-raspberry juice
2 tablespoons Heinz 57 steak sauce
2 tablespoons red raspberry preserves
1/2 teaspoon lemon juice

Sprinkle turkey with salt and pepper. In a large nonstick skillet over medium heat, brown turkey in oil on all sides. Cover and cook for 10-12 minutes or until a thermometer reads 170°. Remove and keep warm.

Combine cornstarch and juice until smooth; add to the pan. Stir in the steak sauce, preserves and lemon juice. Bring to a boil; cook and stir for 1 minute or until thickened. Slice turkey; serve with sauce. YIELD: 2 servings.

PIZZA HOT DISH

FAYTHE ANDERSON ❖ RACINE, WISCONSIN

Here's a spin on pizza everyone will enjoy—especially pasta lovers. The best of both worlds!

    2 eggs
1/2 cup milk
    1 package (7 ounces) elbow macaroni, cooked and drained
    1 pound ground beef
    1 medium onion, chopped
    1 can (10-3/4 ounces) condensed tomato soup, undiluted
    1 teaspoon salt
1/2 teaspoon dried basil
1/2 teaspoon dried oregano
1/4 teaspoon pepper
    2 cups (8 ounces) shredded cheddar cheese

In a large bowl, beat eggs. Add milk and macaroni. Pour into a greased 13-in. x 9-in. baking dish; set aside.

In a large skillet, cook beef and onion over medium heat until meat is no longer pink; drain. Stir in the soup and seasonings.

Spoon over macaroni. Sprinkle with cheese. Bake, uncovered, at 350° for 20-25 minutes or until heated through. YIELD: 12-16 servings.

CHICKEN BUNDLES

LINDA GRABER ❖ ARCHBOLD, OHIO

This quick recipe is special enough to serve to guests. The dill adds a little extra flavor.

    1 package (8 ounces) cream cheese, softened
1/4 cup milk
    1 teaspoon dill weed
1/2 teaspoon salt

1/2 teaspoon pepper
    4 cups cubed cooked chicken
1/2 cup finely chopped celery
    4 green onions with tops, thinly sliced
    3 tubes (8 ounces *each*) refrigerated crescent rolls
1/4 cup butter, melted
1/4 cup seasoned bread crumbs

In a large bowl, beat the cream cheese, milk, dill, salt and pepper until blended. Stir in the chicken, celery and onions.

Unroll crescent roll dough and separate into 12 rectangles, four from each tube; place on a greased baking sheet and press the perforations together. Spoon 1/2 cup of chicken mixture into the center of each rectangle. Bring edges up to the center and pinch to seal. Brush with butter; sprinkle with bread crumbs.

Bake at 350° for 15-20 minutes or until golden brown. YIELD: 6 servings.

SALMON CAKES

IMOGENE HUTTON ❖ BROWNWOOD, TEXAS

Since pinto beans and mashed potatoes were our usual daily fare, salmon was a special treat on Sundays. We ate these cakes as quickly as Mama could cook them—she couldn't get them off the griddle fast enough.

    2 eggs
1/4 cup heavy whipping cream
1/4 cup cornmeal
    2 tablespoons sliced green onions
    2 tablespoons all-purpose flour
1/4 teaspoon baking powder
Pinch pepper
1/2 teaspoon salt, optional
    1 can (14-3/4 ounces) salmon, drained, bones and skin removed
    1 to 2 tablespoons butter

In a small bowl, beat eggs. Stir in the cream, cornmeal, green onions, flour, baking powder, pepper and salt if desired. Flake salmon into bowl; blend gently.

Melt butter in a large nonstick skillet or griddle over medium heat. Drop salmon mixture by 1/3 cupfuls into butter. Fry in batches for 5 minutes on each side or until lightly browned. Serve warm. YIELD: 3-4 servings (six patties).

CAESAR ORANGE ROUGHY

MARY LOU BOYCE ❖ WILMINGTON, DELAWARE
Sprinkled with buttery cracker crumbs, these tender fish fillets are nicely flavored with Caesar salad dressing and shredded cheddar cheese. To top it off, they're speedy and oh-so easy to make.

    2 pounds orange roughy fillets
    1 cup creamy Caesar salad dressing
    2 cups crushed butter-flavored crackers (about 50 crackers)
    1 cup (4 ounces) shredded cheddar cheese

Place the the orange roughy fillets in an ungreased 13-in. x 9-in. baking dish. Drizzle with the salad dressing; sprinkle with the cracker crumbs.

Bake, uncovered, at 400° for 10 minutes. Sprinkle with cheese. Bake 3-5 minutes longer or until fish flakes easily with a fork and cheese is melted. YIELD: 8 servings.

EASY SAUSAGE AND VEGETABLE SKILLET

RUBY WILLIAMS ❖ BOGALUSA, LOUISIANA
This is an old recipe that has been passed down in our family through my sister-in-law. When I was a child, she did most of the cooking in our house, and this was my favorite meal. The variety of vegetables makes this an attractive dish, and the cooking time is minimal.

  1/2 pound Italian sausage links
    1 tablespoon canola oil
    1 cup cubed yellow summer squash (3/4-inch pieces)
  1/2 cup chopped green onions
    2 garlic cloves, minced
1-1/2 cups chopped fresh tomatoes
    2 teaspoons Worcestershire sauce
  1/8 teaspoon cayenne pepper

In a large skillet, cook the sausage over medium heat in the oil until a thermometer reads 160°; drain. Cut into 1/2 inch slices.

Add the sausage, summer squash and green onions to the skillet; cook for 3-4 minutes or until the vegetables are tender. Add the minced garlic and cook 1 minute longer.

Stir in the tomatoes, Worcestershire sauce and cayenne pepper; heat through. YIELD: 2 servings.

2 tablespoons butter, melted
1/3 cup all-purpose flour
1-1/2 cups chicken broth
4 garlic cloves, minced
1 cup heavy whipping cream
1/2 cup minced fresh parsley
2 teaspoons paprika
Salt and pepper to taste
2 pounds large uncooked shrimp, peeled and deveined
Hot cooked noodles or rice

In a small saucepan, melt butter; stir in flour until smooth. Gradually add broth and garlic. Bring to a boil; cook and stir for 2 minutes or until thickened. Remove from the heat. Stir in the cream, parsley, paprika, salt and pepper.

Butterfly shrimp, by cutting lengthwise almost in half, but leaving shrimp attached at opposite side. Spread to butterfly. Place cut side down in a greased 13-in. x 9-in. baking dish. Pour cream sauce over shrimp. Bake, uncovered, at 400° for 15-18 minutes or until shrimp turn pink. Serve with noodles or rice. YIELD: 8 servings.

APRICOT CHICKEN STIR-FRY

LORI LOCKREY ✢ WEST HILL, ONTARIO

This sweet, fruity sauce goes very well with juicy chicken. It's a great dish for two, but the recipe is easily adjusted to serve more if you'd like.

1/2 pound boneless skinless chicken breasts, cut into strips
1 teaspoon canola oil
1 cup fresh snow peas
6 tablespoons apricot preserves
1/4 cup water
1 garlic clove, minced
1-1/2 teaspoons sesame oil
1 teaspoon sesame seeds, toasted
1 teaspoon reduced-sodium soy sauce
1/4 teaspoon ground ginger
1/4 teaspoon Dijon mustard
Hot cooked rice

In a large skillet or wok, stir-fry chicken in canola oil for 3 minutes. Add the snow peas, preserves, water, garlic, sesame oil, sesame seeds, soy sauce, ginger and mustard. Bring to a boil. Reduce heat; simmer, uncovered, for 5-7 minutes or until chicken is no longer pink and vegetables are tender. Serve with rice. YIELD: 2 serving.

SHRIMP IN CREAM SAUCE

JANE BIRCH ✢ EDISON, NEW JERSEY

Looking for a special Christmas Eve entree to delight your busy crowd? My family enjoys this rich shrimp dish on the holiday. I serve it over golden egg noodles.

WILD SALMON WITH HAZELNUTS OVER SPINACH

BARBARA SIDWAY ✢ BAKER CITY, OREGON

We serve only fresh, line-caught wild salmon at our hotel. The crunchy toasted hazelnuts and the nutritious spinach add great flavor.

8 wild salmon fillets (7 ounces *each*)
1/2 pound fresh baby spinach
1 tablespoon plus 1/2 cup butter, *divided*
6 garlic cloves, minced
3 tablespoons lemon juice
1/4 teaspoon salt
1/4 teaspoon pepper
1/3 cup chopped hazelnuts, toasted

Using long-handled tongs, moisten a paper towel with cooking oil and lightly coat the grill rack. Grill salmon skin side down, covered, over medium heat or broil 4 in. from the heat for 12-14 minutes or until the salmon flakes easily with a fork.

Meanwhile, in a large skillet, saute spinach in 1 tablespoon butter until tender; remove from the pan and keep warm. In the same skillet, saute garlic in remaining butter for 1 minute. Stir in the lemon juice, salt and pepper.

Place spinach on serving plates; top with salmon. Drizzle with butter mixture and sprinkle with hazelnuts. YIELD: 8 servings.

BLACK BEAN QUESADILLAS

DIXIE TERRY ✤ GOREVILLE, ILLINOIS

Need a quick snack or appetizer? These bean and cheese quesadillas are the answer. I got the recipe at a Mexican festival held at our children's school. It's been served at our house regularly ever since.

1 cup canned black beans, rinsed and drained
1 green onion, chopped
2 tablespoons chopped red onion
2 tablespoons finely chopped roasted sweet red pepper
1 tablespoon minced fresh cilantro
1 tablespoon lime juice
1 garlic clove, minced
4 flour tortillas (10 inches)
1 cup (4 ounces) shredded Muenster *or* Monterey Jack cheese

In a small bowl, mash beans with a fork; stir in the green onion, red onion, pepper, cilantro, lime juice and garlic. Spread 1/4 cup bean mixture over half of each tortilla; top with 1/4 cup cheese. Fold over.

Cook on a griddle coated with cooking spray over low heat for 1-2 minutes on each side or until cheese is melted. Cut into wedges. YIELD: 4 servings.

QUESADILLAS, OLÉ!

You can create any type of flavor you want in your quesadilla. Add shredded chicken, beef or pork instead of half of the beans. Use pepper jack to add spicy flavor. You can even add another 1/2 teaspoon of minced garlic.

TURKEY SALAD WITH PISTACHIOS

KATHY KITTELL ❖ LENEXA, KANSAS

I found this recipe in my "someday I'll make this" file and declared it a winner. The pickle relish and chopped pistachios give it a unique flavor. Served with garlic bread, it's a complete meal.

3/4 cup fat-free mayonnaise
3 tablespoons sour cream
1 tablespoon sweet pickle relish
1/8 teaspoon salt
1/8 teaspoon pepper
1 cup cubed cooked turkey
1/4 cup chopped green onions
1/4 cup chopped celery
3 tablespoons chopped pistachios

In a large bowl, combine the first five ingredients. Add turkey; toss to coat. Stir in the onions, celery and pistachios. Cover and refrigerate until ready to serve. YIELD: 2 servings.

CHICKEN FAJITA SALAD

LOIS PROUDFIT ❖ EUGENE, OREGON

This recipe came from Texas, which is famous for its Mexican food. I love to cook, even though it's just for me and my husband now. I invite our grown kids over a lot, and they just love this recipe. I'm happy to share it!

---

4 tablespoons canola oil, *divided*
1/2 cup lime juice
2 garlic cloves, minced
1 teaspoon ground cumin
1 teaspoon dried oregano
1 pound boneless skinless chicken breasts, cut into thin strips
1 medium onion, cut into thin wedges
1 medium sweet red pepper, cut into thin strips
2 cans (4 ounces *each*) chopped green chilies
1 cup unblanched almonds, toasted
Shredded lettuce
3 medium tomatoes, cut into wedges
1 medium ripe avocado, peeled and sliced

In a small bowl, combine 2 tablespoons oil, lime juice, garlic, cumin and oregano. Pour half in a large resealable plastic bag; add chicken. Seal bag and turn to coat. Marinate for at least 30 minutes. Cover and refrigerate remaining marinade.

In a large skillet, heat remaining oil on medium-high. Saute onion for 2-3 minutes or until crisp-tender.

Drain and discard the marinade. Add the chicken to skillet; stir-fry until the meat is no longer pink. Add the red pepper, green chilies and reserved marinade; cook 2 minutes or until heated through. Stir in the toasted almonds. Serve salad immediately over shredded lettuce; top with fresh tomatoes and avocado. YIELD: 4-6 servings.

TILAPIA WITH TOMATO-ORANGE RELISH

HELEN CONWELL ❖ PORTLAND, OREGON

The mild flavor and tender texture of tilapia goes beautifully with this colorful, garden-fresh relish made with tomato, orange, red onions and capers. It makes a big impression with only a little work!

---

6 tilapia fillets (6 ounces *each*)
3 tablespoons butter, melted
1/2 teaspoon salt, *divided*
1/2 teaspoon lemon-pepper seasoning
1 medium tomato, seeded and chopped
1 medium orange, peeled, sectioned and chopped
1/3 cup finely chopped red onion
1 tablespoon capers, drained
1-1/2 tablespoons brown sugar
1 tablespoon red wine vinegar

Place the fish in a greased 15-in. x 10-in. x 1-in. baking pan. Drizzle with butter; sprinkle with 1/4 teaspoon salt and the lemon-pepper. Bake at 425° for 10 minutes or until fish flakes easily with a fork.

In a small bowl, combine the tomato, orange, onion, capers, brown sugar, vinegar and remaining salt. Serve with fish. YIELD: 6 servings.

SPAGHETTI WITH ROASTED RED PEPPER SAUCE

DIANE LOMBARDO ❖ NEW CASTLE, PENNSYLVANIA

This pasta recipe, sparked by jarred red peppers, is an excellent company dish. Guests won't believe how easy it is until they try making it. It's as good as any restaurant special, but much more affordable!

---

12 ounces uncooked spaghetti
1 jar (12 ounces) roasted sweet red peppers, drained
2 large tomatoes, seeded and chopped
1 tablespoon red wine vinegar
1 garlic clove, peeled and halved
1/2 teaspoon salt
1/4 teaspoon pepper
1/2 cup olive oil
5 tablespoons grated Parmesan cheese

Cook the spaghetti according to package directions. Meanwhile, in a food processor, combine the roasted red peppers, tomatoes, red wine vinegar, garlic, salt and pepper. Cover and process until blended. While processing, gradually add the olive oil in a steady stream.

Transfer to a small saucepan; bring to a boil. Reduce heat; simmer, uncovered, for 10 minutes. Drain spaghetti; serve with sauce. Sprinkle with cheese. YIELD: 5 servings.

MEMORABLE MEALS

These family-favorite supper spreads always bring simple, satisfying and festive recipes to the table. Best of all, they each come from busy home cooks just like you!

A Taste of the Country

CHERRY DUMPLINGS

GAIL HALE ❖ FILLMORE, NEW YORK

This is my mom's recipe, and I'm happy to share it. The dumplings are out of this world, and they complement the tart cherries.

1 can (14-1/2 ounces) pitted tart cherries, undrained
1 cup sugar, *divided*
1/2 cup water
1 cup all-purpose flour
1 teaspoon baking powder
1/2 teaspoon grated lemon peel
Dash salt
1/3 cup milk
3 tablespoons butter, melted

In a large saucepan, combine the cherries with juice, 3/4 cup sugar and water; bring to a boil. Reduce heat; cover and simmer.

Meanwhile, in a small bowl, combine the flour, baking powder, lemon peel, salt and remaining sugar. Stir in milk and butter just until moistened.

Drop by tablespoonfuls onto simmering cherry mixture. Cover and simmer for 20 minutes or until a toothpick inserted in a dumpling comes out clean (do not lift the cover while simmering). YIELD: 8 servings.

ROASTED ONION & GARLIC SOUP

NANCY MUELLER ❖ MENOMONEE FALLS, WISCONSIN

When it comes to stirring up comfort in a bowl, this low-fat soup made with sweet onions is a surefire cold-weather tonic.

6 medium sweet onions
1 whole garlic bulb
3 cups reduced-sodium chicken broth, *divided*
1/2 cup buttermilk
1 tablespoon minced fresh thyme *or* 1 teaspoon dried thyme
1/2 teaspoon coarsely ground pepper
1/2 cup shredded Swiss cheese

Place the unpeeled onions and garlic bulb in a 15-in. x 10-in. x 1-in. baking pan coated with cooking spray. Spritz with cooking spray. Bake, uncovered, at 450° for 50-60 minutes or until tender.

When cool enough to handle, peel the onions and garlic. Place in a blender; add 1 cup of broth. Cover and process until smooth; transfer to a large saucepan. Add the buttermilk, thyme, pepper and remaining broth; heat through. Garnish with cheese. YIELD: 8 servings (2 quarts).

CARAMEL SWEET POTATOES

MARY JO PATRICK ❖ NAPOLEON, OHIO

The sauce is the star of this recipe. It really does taste like butterscotch. It is a nice side dish for poultry or ham.

6 medium sweet potatoes, peeled and cut into 1-inch chunks
1/2 cup packed brown sugar
1/2 cup corn syrup
1/4 cup milk
2 tablespoons butter
1/2 to 1 teaspoon salt
1/2 teaspoon ground cinnamon

Place sweet potatoes in a Dutch oven; cover with water. Bring to a boil. Reduce heat; cover and simmer for 20 minutes or until crisp-tender.

Drain and transfer to a greased 13-in. x 9-in. baking dish. Bake, uncovered, at 325° for 15 minutes.

Meanwhile, in a small saucepan, combine the remaining ingredients. Bring to a boil; pour over sweet potatoes. Bake 10-15 minutes longer or until glazed, basting frequently. YIELD: 10 servings.

OVEN FRIED CHICKEN

STEPHANIE OTTEN ❖ BYRON CENTER, MICHIGAN

My family loves this chicken recipe. The coating keeps the chicken nice and moist, and with the taste enhanced by marinating, the result is delicious.

    2 cups buttermilk
    2 tablespoons Dijon mustard
    2 teaspoons salt
    2 teaspoons hot pepper sauce
1-1/2 teaspoons garlic powder
    8 bone-in chicken breast halves, skin removed
      (8 ounces *each*)
    2 cups soft bread crumbs
    1 cup cornmeal
    2 tablespoons canola oil
  1/2 teaspoon poultry seasoning
  1/2 teaspoon ground mustard
  1/2 teaspoon paprika
  1/2 teaspoon cayenne pepper
  1/4 teaspoon dried oregano
  1/4 teaspoon dried parsley flakes

In a large resealable plastic bag, combine the buttermilk, mustard, salt, hot pepper sauce and garlic powder; add the chicken. Seal bag and turn to coat; refrigerate for at least 1 hour or overnight.

Drain and discard the marinade. In a large resealable plastic bag, combine the bread crumbs, cornmeal, oil and seasonings. Add the chicken, one piece at a time, and shake to coat. Place on a parchment paper-lined baking sheet. Bake chicken at 400° for 35-40 minutes or until a thermometer reads 170°. YIELD: 8 servings.

MAKING SOFT BREAD CRUMBS

Tear several slices of fresh white, French or whole wheat bread into 1-in. pieces. Place in a food processor or blender; cover and pulse several times to make coarse crumbs. One slice of bread yields about 1/2 cup crumbs.

Grub from the Grill

HONEY-MUSTARD BRATS

LILY JULOW ❖ GAINESVILLE, FLORIDA

The flavor of these brats is enhanced by a sweet mustard glaze, which give them a unique taste. Everyone loves them and declares them delicious!

1/4 cup Dijon mustard
1/4 cup honey
2 tablespoons mayonnaise
1 teaspoon steak sauce
4 uncooked bratwurst links
4 brat buns

In a small bowl, combine the mustard, honey, mayonnaise and steak sauce. Grill bratwurst, covered, over medium heat for 15-20 minutes or until meat is no longer pink, turning and basting frequently with mustard mixture. Serve on buns. YIELD: 4 servings.

GRILLED POTATOES WITH SOUR CREAM SAUCE

CRAIG CARPENTER ❖ CORAOPOLIS, PENNSYLVANIA

These potatoes are tender and good all by themselves, but pairing them with the sauce creates a perfect combination and a side dish compatible with any grilled entree.

2 tablespoons olive oil
1 tablespoon barbecue seasoning
2 garlic cloves, minced
2 teaspoons lemon juice
1-1/2 pounds small potatoes, quartered

SAUCE
2/3 cup ranch salad dressing
4 teaspoons bacon bits
2 teaspoons minced chives
Dash hot pepper sauce

In a large bowl, combine the oil, barbecue seasoning, garlic and lemon juice. Add the potatoes; toss to coat. Place on a double thickness of heavy-duty foil (about 28 in. x 18 in.). Fold foil around the potato mixture and seal tightly.

Grill, covered, over medium heat for 20-25 minutes or until potatoes are tender. In a small bowl, combine the sauce ingredients. Serve with potatoes. YIELD: 5 servings.

EDITOR'S NOTE: This recipe was tested with McCormick's Grill Mates Barbecue Seasoning. Look for it in the spice aisle.

BARBECUED BEANS

MILLIE VICKERY ❖ LENA, ILLINOIS

This is a simple, classic recipe, but cooking it on the grill introduces a subtle flavor.

1 can (16 ounces) kidney beans, rinsed and drained
1 can (15-1/2 ounces) great northern beans, rinsed and drained
1 can (15 ounces) pork and beans
1/2 cup barbecue sauce
2 tablespoons brown sugar
2 teaspoons prepared mustard

In an ungreased 8-in. x 8-in. disposable foil pan, combine all ingredients. Grill, covered, over medium heat for 15-20 minutes or until heated through, stirring occasionally. YIELD: 5 servings.

GRILLED WAFFLE TREATS

CHRIS SEGER ❖ LOMBARD, ILLINOIS

I made these the first time on July 4th. Everyone shared memories of making and eating s'mores while camping.

8 frozen waffles
1 cup miniature marshmallows
1 cup semisweet chocolate chips

Place one waffle on a greased double thickness of heavy-duty foil (about 12 in. square). Sprinkle with 1/4 cup each marshmallows and chocolate chips; top with another waffle. Fold foil around sandwich and seal tightly. Repeat three times.

Grill, covered, over medium heat for 8-10 minutes or until chocolate is melted, turning once. Open foil carefully to allow steam to escape. YIELD: 4 servings.

GRILLING FRESH SAUSAGES

To grill fresh sausages, turn them often and, before serving, cut one in half to be certain it's no longer pink in the center. If you simmer sausages in water first, they take less time to finish on the grill and seem to stay more moist.

Welcome to the Potluck

MOLDED RASPBERRY GELATIN

CHERYL DIXON ✤ MATHIS, TEXAS

I like the blend of flavors in this refreshing dessert. It is light, very easy to make and beautiful on a buffet table.

- 2 packages (3 ounces *each*) raspberry gelatin
- 1 cup boiling water
- 2 cups vanilla ice cream, softened
- 1 cup orange juice
- 2 medium bananas, chopped
- 2 cans (8 ounces *each*) unsweetened crushed pineapple, drained

In a small bowl, dissolve gelatin in boiling water. Stir in ice cream and orange juice until blended. Fold in bananas and pineapple. Spoon into a 6-cup mold coated with cooking spray. Cover and refrigerate until firm. Unmold gelatin onto a serving platter. YIELD: 12 servings.

PANGUITCH POTATOES

LUCILE PROCTOR ✤ PANGUITCH, UTAH

When my husband was in charge of our large pioneer celebration a few years ago, he decided to multiply our family favorite for a crowd. The dish is easy to fix and has become a standby for the event. Here is the original recipe, cheesy and comforting.

- 4 pounds medium potatoes, peeled
- 2-3/4 cups (11 ounces) shredded cheddar cheese
- 1 cup (8 ounces) sour cream
- 2/3 cup buttermilk
- 2 tablespoons plus 1-1/2 teaspoons dried minced onion
- 1/2 teaspoon salt
- 1/4 teaspoon pepper

Place potatoes in a Dutch oven and cover with water. Bring to a boil. Reduce heat; cover and simmer for 12-15 minutes or just until tender. Drain; cool slightly. Grate potatoes.

In a large bowl, combine the remaining ingredients; add potatoes. Stir to combine. Transfer to a greased 13-in. x 9-in. baking dish. Bake, uncovered, at 350° for 35-40 minutes or until heated through. Refrigerate leftovers. YIELD: 15 servings.

CHILLED TURKEY PASTA SALAD

SHERRY CONLEY ✤ NOEL, NOVA SCOTIA

This cheerful pasta salad is a wonderfully new and flavorful way to use leftover turkey. Kids love it when you use multicolored pasta.

- 4-1/2 cups uncooked bow tie pasta
- 2 cans (20 ounces *each*) unsweetened pineapple chunks, undrained
- 2/3 cup red wine vinegar
- 1/4 cup lemon juice
- 1/4 cup honey mustard
- 2 tablespoons olive oil
- 2 teaspoons garlic salt
- 6 cups cubed cooked turkey
- 4 cups chopped fresh broccoli
- 4 celery ribs, chopped
- 1 medium red onion, chopped
- 1 large green pepper, chopped
- 2 cups cubed cheddar cheese

Cook pasta according to package directions. Drain pasta and rinse in cold water.

Drain the pineapple, reserving 1 cup juice; set pineapple aside. For dressing, in a small bowl, whisk the vinegar, lemon juice, honey mustard, olive oil, garlic salt and reserved pineapple juice; set aside.

In a large bowl, combine the pasta, turkey, broccoli, celery, onion, pepper and pineapple. Drizzle with dressing; toss to coat. Cover and refrigerate for at least 2 hours. Just before serving, stir in the cheese. YIELD: 16 servings.

EIGHT-LAYER CASSEROLE

JO PRUSHA ❖ OMAHA, NEBRASKA

My sister shared this original recipe, but I adapted it for my family's taste. I like that it's a nutritious meal in one dish, and when my boys were young, it was a good way to disguise vegetables. This is also a good choice for potlucks.

1 pound frozen home-style egg noodles
2 pounds ground beef
2 cans (15 ounces *each*) tomato sauce
1 tablespoon dried minced onion
2 teaspoons sugar
2 teaspoons *each* Italian seasoning, dried basil and dried parsley flakes
1-1/2 teaspoons garlic powder
1 teaspoon salt
1/2 teaspoon pepper
1 package (8 ounces) cream cheese, softened

1 cup (8 ounces) sour cream
1/2 cup milk
2 packages (10 ounces *each*) frozen chopped spinach, thawed and squeezed dry
1 cup (4 ounces) shredded Colby-Monterey Jack cheese
1 cup (4 ounces) shredded cheddar cheese

Cook noodles according to package directions.

Meanwhile, in a large skillet, cook beef over medium heat until no longer pink; drain. Add the tomato sauce, onion, sugar and seasonings. Bring to a boil. Reduce heat; cover and simmer for 10 minutes. In a small bowl, combine the cream cheese, sour cream and milk.

Place half of the noodles in a greased 13-in. x 9-in. baking dish; top with 3 cups meat mixture. Layer with cream cheese mixture, spinach, and remaining meat mixture and noodles. Sprinkle with cheeses (dish will be full).

Bake, uncovered, at 350° for 40-45 minutes or until bubbly. Let stand for 10 minutes before serving. YIELD: 12 servings.

State Fair Edibles

FRESH-SQUEEZED PINK LEMONADE

CINDY BARTNICKI ✤ MOUNT PROSPECT, ILLINOIS

There's a balance of sweet and tart in this summer drink. It becomes perfectly pink with the addition of grape juice.

    4 cups water, *divided*
    1 cup sugar
    3 lemon peel strips
    1 cup lemon juice (about 5 lemons)
    1 tablespoon grape juice
Lemon slices and maraschino cherries, optional

In a small saucepan, bring 2 cups water, sugar and lemon peel to a boil. Reduce heat; cover and simmer for 5 minutes. Remove from the heat. Discard lemon peel.

In a large pitcher, combine the remaining water, lemon juice, grape juice and sugar mixture. Serve over ice. Garnish with lemon slices and cherries if desired. YIELD: 6 servings.

ADD A SPECIAL TOUCH TO LEMONADE

Freeze sprigs of mint or lemon balm or slivers of lemon zest in each ice cube and drop a few in each glass. Or make pretty cubes of frozen lemonade with maraschino cherries in the center and serve with the lemonade.

TRADITIONAL FUNNEL CAKES

SUSAN TINGLEY ✤ PORTLAND, OREGON

When I was in high school, I made these funnel cakes every Sunday after church for my family. They are crisp and tender, just like the kind we always ate at the state fair.

    2 cups 2% milk
    3 eggs
    1/4 cup sugar
    2 cups all-purpose flour
    2 teaspoons baking powder
Oil for deep-fat frying
Confectioners' sugar
Lingonberry jam or red currant jelly

In a large bowl, combine the milk, eggs and sugar. Combine flour and baking powder; beat into egg mixture until smooth.

In an electric skillet or deep fryer, heat oil to 375°. Cover the bottom of a funnel spout with your finger; ladle 1/2 cup batter into funnel. Holding the funnel several inches above the skillet release finger and move the funnel in a spiral motion until all of the batter is released (scraping funnel with a rubber spatula if needed).

Fry for 1-2 minutes on each side or until golden brown. Drain on paper towels. Repeat with remaining batter. Dust with confectioners' sugar. Serve warm with jam. YIELD: 8 servings.

MINIATURE CORN DOGS

DEB PERRY ❖ BLUFFTON, INDIANA

These little corn dogs add delicious fun to breakfast or brunch. The little snacks are also great for appetizer parties and other get-togethers. Kids and adults alike love to pop them into their mouths. Expect them to disappear fast!

1 cup all-purpose flour
2 tablespoons cornmeal
1-1/2 teaspoons baking powder
1/4 teaspoon salt
Dash onion powder
3 tablespoons shortening
3/4 cup 2% milk
1 egg
1 package (16 ounces) miniature smoked sausages
Oil for deep-fat frying
Spicy ketchup

In a small bowl combine the flour, cornmeal, baking powder, salt and onion powder; cut in shortening until crumbly. Whisk milk and egg; stir into flour mixture just until moistened. Dip sausages into batter.

In an electric skillet or deep fryer, heat oil to 375°. Fry sausages, in batches, for 2-3 minutes or until golden brown. Drain on paper towels. Serve with ketchup. YIELD: about 3-1/2 dozen.

GRILLED CORN WITH THYME

FRIEDA BLIESNER ❖ ADELL, WISCONSIN

The simple addition of thyme and lemon juice brings a unique flavor to corn. Grilled in the husks, the kernels are moist and tender.

4 large ears sweet corn in husks
3 tablespoons butter, softened
2 teaspoons lemon juice
1 teaspoon minced fresh thyme *or* 1/4 teaspoon dried thyme
1/4 teaspoon salt
1/4 teaspoon pepper

Carefully peel back corn husks to within 1 in. of bottoms; remove silk. Combine the remaining ingredients; spread over corn. Rewrap corn in husks and secure with kitchen string. Place in a Dutch oven; cover with cold water. Soak for 20 minutes; drain.

Grill corn, covered, over medium heat for 25-30 minutes or until tender, turning often. YIELD: 4 servings.

BACON & CHEESE SALAD

JOHN DALE WHEELER ❖ ST. CHARLES, MISSOURI

I ordered this salad at a restaurant. The kitchen staff wouldn't share the salad dressing recipe, so I created my own. It took several tries, using different spices and vinegars, but this is close. Adding the bacon was my idea.

- 8 cups torn leaf lettuce
- 10 bacon strips, cooked and crumbled
- 6 green onions, thinly sliced
- 1 cup (4 ounces) shredded part-skim mozzarella cheese
- 1/2 cup shredded Parmesan cheese
- 1 jar (2 ounces) diced pimientos, drained
- 1/2 cup olive oil
- 1/4 cup apple cider *or* juice
- 7-1/2 teaspoons sugar
- 1/2 teaspoon garlic powder
- 1/4 teaspoon salt
- 1/4 teaspoon coarsely ground pepper
- 1 cup salad croutons

In a large bowl, combine the lettuce, bacon, green onions, cheeses and pimientos.

In a small bowl, whisk the oil, cider, sugar, garlic powder, salt and pepper. Pour over salad; toss to coat. Sprinkle with croutons. YIELD: 8 servings.

BANANA SPLIT DESSERT

JOAN ANTONEN ❖ ARLINGTON, SOUTH DAKOTA

I came across this recipe in the paper many years ago, and it has since become a favorite in our household. Whenever my family finds out there is Banana Split Dessert in the freezer, it doesn't last long!

- 1-2/3 cups graham cracker crumbs
- 1/4 cup sugar
- 1/4 cup butter, melted
- 5 medium firm bananas
- 1/2 gallon Neapolitan *or* vanilla ice cream (block carton)
- Hot fudge ice cream topping, warmed, optional

In a small bowl, combine cracker crumbs and sugar; stir in butter. Press onto the bottom of an ungreased 13-in. x 9-in. baking pan. Bake at 350° for 8-10 minutes or until set. Cool completely on a wire rack.

Cut bananas into slices and layer over crust. Cut ice cream widthwise into 3/4-in. slices; place over bananas. Spread edges of ice cream slices to cover bananas and form a smooth layer. Freeze until firm.

Remove from the freezer 10 minutes before serving. Serve with hot fudge topping if desired. YIELD: 12 servings.

TARRAGON-CREAM CHICKEN

TERI LINDQUIST ❖ GURNEE, ILLINOIS

I put together this recipe based on ingredients on hand. I experimented until my family declared that it was perfect!

- 8 boneless skinless chicken breast halves (4 ounces *each*)
- 8 slices deli ham
- 8 slices Swiss cheese (3/4 ounce *each*)
- 1 can (10-3/4 ounces) condensed cream of chicken soup, undiluted
- 1/2 cup white wine *or* chicken broth
- 1/2 cup sour cream
- 2 teaspoons dried tarragon
- 1/4 teaspoon salt
- 1/8 teaspoon pepper
- 2 cups crushed corn bread stuffing
- 1 tablespoon minced fresh parsley

Arrange chicken in a greased 13-in. x 9-in. baking dish. Place a slice of ham and cheese on each chicken breast. In a small saucepan, combine the soup, wine, sour cream, tarragon, salt and pepper; heat through. Pour over chicken.

Cover and bake at 325° for 25 minutes. Uncover; sprinkle with the stuffing and parsley. Bake 10-15 minutes longer or until a thermometer reads 170°. Let stand for 10 minutes before serving. YIELD: 8 servings.

CARROTS LYONNAISE

ELIZABETH PLANTS ❖ KIRKWOOD, MISSOURI

This recipe from a junior high home economics class was brought home by my sister, Laurie. My family liked it so much that it became a part of our Christmas dinner tradition. The term "lyonnaise" refers to the city of Lyon, France, and usually indicates that the center-stage ingredient has been cooked with onions.

- 2 pounds fresh carrots, julienned
- 1 medium onion, thinly sliced
- 1/3 cup butter
- 2 tablespoons all-purpose flour
- 2 teaspoons chicken bouillon granules
- 1/4 teaspoon salt
- 1/8 teaspoon pepper
- 1 cup water

In a Dutch oven, bring 1 in. of water to a boil. Add the julienned carrots; place a lid on the Dutch oven and cook for 5-8 minutes or until crisp-tender.

Meanwhile, in a large skillet, saute the sliced onion in butter until tender. Stir in the flour, bouillon granules, salt and pepper until blended; gradually add the water. Bring to a boil; cook and stir for 2 minutes or until thickened. Drain the carrots and stir stir into the sauce. YIELD: 8 servings.

It's a Slumber Party!

ORANGE SMOOTHIES

GLENNA TOOMAN ❖ BOISE, IDAHO

I've had this recipe for more than 30 years. I led a 4-H club at the time, and one of the girls made this as a demonstration for a project we were doing on milk and milk products. Everyone loved it, and we all copied the recipe.

  1 cup water
  1 cup milk
  1 can (6 ounces) frozen orange juice concentrate, thawed
  10 to 12 ice cubes
  1/2 cup marshmallow creme
  1/4 cup sugar

In a blender, combine all ingredients; cover and process until smooth. Pour into chilled glasses; serve immediately. YIELD: 6 servings.

CREAMY PEPPER DIP

WENDY OLER ❖ WINNIPEG, MANITOBA

This is a wonderfully versatile recipe, which I first tested as a vegetable dip with veggies, potato chips or bread sticks. But my favorite use is as a topping for baked potatoes in place of sour cream.

  1 package (8 ounces) cream cheese, softened
  2 cups mayonnaise
  1 cup buttermilk
  2 teaspoons garlic salt
  2 teaspoons onion powder
  3/4 teaspoon pepper
Assorted fresh vegetables *and/or* ridged potato chips

In a large bowl, beat the cream cheese, mayonnaise, buttermilk and seasonings until smooth. Chill until serving. Serve with vegetables and/or potato chips. YIELD: 4 cups.

CLASSIC PEPPERONI PIZZA

THERESA STEWART ❖ NEW OXFORD, PENNSYLVANIA

My friend Joan gave me this recipe before I got married. It is a basic pizza recipe—easy to make—and toppings can be added to suit anyone.

  1 package (1/4 ounce) active dry yeast
  1 cup warm water (110° to 115°)
  2 tablespoons olive oil
  1 teaspoon sugar
  1 teaspoon salt
2-1/2 cups all-purpose flour
SAUCE
  1 can (8 ounces) tomato sauce
  1 small onion, chopped
  1 garlic clove, minced
  1/4 teaspoon salt
  1/8 teaspoon pepper
TOPPINGS
  1/4 cup grated Parmesan cheese
  2 teaspoons dried oregano
  1 package (3 ounces) sliced pepperoni
  2 cups (8 ounces) shredded part-skim mozzarella cheese

In a large bowl, dissolve yeast in warm water. Add the oil, sugar, salt and 2 cups flour. Beat until smooth. Stir in enough remaining flour to form a soft dough (dough will be sticky).

Turn onto a lightly floured surface; knead until smooth and elastic, about 6-8 minutes. Place in a greased bowl, turning once to grease the top. Cover and let dough rest in a warm place for 10 minutes.

Divide dough in half. On a floured surface, roll out each portion into a 10-in. circle. Transfer to two greased 12-in. pizza pans; build up edges slightly. Bake at 425° for 10-12 minutes or until golden brown.

Meanwhile, in a small bowl, combine the tomato sauce, onion, garlic, salt and pepper; spread over crust. Sprinkle with Parmesan cheese and oregano. Arrange pepperoni over top; sprinkle with mozzarella cheese. Bake 10-15 minutes longer or until cheese is melted. YIELD: 2 pizzas (6 slices each).

PEANUT BUTTER SNACK CAKES

JENNY NOEL ✦ CRANSTON, RHODE ISLAND

My aunt introduced this cake to my family, and it has since became a favorite. It was simple enough to make for dorm study breaks in college and was the most-requested snack.

    2 cups sugar
    1 cup 2% milk
    4 eggs
    2 tablespoons canola oil, *divided*
    1 teaspoon vanilla extract
    2 cups all-purpose flour
1/4 teaspoon salt

    1 cup creamy peanut butter
1-1/3 cups milk chocolate chips

In a small bowl, beat the sugar, milk, eggs, 1 tablespoon oil and vanilla until well blended. Combine flour and salt; gradually beat into sugar mixture.

Transfer to a greased 15 in. x 10-in. x 1-in. baking pan. Bake at 350° for 15-20 minutes or until a toothpick inserted near the center comes out clean. Place on a wire rack. Drop peanut butter by tablespoonfuls onto cake; gently spread evenly. Cool completely. Refrigerate for 30 minutes.

Melt chocolate chips with remaining oil; stir until smooth. Spread over peanut butter layer. Refrigerate until set. Let stand at room temperature for 20 minutes before cutting into bars. Refrigerate leftovers. YIELD: 3 dozen.

MEASURING CUPS ON HAND
For convenience, keep one set of metal measuring cups in your flour canister and a second set in the sugar canister. This way, you won't be searching for them, and they needn't be washed each time.

Substitutions & Equivalents

EQUIVALENT MEASURES

3 teaspoons	= 1 tablespoon	16 tablespoons	= 1 cup
4 tablespoons	= 1/4 cup	2 cups	= 1 pint
5-1/3 tablespoons	= 1/3 cup	4 cups	= 1 quart
8 tablespoons	= 1/2 cup	4 quarts	= 1 gallon

FOOD EQUIVALENTS

GRAINS

Macaroni	1 cup (3-1/2 ounces) uncooked	= 2-1/2 cups cooked
Noodles, Medium	3 cups (4 ounces) uncooked	= 4 cups cooked
Popcorn	1/3 to 1/2 cup unpopped	= 8 cups popped
Rice, Long Grain	1 cup uncooked	= 3 cups cooked
Rice, Quick-Cooking	1 cup uncooked	= 2 cups cooked
Spaghetti	8 ounces uncooked	= 4 cups cooked

CRUMBS

Bread	1 slice	= 3/4 cup soft crumbs, 1/4 cup fine dry crumbs
Graham Crackers	7 squares	= 1/2 cup finely crushed
Buttery Round Crackers	12 crackers	= 1/2 cup finely crushed
Saltine Crackers	14 crackers	= 1/2 cup finely crushed

FRUITS

Bananas	1 medium	= 1/3 cup mashed
Lemons	1 medium	= 3 tablespoons juice, 2 teaspoons grated peel
Limes	1 medium	= 2 tablespoons juice, 1-1/2 teaspoons grated peel
Oranges	1 medium	= 1/4 to 1/3 cup juice, 4 teaspoons grated peel

VEGETABLES

Cabbage	1 head	= 5 cups shredded	Green Pepper	1 large	= 1 cup chopped
Carrots	1 pound	= 3 cups shredded	Mushrooms	1/2 pound	= 3 cups sliced
Celery	1 rib	= 1/2 cup chopped	Onions	1 medium	= 1/2 cup chopped
Corn	1 ear fresh	= 2/3 cup kernels	Potatoes	3 medium	= 2 cups cubed

NUTS

Almonds	1 pound	= 3 cups chopped	Pecan Halves	1 pound	= 4-1/2 cups chopped
Ground Nuts	3-3/4 ounces	= 1 cup	Walnuts	1 pound	= 3-3/4 cups chopped

EASY SUBSTITUTIONS

When you need...   Use...

When you need...		Use...
Baking Powder	1 teaspoon	1/2 teaspoon cream of tartar + 1/4 teaspoon baking soda
Buttermilk	1 cup	1 tablespoon lemon juice or vinegar + enough milk to measure 1 cup (let stand 5 minutes before using)
Cornstarch	1 tablespoon	2 tablespoons all-purpose flour
Honey	1 cup	1-1/4 cups sugar + 1/4 cup water
Half-and-Half Cream	1 cup	1 tablespoon melted butter + enough whole milk to measure 1 cup
Onion	1 small, chopped (1/3 cup)	1 teaspoon onion powder or 1 tablespoon dried minced onion
Tomato Juice	1 cup	1/2 cup tomato sauce + 1/2 cup water
Tomato Sauce	2 cups	3/4 cup tomato paste + 1 cup water
Unsweetened Chocolate	1 square (1 ounce)	3 tablespoons baking cocoa + 1 tablespoon shortening or oil
Whole Milk	1 cup	1/2 cup evaporated milk + 1/2 cup water

COOKING TERMS

Here's a quick reference for some of the cooking terms used in *The Best of Country Cooking* recipes:

BASTE To moisten food with melted butter, pan drippings, marinades or other liquid to add more flavor and juiciness.

BEAT A rapid movement to combine ingredients using a fork, spoon, wire whisk or electric mixer.

BLEND To combine ingredients until *just* mixed.

BOIL To heat liquids until bubbles form that cannot be "stirred down." In the case of water, the temperature will reach 212°.

BONE To remove all meat from the bone before cooking.

CREAM To beat ingredients together to a smooth consistency, usually in the case of butter and sugar for baking.

DASH A small amount of seasoning, less than 1/8 teaspoon. If using a shaker, a dash would comprise a quick flip of the container.

DREDGE To coat foods with flour or other dry ingredients. Most often done with pot roasts and stew meat before browning.

FOLD To incorporate several ingredients by careful and gentle turning with a spatula. Used generally with beaten egg whites or whipped cream when mixing into the rest of the ingredients to keep the batter light.

JULIENNE To cut foods into long thin strips much like matchsticks. Used most often for salads and stir-fry dishes.

MINCE To cut into very fine pieces. Used often for garlic or fresh herbs.

PARBOIL To cook partially, usually used in the case of chicken, sausages and vegetables.

PARTIALLY SET Describes the consistency of gelatin after it has been chilled for a short amount of time. Mixture should resemble the consistency of egg whites.

PUREE To process foods to a smooth mixture. Can be prepared in an electric blender, food processor, food mill or sieve.

SAUTE To fry quickly in a small amount of fat, stirring almost constantly. Most often done with onions, mushrooms and other chopped vegetables.

SCORE To cut slits partway through the outer surface of foods. Often used with ham or flank steak.

STIR-FRY To cook meats and/or vegetables with a constant stirring motion in a small amount of oil in a wok or skillet over high heat.

GENERAL RECIPE INDEX

APPETIZERS & SNACKS

COLD APPETIZERS
Cheese and Grape Appetizers, 13
Quick Kraut Snacks, 6
Secret-Ingredient Stuffed Eggs, 17
Sesame Omelet Spinach Spirals, 10

DIPS & SPREADS
Aunt Shirley's Liver Pate, 17
Big Dipper Salsa, 8
Cajun Shrimp Spread, 10
Crab Pesto Cheesecake, 11
Creamy Pepper Dip, 178
Fast Clam Dip, 6
Mexican Layer Dip, 9

HOT APPETIZERS
Artichoke-Cheese French Bread, 7
Brunch Tidbits Bread, 6
Cheesy Olive Snacks, 17
Crabmeat-Cheese Appetizers, 14
Fried Corn Balls, 14
Ham 'n' Cheese Puffs, 13
Hot Wings, 16
Miniature Corn Dogs, 175
Mock Chicken Legs, 16
Norwegian Meatballs, 12
Snappy Cocktail Meatballs, 8
Swiss Cheese Bread, 8
Three-Cheese Fondue, 15
Zucchini Fries for 2, 137

APPLES
Apple and Gorgonzola Salad, 35
Apple-Bacon Mini Loaves, 140
Apple Camembert Salad, 34
Apple Cider Cinnamon Rolls, 97
Apple Kolaches, 131
Apple Pear Crisp, 144
Apple Pecan Cheesecake, 114
Apple Upside-Down Cake, 130
Apple Venison Meat Loaf, 56
Buttery Apple Biscuits, 91
Picnic Sweet Potato Salad, 34
Plum Apple Butter, 82
Quick Cran-Apple Relish, 83
Sour Cream Apple Squares, 110
Trail Mix Apple Salad, 151
Turkey Waldorf Salad, 35
Walnut-Apple Snack Cake, 122

APRICOTS
Apricot Chicken Stir-Fry, 162
Apricot-Ginger Acorn Squash, 75
Glazed Apricot Coffee Cake, 94
Holiday Baked Ham, 50

ARTICHOKES
Artichoke-Cheese French Bread, 7
Chicken with Artichokes and
  Shrimp, 140
Crab Pesto Cheesecake, 11

ASPARAGUS
Asparagus with Blue Cheese, 78
Mac 'n' Cheese with Ham, 55

BACON
Apple-Bacon Mini Loaves, 140
Bacon & Cheese Salad, 176
Bacon and Garlic Green Beans, 79
Bacon Breakfast Sandwiches, 33
Bacon Broccoli Salad, 39
Bacon Cheeseburgers for 2, 136
Northwest Seafood Corn
  Chowder, 38
Picnic Sweet Potato Salad, 34
Quick Spaghetti Carbonara, 156
Spinach-Onion Salad with Hot
  Bacon Dressing, 32

BANANAS & PLANTAINS
Banana Split Dessert, 176
Broiled Banana Crisp, 115
Cantaloupe Banana Smoothies, 12
Chocolate-Almond Banana
  Splits, 150
Chocolate Chip Banana Bread, 92
Cranberry Banana Coffee Cake, 95
Matoke in Peanut Sauce, 76
Molded Raspberry Gelatin, 172
Peanut Butter 'n' Banana
  Pudding, 118

BARS & BROWNIES
Caramel Cashew Brownies, 103
Championship Chocolate Chip
  Bars, 108
Chocolate-Berry Bars, 111
Coconut-Lemon Cheesecake
  Dessert, 106
Napoleon Cremes, 105
Peanut Butter Fingers, 111
Peanut Butter Snack Cakes, 179

Plantation Bars, 108
Sour Cream Apple Squares, 110

BEANS & LEGUMES
Barbecued Beans, 170
Black Bean Quesadillas, 163
Cilantro Bean Burgers, 23
Cobre Valley Casserole, 70
Colorado Lamb Chili, 41
Mexican Layer Dip, 9
Radish & Garbanzo Bean Salad, 40
Skillet Cassoulet, 159
Southwestern Potpie with
  Cornmeal Biscuits, 48
The Best Derned Southwestern
  Casserole, 62

BEEF
Beef 'n' Cheese Braid, 33
Beef Tips & Caramelized Onion
  Casserole, 45
Braised Beef with Mushrooms, 144
Curried Beef, 59
Green Chili Beef Burritos, 44
Hearty Oxtail Soup, 38
Liver Dumplings, 28
Old-Fashioned Swiss Steak, 68
Pan-Fried Venison Steak, 156
Peppered Filets with Cherry Port
  Sauce for 2, 138
Ribeyes with Chili Butter, 155
Slow-Cooked Pot Roast, 64
Special Beef Wraps, 29
Steak au Poivre for 2, 139
Thai Steak Salad, 138

BEETS
Beet Salad with Orange-Walnut
  Dressing, 31
Best Chilled Beets, 82

BEVERAGES

COLD BEVERAGES
Cantaloupe Banana Smoothies, 12
Chocolate Soda, 9
Cool Lime Pie Frappes, 14
Dairy Hollow House Herbal
  Cooler, 16
Fresh-Squeezed Pink Lemonade, 174
Homemade Cream Soda, 13
Orange Smoothies, 178

Raspberry-Lemon Spritzer, 134
HOT BEVERAGE
Hot Tomato Drink, 136

BISCUITS & SCONES
Buttery Apple Biscuits, 91
Potato Biscuits, 86

BLACKBERRIES
Blackberry Whole Wheat Coffee
Cake, 94
Mixed Berry Sundaes for 2, 137

BLUE RIBBON RECIPES
APPETIZERS
Crab Pesto Cheesecake, 11
Secret-Ingredient Stuffed Eggs, 17
Sesame Omelet Spinach Spirals, 10
Three-Cheese Fondue, 15
BREAD & ROLLS
Apple Cider Cinnamon Rolls, 97
Cheddar Cheese Batter Bread, 90
CASSEROLES
Beef Tips & Caramelized Onion
Casserole, 45
Classic Cottage Pie, 62
Roasted Eggplant Lasagna, 63
Shrimp and Fontina Casserole, 63
Southwestern Potpie with
Cornmeal Biscuits, 48
The Best Derned Southwestern
Casserole, 62
DESSERTS
Apple Kolaches, 131
Apple Upside-Down Cake, 130
Brown Sugar Angel Food Cake, 122
Cranberry Buttermilk Sherbet, 127
Rhubarb Ice Cream, 126
Triple-Layer Lemon Cake, 119
MAIN DISHES
Chicken Alfredo Stuffed Shells, 58
Chicken with Cranberry-Balsamic
Sauce, 53
Grilled Stuffed Salmon, 50
Jerk Pork & Pineapple Kabobs, 66
Marinated Pork with Caramelized
Fennel, 67
Pecan Pork Medallions with
Cambozola Cream, 69
Peppered Filets with Cherry Port
Sauce for 2, 138
Pork Tenderloin with Pear Cream
Sauce, 47
Slow-Cooked Pot Roast, 64
Spanish Turkey Tenderloins, 64
Steak au Poivre for 2, 139

SALADS
Ramen-Veggie Chicken Salad, 27
Turkey Waldorf Salad, 35
SANDWICHES
Grilled Turkey Pitas, 39
Onion Italian Sausage, 22
SIDE DISHES
Glazed Carrots and Green
Beans, 80
Pepper Jack Mac, 74
Winter Vegetable Gratin, 80
SOUP
Winning Cream of Leek Soup, 36

BLUEBERRIES
Blueberry Muffins, 93
Easy Lemon-Blueberry Jam, 82
Mixed Berry Sundaes for 2, 137
Rosemary Pork with Berry Port
Sauce, 65

BREADS & ROLLS
*(also see Appetizers & Snacks; Biscuits
& Scones; Cakes & Coffee Cakes;
Muffins)*
Apple-Bacon Mini Loaves, 140
Apple Cider Cinnamon Rolls, 97
Beef 'n' Cheese Braid, 33
Cheddar Cheese Batter Bread, 90
Chocolate Chip Banana
Bread, 92
Cinnamon Cherry Rolls, 91
Cranberry Orange Walnut
Bread, 88
Easy Orange Rolls, 96
Glazed Cranberry Sweet Potato
Bread, 99
Grandma's Cinnamon Rolls, 90
Homemade Bread, 86
Icebox Butterhorns, 99
Moist Corn Bread, 96
Mom's Brown Bread, 88
Poppy Seed Bread, 87
Potato Rolls, 92
Rose Rolls, 89
Sourdough English Muffins, 98
Sourdough Starter, 98
Swiss Cheese Bread, 8

BROCCOLI
Bacon Broccoli Salad, 39
Broccoli & Horseradish Sauce, 75
Broccoli Beef Pie, 47
Broccoli Chicken Tortellini, 156
Broccoli-Potato Mash, 143
Chicken in the Garden, 48
Chilled Turkey Pasta Salad, 172

BRUSSELS SPROUTS
Lemon Brussels Sprouts, 78
Mashed Potatoes 'n' Brussels
Sprouts, 77

CABBAGE & SAUERKRAUT
German Vegetable Soup, 24
Quick Kraut Snacks, 6
Sweetheart Slaw, 148

CAKES & COFFEE CAKES
(also see Cheesecakes)
Apple Upside-Down Cake, 130
Blackberry Whole Wheat Coffee
Cake, 94
Brown Sugar Angel Food
Cake, 122
Chewy Date Torte, 116
Chocolate Sheet Cake, 115
Coconut-Filled Fudge Cake, 149
Cranberry Banana Coffee Cake, 95
Glazed Apricot Coffee Cake, 94
Graham-Streusel Coffee Cake, 94
Icebox Cake, 123
Lemon Coconut Cupcakes, 123
Old-Fashioned Fudge Cake, 140
Peanut Butter Snack Cakes, 179
Toffee-Mocha Cream Cake, 128
Triple-Layer Lemon Cake, 119
Walnut-Apple Snack Cake, 122

CANDIES
Birch Pretzel Logs, 105
Cherry Walnut Balls, 104
Chocolate Cashew Clusters, 102
Kids' Sushi, 106
Mocha Almond Fudge, 102
Napoleon Cremes, 105

CARROTS
Carrots Lyonnaise, 177
Glazed Carrots and Green
Beans, 80

CASSEROLES
MAIN DISHES
Baked Spinach Supreme, 54
Beef Tips & Caramelized Onion
Casserole, 45
Broccoli Beef Pie, 47
California Egg Bake, 136
Chick-A-Roni, 53
Chicken Alfredo Stuffed Shells, 58
Chicken 'n' Chilies Casserole, 66
Chicken Casserole, 55
Chicken in the Garden, 48
Classic Cottage Pie, 62

CASSEROLES (continued)

Cobre Valley Casserole, 70
Eight-Layer Casserole, 173
Mac 'n' Cheese with Ham, 55
Overnight Chicken Casserole, 60
Pizza Casserole, 58
Pizza Hot Dish, 160
Poor Man's Dinner, 68
Pronto Pinwheels, 52
Roasted Eggplant Lasagna, 63
Shrimp and Fontina Casserole, 63
Southwestern Potpie with
  Cornmeal Biscuits, 48
The Best Derned Southwestern
  Casserole, 62

SIDE DISHES
German Noodle Bake, 81
Gruyere Potato Bake, 77
Pepper Jack Mac, 74

CAULIFLOWER
Cauliflower and Ham Chowder, 32

CHEESE

APPETIZERS
Artichoke-Cheese French Bread, 7
Brunch Tidbits Bread, 6
Cheese and Grape Appetizers, 13
Cheesy Olive Snacks, 17
Crab Pesto Cheesecake, 11
Crabmeat-Cheese Appetizers, 14
Mexican Layer Dip, 9
Swiss Cheese Bread, 8
Three-Cheese Fondue, 15

BREADS
Beef 'n' Cheese Braid, 33
Cheddar Cheese Batter Bread, 90

MAIN DISHES
Chicken Alfredo Stuffed Shells, 58
Chicken Cordon Bleu, 143
Ham 'n' Swiss Ring, 46
Mac 'n' Cheese with Ham, 55
Pecan Pork Medallions with
  Cambozola Cream, 69
Shrimp and Fontina Casserole, 63
Three-Cheese Spinach Calzones, 61

SALADS & SIDE DISHES
Apple and Gorgonzola Salad, 35
Apple Camembert Salad, 34
Asparagus with Blue Cheese, 78
Bacon & Cheese Salad, 176
Cheddar-Topped Mashed
  Potatoes, 144
Gruyere Potato Bake, 77
Panguitch Potatoes, 172
Pepper Jack Mac, 74

SANDWICH
Ham 'n' Cheese Melts, 36

CHEESECAKES
Apple Pecan Cheesecake, 114
Coconut-Lemon Cheesecake
  Dessert, 106
Crab Pesto Cheesecake, 11

CHERRIES
Cherry-Chicken Pasta Salad, 28
Cherry Dumplings, 168
Cherry Supreme Dessert, 130
Cherry Walnut Balls, 104
Cinnamon Cherry Rolls, 91
Pecan Pork Medallions with
  Cambozola Cream, 69
Peppered Filets with Cherry Port
  Sauce for 2, 138
Rosemary Pork with Berry Port
  Sauce, 65
Rose Rolls, 89

CHICKEN

APPETIZERS
Aunt Shirley's Liver Pate, 17
Hot Wings, 16

MAIN DISHES
Apricot Chicken Stir-Fry, 162
Broccoli Chicken Tortellini, 156
Chick-A-Roni, 53
Chicken Alfredo Stuffed Shells, 58
Chicken 'n' Chilies Casserole, 66
Chicken Bundles, 160
Chicken Casserole, 55
Chicken Cordon Bleu, 143
Chicken in the Garden, 48
Chicken with Artichokes and
  Shrimp, 140
Chicken with Cranberry-Balsamic
  Sauce, 53
Herbed Chicken, 59
Oven Fried Chicken, 169
Overnight Chicken Casserole, 60
Pineapple Chicken, 154
Tarragon-Cream Chicken, 177

SALADS
Cherry-Chicken Pasta Salad, 28
Chicken and Pineapple Salad, 30
Chicken Fajita Salad, 164
Chicken Salad Supreme, 32
Ramen-Veggie Chicken Salad, 27

SOUP
Harvest Chicken Rice Soup, 22

CHOCOLATE
Birch Pretzel Logs, 105

Championship Chocolate Chip
  Bars, 108
Chocolate-Almond Banana
  Splits, 150
Chocolate Bavarian with
  Strawberry Cream, 129
Chocolate-Berry Bars, 111
Chocolate Cashew Clusters, 102
Chocolate Chip Banana Bread, 92
Chocolate Peanut Cookies, 134
Chocolate Sheet Cake, 115
Chocolate Soda, 9
Coconut-Filled Fudge Cake, 149
Mocha Almond Fudge, 102
Napoleon Cremes, 105
Old-Fashioned Fudge Cake, 140
Orange Cocoa Sandies, 146

COCONUT
Coconut-Filled Fudge Cake, 149
Coconut-Lemon Cheesecake
  Dessert, 106
Lemon Coconut Cupcakes, 123

COFFEE
Mocha Almond Fudge, 102
Old Fashioned Coffee Pudding, 120
Toffee-Mocha Cream Cake, 128

CONDIMENTS
Easy Lemon-Blueberry Jam, 82
Green Onion Tartar Sauce, 76
Lemon & Rosemary Steak Rub, 77
Plum Apple Butter, 82
Quick Cran-Apple Relish, 83
Vanilla Glaze, 89

COOKIES
Almond Rusks, 110
Berliner Kranz Cookies, 109
Chocolate Cashew Clusters, 102
Chocolate Peanut Cookies, 134
Cutout Wedding Cookies, 107
Grandma's Sugar Cookies, 108
Maple Oatmeal Cookies, 104
Orange Cocoa Sandies, 146
Original Brown Butter
  Refrigerator Cookies, 104
Pfeffernuesse, 111
Piggy Pops, 109
Pumpkin Whoopie Pies, 102

CORN & CORNMEAL
Cornmeal-Crusted Walleye, 46
Creamed Corn with Peas, 146
Fried Corn Balls, 14
Grilled Corn with Thyme, 175

Miniature Corn Dogs, 175
Moist Corn Bread, 96
Northwest Seafood Corn
  Chowder, 38
Southwestern Potpie with
  Cornmeal Biscuits, 48
Zesty Jalapeno Corn Muffins, 87

CORNISH HENS
Garlic-Rosemary Cornish Hen, 52

CRANBERRIES
Chicken with Cranberry-Balsamic
  Sauce, 53
Cranberry Banana Coffee Cake, 95
Cranberry Buttermilk Sherbet, 127
Cranberry Orange Walnut
  Bread, 88
Glazed Cranberry Sweet Potato
  Bread, 99
Pears and Cranberries Poached in
  Wine, 124
Quick Cran-Apple Relish, 83

DATES
Cherry Walnut Balls, 104
Chewy Date Torte, 116
Date Pecan Pie, 117
Fruitcake Pie, 118

DESSERTS
(also see Bars & Brownies; Cakes &
Coffee Cakes; Candies; Cheesecakes;
Chocolate; Cookies; Ice Cream & More;
Pies & Tarts)
Amaretto Peach Parfaits, 121
Apple Kolaches, 131
Apple Pear Crisp, 144
Broiled Banana Crisp, 115
Brown Rice Pudding, 117
Cherry Dumplings, 168
Cherry Supreme Dessert, 130
Chewy Date Torte, 116
Chocolate Bavarian with
  Strawberry Cream, 129
Fresh Strawberry Dessert, 124
Gingersnap Pear Trifles, 146
Grilled Waffle Treats, 170
Lemon Delight Dessert, 130
Lemon Velvet Dessert, 121
Maple Syrup Cream, 120
Molded Raspberry Gelatin, 172
Old Fashioned Coffee Pudding, 120
Peanut Butter 'n' Banana
  Pudding, 118
Pears and Cranberries Poached in
  Wine, 124
Traditional Funnel Cakes, 174

EGGS
Bacon Breakfast Sandwiches, 33
Baked Spinach Supreme, 54
California Egg Bake, 136
Florentine Frittata for Two, 150
Secret-Ingredient Stuffed Eggs, 17
Sesame Omelet Spinach Spirals, 10

FISH & SEAFOOD
APPETIZERS
Cajun Shrimp Spread, 10
Crabmeat-Cheese Appetizers, 14
Crab Pesto Cheesecake, 11
Fast Clam Dip, 6
MAIN DISHES
Broiled Fish, 155
Caesar Orange Roughy, 161
Chicken with Artichokes and
  Shrimp, 140
Cornmeal-Crusted Walleye, 46
Crab-Stuffed Flounder with
  Herbed Aioli, 71
Herbed Shrimp Skillet, 158
Homemade Macadamia Crusted
  Tilapia, 148
Grilled Stuffed Salmon, 50
Salmon Cakes, 160
Salmon with Caribbean Salsa, 71
Salmon with Gingered Rhubarb
  Compote, 67
Salmon with Pineapple Sauce, 154
Salmon with Tarragon Sauce, 157
Shrimp and Fontina Casserole, 63
Shrimp in Cream Sauce, 162
Smoked Shrimp & Wild
  Mushroom Fettuccine, 60
Tilapia with Tomato-Orange
  Relish, 165
Wild Salmon with Hazelnuts Over
  Spinach, 162
SOUP & SANDWICH
Northwest Seafood Corn
  Chowder, 38
Vegetable Tuna Sandwiches, 24

GARLIC
Bacon and Garlic Green Beans, 79
Garlic Ranch Potato Salad, 29
Garlic-Rosemary Cornish Hen, 52
Roasted Onion & Garlic Soup, 168

GREEN BEANS
Bacon and Garlic Green
  Beans, 79
Glazed Carrots and Green
  Beans, 80

GRILLED RECIPES
DESSERT
Grilled Waffle Treats, 170
MAIN DISHES
Grilled Stuffed Salmon, 50
Jerk Pork & Pineapple Kabobs, 66
Peppered Filets with Cherry Port
  Sauce for 2, 138
Pork Tenderloin Nectarine
  Salad, 44
Priceless BBQ Ribs, 56
Ribeyes with Chili Butter, 155
Smoked Shrimp & Wild
  Mushroom Fettuccine, 60
Spanish Turkey Tenderloins, 64
Sweet Mustard Chops, 56
Wild Salmon with Hazelnuts Over
  Spinach, 162
SALADS & SIDE DISHES
Barbecued Beans, 170
Grilled Corn with Thyme, 175
Grilled Potatoes with Sour Cream
  Sauce, 170
Grilled Vegetable Ranch Salad, 24
Ramen-Veggie Chicken Salad, 27
SANDWICHES & BURGERS
Grilled Turkey Pitas, 39
Honey-Mustard Brats, 170
Special Beef Wraps, 29
Tasty Italian Burgers, 26
Thai Turkey Burgers, 21

GROUND BEEF
Bacon Cheeseburgers for 2, 136
Broccoli Beef Pie, 47
Calico Main Dish Soup, 26
Classic Cottage Pie, 62
Cobre Valley Casserole, 70
Eight-Layer Casserole, 173
Meaty Mexican Sandwiches, 20
Mexican Layer Dip, 9
Norwegian Meatballs, 12
Pasa De Shuto, 154
Pizza Casserole, 58
Pizza Hot Dish, 160
Poor Man's Dinner, 68
Pronto Pinwheels, 52
Snappy Cocktail Meatballs, 8

HAM
Cauliflower and Ham
  Chowder, 32
Chicken Cordon Bleu, 143
Ham 'n' Cheese Melts, 36
Ham 'n' Cheese Puffs, 13
Ham 'n' Swiss Ring, 46
Hasty Heartland Dinner, 64

HAM (continued)

Holiday Baked Ham, 50
Mac 'n' Cheese with Ham, 55
Skillet Cassoulet, 159

ICE CREAM & MORE

Banana Split Dessert, 176
Chocolate-Almond Banana
  Splits, 150
Chocolate Soda, 9
Citrus Melon Sorbet, 142
Cranberry Buttermilk Sherbet, 127
Mango Ice Cream, 126
Molded Raspberry Gelatin, 172
Peach Ice, 126
Peach Ice Cream, 127
Rhubarb Ice Cream, 126
Yogurt Ice Pops, 114

LAMB

Classic Cottage Pie, 62
Colorado Lamb Chili, 41
Pan-Seared Lamb Chops, 158
Roast Leg of Lamb with
  Rosemary, 51

LEMONS & LIMES

Coconut-Lemon Cheesecake
  Dessert, 106
Cool Lime Pie Frappes, 14
Easy Lemon-Blueberry Jam, 82
Fresh-Squeezed Pink
  Lemonade, 174
Lemon & Rosemary Steak
  Rub, 77
Lemon Brussels Sprouts, 78
Lemon Coconut Cupcakes, 123
Lemon Delight Dessert, 130
Lemon Velvet Dessert, 121
Raspberry-Lemon Spritzer, 134
Simple Lime Gelatin Salad, 41
Triple-Layer Lemon Cake, 119

MAPLE

Maple Oatmeal Cookies, 104
Maple Syrup Cream, 120

MEATBALLS & MEAT LOAF

Apple Venison Meat Loaf, 56
Norwegian Meatballs, 12
Red Pepper Meat Loaf, 147
Snappy Cocktail Meatballs, 8

MELONS

Cantaloupe Banana Smoothies, 12
Citrus Melon Sorbet, 142

MUFFINS

Blueberry Muffins, 93
Butter Pecan Muffins, 96
Quick Muffin Mix, 93
Sourdough English Muffins, 98
Zesty Jalapeno Corn Muffins, 87

MUSHROOMS

Braised Beef with Mushrooms, 144
Pork Chops with Mushroom
  Gravy, 49
Slow-Cooked Pot Roast, 64
Smoked Shrimp & Wild
  Mushroom Fettuccine, 60

NUTS (also see Peanut Butter)

Almond Rusks, 110
Apple Pecan Cheesecake, 114
Butter Pecan Muffins, 96
Caramel Cashew Brownies, 103
Cherry Walnut Balls, 104
Chocolate-Almond Banana
  Splits, 150
Chocolate Cashew Clusters, 102
Chocolate Peanut Cookies, 134
Cranberry Orange Walnut
  Bread, 88
Date Pecan Pie, 117
Homemade Macadamia Crusted
  Tilapia, 148
Matoke in Peanut Sauce, 76
Mocha Almond Fudge, 102
Turkey Salad with Pistachios, 164
Walnut-Apple Snack Cake, 122

ONIONS

Beef Tips & Caramelized Onion
  Casserole, 45
Green Onion Tartar Sauce, 76
Onion Italian Sausage, 22
Roasted Onion & Garlic Soup, 168
Spinach-Onion Salad with Hot
  Bacon Dressing, 32
Winning Cream of Leek Soup, 36

ORANGES

Beet Salad with Orange-Walnut
  Dressing, 31
Cranberry Orange Walnut
  Bread, 88
Easy Orange Rolls, 96
Orange Cocoa Sandies, 146
Orange Smoothies, 178
Spiced Orange Gelatin Salad, 36
Tilapia with Tomato-Orange
  Relish, 165
Watercress & Orange Salad, 37

OVEN ENTREES (also see Casseroles; Meatballs & Meat Loaf)

Braised Pork with Tomatillos, 54
Broiled Fish, 155
Caesar Orange Roughy, 161
Chicken Bundles, 160
Chicken Cordon Bleu, 143
Chicken with Cranberry-Balsamic
  Sauce, 53
Classic Pepperoni Pizza, 178
Cornmeal-Crusted Walleye, 46
Crab-Stuffed Flounder with
  Herbed Aioli, 71
Garlic-Rosemary Cornish Hen, 52
Ham 'n' Swiss Ring, 46
Holiday Baked Ham, 50
Holiday Pork Roast, 51
Marinated Pork with Caramelized
  Fennel, 67
Norwegian Meatballs, 12
Old-Fashioned Swiss Steak, 68
Oven Fried Chicken, 169
Pesto Veggie Pizza, 70
Pork Tenderloin with Pear Cream
  Sauce, 47
Roast Leg of Lamb with
  Rosemary, 51
Rosemary Pork with Berry Port
  Sauce, 65
Salmon with Caribbean Salsa, 71
Salmon with Gingered Rhubarb
  Compote, 67
Salmon with Pineapple Sauce, 154
Shrimp in Cream Sauce, 162
Tarragon-Cream Chicken, 177
Three-Cheese Spinach Calzones, 61
Tilapia with Tomato-Orange
  Relish, 165
Unstuffed Pork Chops, 68

PASTA & NOODLES

Big-Batch Marinara Sauce, 57
Broccoli Chicken Tortellini, 156
Cherry-Chicken Pasta Salad, 28
Chick-A-Roni, 53
Chicken Alfredo Stuffed Shells, 58
Chilled Turkey Pasta Salad, 172
Eight-Layer Casserole, 173
German Noodle Bake, 81
Mac 'n' Cheese with Ham, 55
Pasa De Shuto, 154
Pepper Jack Mac, 74
Pizza Casserole, 58
Pizza Hot Dish, 160
Roasted Eggplant Lasagna, 63
Quick Spaghetti Carbonara, 156
Smoked Shrimp & Wild
  Mushroom Fettuccine, 60

Spaghetti with Roasted Red
   Pepper Sauce, 165

PEACHES
Amaretto Peach Parfaits, 121
Peach Ice, 126
Peach Ice Cream, 127
Rustic Peach Tart with Raspberry
   Drizzle, 125
Yogurt Ice Pops, 114

PEANUT BUTTER
Chocolate Peanut Cookies, 134
Peanut Butter 'n' Banana
   Pudding, 118
Peanut Butter Fingers, 111
Peanut Butter Snack Cakes, 179
Plantation Bars, 108

PEARS
Apple Pear Crisp, 144
Gingersnap Pear Trifles, 146
Pears and Cranberries Poached in
   Wine, 124
Pork Tenderloin with Pear Cream
   Sauce, 47

PEPPERONI
Classic Pepperoni Pizza, 178
Pizza Casserole, 58

PEPPERS & CHILIS
Chicken 'n' Chilies Casserole, 66
Chicken Fajita Salad, 164
Creamy Pepper Dip, 178
Green Chili Beef Burritos, 44
Red Pepper Meat Loaf, 147
Ribeyes with Chili Butter, 155
Spaghetti with Roasted Red
   Pepper Sauce, 165

PIES & TARTS (also see Casseroles for savory pies)
Date Pecan Pie, 117
Fruitcake Pie, 118
Pineapple Chiffon Pie, 128
Pineapple Cream Pie, 116
Rhubarb Cheese Pie, 128
Rustic Peach Tart with Raspberry
   Drizzle, 125

PINEAPPLE
Chicken and Pineapple Salad, 30
Creamy Cloud Nine Salad, 30
Jerk Pork & Pineapple Kabobs, 66
Pineapple Chicken, 154
Pineapple Chiffon Pie, 128

Pineapple Cream Pie, 116
Salmon with Pineapple Sauce, 154

PIZZA
Classic Pepperoni Pizza, 178
Pesto Veggie Pizza, 70
Pizza Casserole, 58

PORK (also see Bacon; Ham; Pepperoni; Sausage)
Braised Pork with Tomatillos, 54
Holiday Pork Roast, 51
Jerk Pork & Pineapple Kabobs, 66
Marinated Pork with Caramelized
   Fennel, 67
Meaty Mexican Sandwiches, 20
Mock Chicken Legs, 16
Norwegian Meatballs, 12
Pasa De Shuto, 154
Pecan Pork Medallions with
   Cambozola Cream, 69
Pork Chops with Mushroom
   Gravy, 49
Pork Tenderloin Nectarine
   Salad, 44
Pork Tenderloin with Pear Cream
   Sauce, 47
Priceless BBQ Ribs, 56
Red Pepper Meat Loaf, 147
Rosemary Pork with Berry Port
   Sauce, 65
Southwestern Potpie with
   Cornmeal Biscuits, 48
Sweet Mustard Chops, 56
Unstuffed Pork Chops, 68

POTATOES (see also Sweet Potatoes)
Baked Potato Slices, 78
Broccoli-Potato Mash, 143
Cheddar-Topped Mashed
   Potatoes, 144
Classic Cottage Pie, 62
Garlic Ranch Potato Salad, 29
Gruyere Potato Bake, 77
Hasty Heartland Dinner, 64
Home-Style Mashed Potatoes, 147
Grilled Potatoes with Sour Cream
   Sauce, 170
Mashed Potatoes 'n' Brussels
   Sprouts, 77
Mother's Potato Soup, 21
Oven-Fried Parmesan Potatoes, 148
Panguitch Potatoes, 172
Potato Biscuits, 86
Potato Rolls, 92
Potato-Stuffed Tomatoes, 83

RASPBERRIES
Mixed Berry Sundaes for 2, 137
Molded Raspberry Gelatin, 172
Raspberry-Lemon Spritzer, 134
Rustic Peach Tart with Raspberry
   Drizzle, 125

RHUBARB
Rhubarb Cheese Pie, 128
Rhubarb Ice Cream, 126
Salmon with Gingered Rhubarb
   Compote, 67

RICE
Brown Rice Pudding, 117
Ginger Fried Rice, 74
Harvest Chicken Rice Soup, 22

SALADS
FRUIT & GELATIN
Apple and Gorgonzola Salad, 35
Creamy Cloud Nine Salad, 30
Simple Lime Gelatin Salad, 41
Spiced Orange Gelatin Salad, 36
Summertime Strawberry
   Salad, 134
Trail Mix Apple Salad, 151
GREEN SALADS & COLESLAW
Apple Camembert Salad, 34
Bacon & Cheese Salad, 176
Beet Salad with Orange-Walnut
   Dressing, 31
Mixed Greens with Creamy Honey
   Mustard Dressing, 142
Salad Greens with Honey Mustard
   Vinaigrette, 140
Spinach-Onion Salad with Hot
   Bacon Dressing, 32
Sweetheart Slaw, 148
Tossed Salad with Simple
   Vinaigrette, 151
Watercress & Orange Salad, 37
MAIN DISH SALADS
Chicken and Pineapple Salad, 30
Chicken Fajita Salad, 164
Chicken Salad Supreme, 32
Chilled Turkey Pasta Salad, 172
Greek Salad Pitas, 150
Pork Tenderloin Nectarine
   Salad, 44
Ramen-Veggie Chicken Salad, 27
Thai Steak Salad, 138
Turkey Salad with Pistachios, 164
Turkey Waldorf Salad, 35
PASTA & GRAIN SALADS
Cherry-Chicken Pasta Salad, 28

SALADS (continued)
Chilled Turkey Pasta Salad, 172
Quinoa Vegetable Salad, 26
Tabbouleh Salad, 40

POTATO SALADS
Garlic Ranch Potato Salad, 29
Picnic Sweet Potato Salad, 34

VEGETABLE SALADS
Bacon Broccoli Salad, 39
Grilled Vegetable Ranch Salad, 24
Radish & Garbanzo Bean Salad, 40
Summer Garden Salad, 25

SALSA
Big Dipper Salsa, 8
Salmon with Caribbean Salsa, 71

SANDWICHES & BURGERS

BURGERS
Bacon Cheeseburgers for 2, 136
Cilantro Bean Burgers, 23
Tasty Italian Burgers, 26
Thai Turkey Burgers, 21

COLD SANDWICHES
Greek Salad Pitas, 150
Italian Chicken Salad
    Sandwiches, 135
Vegetable Tuna Sandwiches, 24

HOT SANDWICHES
Bacon Breakfast Sandwiches, 33
Grilled Turkey Pitas, 39
Ham 'n' Cheese Melts, 36
Honey-Mustard Brats, 170
Meaty Mexican Sandwiches, 20
Onion Italian Sausage, 22
Special Beef Wraps, 29

SAUSAGE
Easy Sausage and Vegetable
    Skillet, 161
Honey-Mustard Brats, 170
Miniature Corn Dogs, 175
Onion Italian Sausage, 22
Pasa De Shuto, 154
Quick Kraut Snacks, 6
The Best Derned Southwestern
    Casserole, 62

SIDE DISHES
(also see Condiments)

BEANS & RICE
Barbecued Beans, 170

PASTA & RICE
German Noodle Bake, 81
Ginger Fried Rice, 74
Pepper Jack Mac, 74

POTATOES & SWEET POTATOES
Baked Potato Slices, 78
Broccoli-Potato Mash, 143
Caramel Sweet Potatoes, 168
Cheddar-Topped Mashed
    Potatoes, 144
Grilled Potatoes with Sour Cream
    Sauce, 170
Gruyere Potato Bake, 77
Home-Style Mashed Potatoes, 147
Mashed Potatoes 'n' Brussels
    Sprouts, 77
Oven-Fried Parmesan Potatoes, 148
Panguitch Potatoes, 172
Potato-Stuffed Tomatoes, 83
Winter Vegetable Gratin, 80

VEGETABLES
Apricot-Ginger Acorn Squash, 75
Asparagus with Blue Cheese, 78
Bacon and Garlic Green Beans, 79
Best Chilled Beets, 82
Broccoli & Horseradish Sauce, 75
Carrots Lyonnaise, 177
Creamed Corn with Peas, 146
Glazed Carrots and Green
    Beans, 80
Grilled Corn with Thyme, 175
Lemon Brussels Sprouts, 78
Matoke in Peanut Sauce, 76
Vegetable Skillet, 144
Vegetable Ribbons, 81

SLOW COOKER RECIPES
Green Chili Beef Burritos, 44
Slow-Cooked Pot Roast, 64

SOUPS & CHILI
Calico Main Dish Soup, 26
Cauliflower and Ham Chowder, 32
Colorado Lamb Chili, 41
German Vegetable Soup, 24
Golden Squash Soup, 22
Harvest Chicken Rice Soup, 22
Hearty Oxtail Soup, 38
Liver Dumplings, 28
Mother's Potato Soup, 21
Northwest Seafood Corn
    Chowder, 38
Roasted Onion & Garlic Soup, 168
Vegetable Soup with
    Dumplings, 20
Winning Cream of Leek Soup, 36

SPINACH
Baked Spinach Supreme, 54
Cajun Shrimp Spread, 10
Eight-Layer Casserole, 173

Florentine Frittata for Two, 150
Quinoa Vegetable Salad, 26
Sesame Omelet Spinach Spirals, 10
Spinach-Onion Salad with Hot
    Bacon Dressing, 32
Three-Cheese Spinach Calzones, 61
Wild Salmon with Hazelnuts Over
    Spinach, 162

STOVETOP ENTREES
(also see Pasta & Noodles; Sandwiches & Burgers; Soups & Chili)
Apricot Chicken Stir-Fry, 162
Big-Batch Marinara Sauce, 57
Black Bean Quesadillas, 163
Braised Beef with Mushrooms, 144
Broccoli Chicken Tortellini, 156
Chicken Fajita Salad, 164
Chicken with Artichokes and
    Shrimp, 140
Curried Beef, 59
Easy Sausage and Vegetable
    Skillet, 161
Herbed Shrimp Skillet, 158
Homemade Macadamia Crusted
    Tilapia, 148
Onion Italian Sausage, 22
Pan-Fried Venison Steak, 156
Pan-Seared Lamb Chops, 158
Pasa De Shuto, 154
Pecan Pork Medallions with
    Cambozola Cream, 69
Pineapple Chicken, 154
Pork Chops with Mushroom
    Gravy, 49
Priceless BBQ Ribs, 56
Quick Spaghetti Carbonara, 156
Salmon Cakes, 160
Skillet Cassoulet, 159
Smoked Shrimp & Wild
    Mushroom Fettuccine, 60
Spaghetti with Roasted Red
    Pepper Sauce, 165
Steak au Poivre for 2, 139
Turkey Tenderloins with
    Raspberry BBQ Sauce, 159

STRAWBERRIES
Chocolate Bavarian with
    Strawberry Cream, 129
Fresh Strawberry Dessert, 124
Mixed Berry Sundaes for 2, 137
Summertime Strawberry
    Salad, 134
Sweetheart Slaw, 148

SWEET POTATOES
Caramel Sweet Potatoes, 168

Glazed Cranberry Sweet Potato
Bread, 99
Picnic Sweet Potato Salad, 34

TOMATILLOS
Braised Pork with Tomatillos, 54

TOMATOES
Big-Batch Marinara Sauce, 57
Big Dipper Salsa, 8
Hot Tomato Drink, 136
Potato-Stuffed Tomatoes, 83
Tilapia with Tomato-Orange
Relish, 165

TURKEY
Chilled Turkey Pasta Salad, 172
Grilled Turkey Pitas, 39
Red Pepper Meat Loaf, 147
Skillet Cassoulet, 159
Spanish Turkey Tenderloins, 64
Tasty Italian Burgers, 26

Thai Turkey Burgers, 21
Turkey Salad with Pistachios, 164
Turkey Tenderloins with
Raspberry BBQ Sauce, 159
Turkey Waldorf Salad, 35

VEGETABLES
(also see specific kinds)
Easy Sausage and Vegetable
Skillet, 161
German Vegetable Soup, 24
Grilled Vegetable Ranch Salad, 24
Pasa De Shuto, 154
Pesto Veggie Pizza, 70
Quinoa Vegetable Salad, 26
Ramen-Veggie Chicken Salad, 27
Roasted Eggplant Lasagna, 63
Summer Garden Salad, 25
Vegetable Ribbons, 81
Vegetable Skillet, 144
Vegetable Soup with
Dumplings, 20

Vegetable Tuna Sandwiches, 24
Winter Vegetable Gratin, 80

VEAL
Mock Chicken Legs, 16

VENISON
Apple Venison Meat Loaf, 56
Pan-Fried Venison Steak, 156

WINTER SQUASH
Apricot-Ginger Acorn Squash, 75
Golden Squash Soup, 22

YOGURT
Cantaloupe Banana Smoothies, 12
Cool Lime Pie Frappes, 14
Mixed Berry Sundaes for 2, 137
Yogurt Ice Pops, 114

ZUCCHINI
Zucchini Fries for 2, 137

ALPHABETICAL RECIPE INDEX

A

Almond Rusks, 110
Amaretto Peach Parfaits, 121
Apple and Gorgonzola Salad, 35
Apple Camembert Salad, 34
Apple Cider Cinnamon Rolls, 97
Apple Kolaches, 131
Apple Pear Crisp, 144
Apple Pecan Cheesecake, 114
Apple Upside-Down Cake, 130
Apple Venison Meat Loaf, 56
Apple-Bacon Mini Loaves, 140
Apricot Chicken Stir-Fry, 162
Apricot-Ginger Acorn Squash, 75
Artichoke-Cheese French Bread, 7
Asparagus with Blue Cheese, 78
Aunt Shirley's Liver Pate, 17

B

Bacon & Cheese Salad, 176
Bacon and Garlic Green Beans, 79
Bacon Breakfast Sandwiches, 33
Bacon Broccoli Salad, 39
Bacon Cheeseburgers for 2, 136
Baked Potato Slices, 78
Baked Spinach Supreme, 54
Banana Split Dessert, 176
Barbecued Beans, 170
Beef 'n' Cheese Braid, 33
Beef Tips & Caramelized Onion
   Casserole, 45
Beet Salad with Orange-Walnut
   Dressing, 31
Berliner Kranz Cookies, 109
Best Chilled Beets, 82
Big-Batch Marinara Sauce, 57
Big Dipper Salsa, 8
Birch Pretzel Logs, 105
Black Bean Quesadillas, 163
Blackberry Whole Wheat Coffee
   Cake, 94
Blueberry Muffins, 93
Braised Beef with Mushrooms, 144
Braised Pork with Tomatillos, 54
Broccoli & Horseradish Sauce, 75
Broccoli Beef Pie, 47
Broccoli Chicken Tortellini, 156
Broccoli-Potato Mash, 143
Broiled Banana Crisp, 115
Broiled Fish, 155
Brown Rice Pudding, 117

Brown Sugar Angel Food
   Cake, 122
Brunch Tidbits Bread, 6
Butter Pecan Muffins, 96
Buttery Apple Biscuits, 91

C

Caesar Orange Roughy, 161
Cajun Shrimp Spread, 10
Calico Main Dish Soup, 26
California Egg Bake, 136
Cantaloupe Banana Smoothies, 12
Caramel Cashew Brownies, 103
Caramel Sweet Potatoes, 168
Carrots Lyonnaise, 177
Cauliflower and Ham Chowder, 32
Championship Chocolate Chip
   Bars, 108
Cheddar Cheese Batter Bread, 90
Cheddar-Topped Mashed
   Potatoes, 144
Cheese and Grape Appetizers, 13
Cheesy Olive Snacks, 17
Cherry-Chicken Pasta Salad, 28
Cherry Dumplings, 168
Cherry Supreme Dessert, 130
Cherry Walnut Balls, 104
Chewy Date Torte, 116
Chick-A-Roni, 53
Chicken Alfredo Stuffed
   Shells, 58
Chicken 'n' Chilies Casserole, 66
Chicken and Pineapple Salad, 30
Chicken Bundles, 160
Chicken Casserole, 55
Chicken Cordon Bleu, 143
Chicken Fajita Salad, 164
Chicken in the Garden, 48
Chicken Salad Supreme, 32
Chicken with Artichokes and
   Shrimp, 140
Chicken with Cranberry-Balsamic
   Sauce, 53
Chilled Turkey Pasta Salad, 172
Chocolate-Almond Banana
   Splits, 150
Chocolate Bavarian with
   Strawberry Cream, 129
Chocolate-Berry Bars, 111
Chocolate Cashew Clusters, 102
Chocolate Chip Banana Bread, 92
Chocolate Peanut Cookies, 134

Chocolate Sheet Cake, 115
Chocolate Soda, 9
Cilantro Bean Burgers, 23
Cinnamon Cherry Rolls, 91
Citrus Melon Sorbet, 142
Classic Cottage Pie, 62
Classic Pepperoni Pizza, 178
Cobre Valley Casserole, 70
Coconut-Filled Fudge Cake, 149
Coconut-Lemon Cheesecake
   Dessert, 106
Colorado Lamb Chili, 41
Cool Lime Pie Frappes, 14
Cornmeal-Crusted Walleye, 46
Crab Pesto Cheesecake, 11
Crab-Stuffed Flounder with
   Herbed Aioli, 71
Crabmeat-Cheese Appetizers, 14
Cranberry Banana Coffee
   Cake, 95
Cranberry Buttermilk
   Sherbet, 127
Cranberry Orange Walnut
   Bread, 88
Creamed Corn with Peas, 146
Creamy Cloud Nine Salad, 30
Creamy Pepper Dip, 178
Curried Beef, 59
Cutout Wedding Cookies, 107

D

Dairy Hollow House Herbal
   Cooler, 16
Date Pecan Pie, 117

E

Easy Lemon-Blueberry Jam, 82
Easy Orange Rolls, 96
Easy Sausage and Vegetable
   Skillet, 161
Eight-Layer Casserole, 173

F

Fast Clam Dip, 6
Florentine Frittata for Two, 150
Fresh-Squeezed Pink
   Lemonade, 174
Fresh Strawberry Dessert, 124
Fried Corn Balls, 14
Fruitcake Pie, 118

G

Garlic Ranch Potato Salad, 29
Garlic-Rosemary Cornish
   Hen, 52
German Noodle Bake, 81
German Vegetable Soup, 24
Ginger Fried Rice, 74
Gingersnap Pear Trifles, 146
Glazed Apricot Coffee Cake, 94
Glazed Carrots and Green
   Beans, 80
Glazed Cranberry Sweet Potato
   Bread, 99
Golden Squash Soup, 22
Graham-Streusel Coffee Cake, 94
Grandma's Cinnamon Rolls, 90
Grandma's Sugar Cookies, 108
Greek Salad Pitas, 150
Green Chili Beef Burritos, 44
Green Onion Tartar Sauce, 76
Grilled Corn with Thyme, 175
Grilled Potatoes with Sour Cream
   Sauce, 170
Grilled Stuffed Salmon, 50
Grilled Turkey Pitas, 39
Grilled Vegetable Ranch
   Salad, 24
Grilled Waffle Treats, 170
Gruyere Potato Bake, 77

H

Ham 'n' Cheese Melts, 36
Ham 'n' Cheese Puffs, 13
Ham 'n' Swiss Ring, 46
Harvest Chicken Rice Soup, 22
Hasty Heartland Dinner, 64
Hearty Oxtail Soup, 38
Herbed Chicken, 59
Herbed Shrimp Skillet, 158
Holiday Baked Ham, 50
Holiday Pork Roast, 51
Home-Style Mashed
   Potatoes, 147
Homemade Bread, 86
Homemade Cream Soda, 13
Homemade Macadamia Crusted
   Tilapia, 148
Honey-Mustard Brats, 170
Hot Tomato Drink, 136
Hot Wings, 16

I

Icebox Butterhorns, 99
Icebox Cake, 123
Italian Chicken Salad
   Sandwiches, 135

J

Jerk Pork & Pineapple Kabobs, 66

K

Kids' Sushi, 106

L

Lemon & Rosemary Steak Rub, 77
Lemon Brussels Sprouts, 78
Lemon Coconut Cupcakes, 123
Lemon Delight Dessert, 130
Lemon Velvet Dessert, 121
Liver Dumplings, 28

M

Mac 'n' Cheese with Ham, 55
Mango Ice Cream, 126
Maple Oatmeal Cookies, 104
Maple Syrup Cream, 120
Marinated Pork with Caramelized
   Fennel, 67
Mashed Potatoes 'n' Brussels
   Sprouts, 77
Matoke in Peanut Sauce, 76
Meaty Mexican Sandwiches, 20
Mexican Layer Dip, 9
Miniature Corn Dogs, 175
Mixed Berry Sundaes for 2, 137
Mixed Greens with Creamy Honey
   Mustard Dressing, 142
Mocha Almond Fudge, 102
Mock Chicken Legs, 16
Moist Corn Bread, 96
Molded Raspberry Gelatin, 172
Mom's Brown Bread, 88
Mother's Potato Soup, 21

N

Napoleon Cremes, 105
Northwest Seafood Corn
   Chowder, 38
Norwegian Meatballs, 12

O

Old Fashioned Coffee Pudding, 120
Old-Fashioned Fudge Cake, 140
Old-Fashioned Swiss Steak, 68
Onion Italian Sausage, 22
Orange Cocoa Sandies, 146
Orange Smoothies, 178
Original Brown Butter
   Refrigerator Cookies, 104
Oven Fried Chicken, 169
Oven-Fried Parmesan
   Potatoes, 148
Overnight Chicken Casserole, 60

P

Pan-Fried Venison Steak, 156
Pan-Seared Lamb Chops, 158
Panguitch Potatoes, 172
Pasa De Shuto, 154
Peach Ice, 126
Peach Ice Cream, 127
Peanut Butter 'n' Banana
   Pudding, 118
Peanut Butter Fingers, 111
Peanut Butter Snack Cakes, 179
Pears and Cranberries Poached in
   Wine, 124
Pecan Pork Medallions with
   Cambozola Cream, 69
Pepper Jack Mac, 74
Peppered Filets with Cherry Port
   Sauce for 2, 138
Pesto Veggie Pizza, 70
Pfeffernuesse, 111
Picnic Sweet Potato Salad, 34
Piggy Pops, 109
Pineapple Chicken, 154
Pineapple Chiffon Pie, 128
Pineapple Cream Pie, 116
Pizza Casserole, 58
Pizza Hot Dish, 160
Plantation Bars, 108
Plum Apple Butter, 82
Poor Man's Dinner, 68
Poppy Seed Bread, 87
Pork Chops with Mushroom
   Gravy, 49
Pork Tenderloin Nectarine
   Salad, 44
Pork Tenderloin with Pear Cream
   Sauce, 47
Potato Biscuits, 86
Potato Rolls, 92
Potato-Stuffed Tomatoes, 83
Priceless BBQ Ribs, 56
Pronto Pinwheels, 52
Pumpkin Whoopie Pies, 102

Q

Quick Cran-Apple Relish, 83
Quick Kraut Snacks, 6
Quick Muffin Mix, 93
Quick Spaghetti Carbonara, 156
Quinoa Vegetable Salad, 26

R

Radish & Garbanzo Bean
   Salad, 40
Ramen-Veggie Chicken Salad, 27
Raspberry-Lemon Spritzer, 134

Red Pepper Meat Loaf, 147
Rhubarb Cheese Pie, 128
Rhubarb Ice Cream, 126
Ribeyes with Chili Butter, 155
Roast Leg of Lamb with
   Rosemary, 51
Roasted Eggplant Lasagna, 63
Roasted Onion & Garlic Soup, 168
Rose Rolls, 89
Rosemary Pork with Berry Port
   Sauce, 65
Rustic Peach Tart with Raspberry
   Drizzle, 125

S

Salad Greens with Honey Mustard
   Vinaigrette, 140
Salmon Cakes, 160
Salmon with Caribbean Salsa, 71
Salmon with Gingered Rhubarb
   Compote, 67
Salmon with Pineapple Sauce, 154
Salmon with Tarragon Sauce, 157
Secret-Ingredient Stuffed Eggs, 17
Sesame Omelet Spinach
   Spirals, 10
Shrimp and Fontina Casserole, 63
Shrimp in Cream Sauce, 162
Simple Lime Gelatin Salad, 41
Skillet Cassoulet, 159
Slow-Cooked Pot Roast, 64
Smoked Shrimp & Wild
   Mushroom Fettuccine, 60
Snappy Cocktail Meatballs, 8
Sour Cream Apple Squares, 110

Sourdough English Muffins, 98
Sourdough Starter, 98
Southwestern Potpie with
   Cornmeal Biscuits, 48
Spaghetti with Roasted Red
   Pepper Sauce, 165
Spanish Turkey Tenderloins, 64
Special Beef Wraps, 29
Spiced Orange Gelatin Salad, 36
Spinach-Onion Salad with Hot
   Bacon Dressing, 32
Steak au Poivre for 2, 139
Summer Garden Salad, 25
Summertime Strawberry
   Salad, 134
Sweet Mustard Chops, 56
Sweetheart Slaw, 148
Swiss Cheese Bread, 8

T

Tabbouleh Salad, 40
Tarragon-Cream Chicken, 177
Tasty Italian Burgers, 26
Thai Steak Salad, 138
Thai Turkey Burgers, 21
The Best Derned Southwestern
   Casserole, 62
Three-Cheese Fondue, 15
Three-Cheese Spinach
   Calzones, 61
Tilapia with Tomato-Orange
   Relish, 165
Toffee-Mocha Cream Cake, 128
Tossed Salad with Simple
   Vinaigrette, 151

Traditional Funnel Cakes, 174
Trail Mix Apple Salad, 151
Triple-Layer Lemon Cake, 119
Turkey Salad with Pistachios, 164
Turkey Tenderloins with
   Raspberry BBQ Sauce, 159
Turkey Waldorf Salad, 35

U

Unstuffed Pork Chops, 68

V

Vanilla Glaze, 89
Vegetable Ribbons, 81
Vegetable Skillet, 144
Vegetable Soup with
   Dumplings, 20
Vegetable Tuna Sandwiches, 24

W

Walnut-Apple Snack Cake, 122
Watercress & Orange Salad, 37
Wild Salmon with Hazelnuts Over
   Spinach, 162
Winning Cream of Leek Soup, 36
Winter Vegetable Gratin, 80

Y

Yogurt Ice Pops, 114

Z

Zesty Jalapeno Corn
   Muffins, 87
Zucchini Fries for 2, 137